Reading one 2

Step-up

박지성

고려대학교 언어학과 및 영어영문학과 졸업

[현] 해커스 편입
[현] 대치동/목동 중고등 내신강사

- 세계유명 여성리더들의 명연설문 베스트 30 (반석출판사)
- 바로바로 하루 10분 일상 영어 (반석출판사)
- 고등영어 서술형 기본편 (오스틴 북스)
- 고등영어 서술형 실전편 (오스틴 북스)
- chatGPT를 활용한 영어문제 창작하기 (오스틴 북스)
- 리딩 이노베이터 기본편/실전편 (JH Press)

검수 **구은서**

외고전문 (현) 벌벌아카데미 원장

Reading A one ❷ Step-up

저 자 박지성
발행인 고본화
발 행 반석출판사
2024년 8월 10일 초판 1쇄 인쇄
2024년 8월 15일 초판 1쇄 발행
홈페이지 www.bansok.co.kr
이메일 bansok@bansok.co.kr
블로그 blog.naver.com/bansokbooks

07547 서울시 강서구 양천로 583. B동 1007호
       (서울시 강서구 염창동 240-21번지 우림블루나인 비즈니스센터 B동 1007호)
대표전화 02) 2093-3399 **팩 스** 02) 2093-3393
출 판 부 02) 2093-3395 **영업부** 02) 2093-3396
등록번호 제315-2008-000033호

ISBN 978-89-7172-992-2 (13740)

반석출판사

달리기를 하는 사람들은 일정 시간 몸을 움직여 이룰 수 있는 행복감 또는 쾌감을 Runner's high라 표현한다. 사실 의학적으로 보면, 외부 자극이 있는 상황에서 신체에 의도적으로 다소 무리한 스트레스를 지속적으로 유발할 때 느끼는 일종의 도취감이라고 볼 수 있다. 이에 상응하는 정신적 도취감을 Reader's high라고 하는데, 같은 맥락에서 스트레스를 유발하는 정신적 연마의 과정에서 발생하는 희락이라고 말할 수 있다.

학습자가 이러한 Reader's high를 느낄 수 있도록 이끌어주는 요소는 무엇보다 학습자 정신에 가하는 의도적 스트레스를 감당할 수 있는 학습능력을 스스로 갖출 수 있도록 환경을 조성해 주는 동시에 지적 흥미를 꾸준하게 유발시킬 수 있는 일정 수준 이상의 학습적 스트레스를 제공하는 학습물(Study Material)이 중요하다. 심리치료사인 롤프 메르클레가 "천재는 노력하는 사람을 이길 수 없고 노력하는 사람은 즐기는 사람을 이길 수 없다."라고 말한 것에 빗대자면 Reader's high를 느낀 학습자의 학업 성취도는 높을 수밖에 없다.

본서는 저자가 10년에 걸쳐 외고와 자사고 내신 대비를 해 오면서 다뤘던 내용 중에서 학습의 지적 고양을 끌어올릴 수 있는 선별된 양질의 자료만을 담았다. 물론, 수록된 작품 자체만으로도 문학이 주는 순수한 즐거움(pleasure)을 느낄 수 있겠지만, 입시라는 틀의 범위에서 지적 "스트레스"를 통한 Runner's high를 느낄 수 있도록 다양한 형식의 이해도 문제와 평가문제로 알차게 구성했다.

특히, 본서는 일선의 외고와 자사고 내신에서 주/부교재와 보충자료(Supplementary Reading)를 통해 다루는 단편소설(또는 일부 발췌문), 연설문, 시, 그리고 다양한 분야의 비문학 글 중에서 필독서(Must-read)라 견줄 수 있는 글만을 엄선하고, 어휘정리, 구문분석, 배경지식, 실전 평가문제를 모두 담아낸 외고·자사고 대비에 최적화된 수험서임을 자부한다.

자신의 꿈을 실천하기 위해 한 단계 더 높은 곳을 향해 용감히 도전하는 외고·자사고 wanna-be에게 본서가 디딤돌 역할을 해 줄 수 있기를 바란다.

저자 박지성

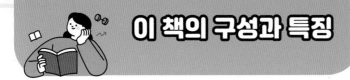

이 책의 구성과 특징

본 책은 6개의 UNIT과 각 UNIT은 5개 PART로 구성되어 있다.

PART 1 Voca Master
PART 2 Text Reading
PART 3 Voca Check
PART 4 Reading Comprehension
PART 5 Sentence Completion

각 PART의 세부 구성은 다음과 같다.

PART 1 Voca Master

PART 1에선 각 UNIT에서 다루는 작품 또는 Article에서 나오는 중요 단어를 먼저 학습할 수 있도록 구성했다. 특히, 각 단어의 영영풀이와 함께 예문 속 활용을 통해 미묘한 문맥적 뉘앙스까지 파악할 수 있도록 구성했다.

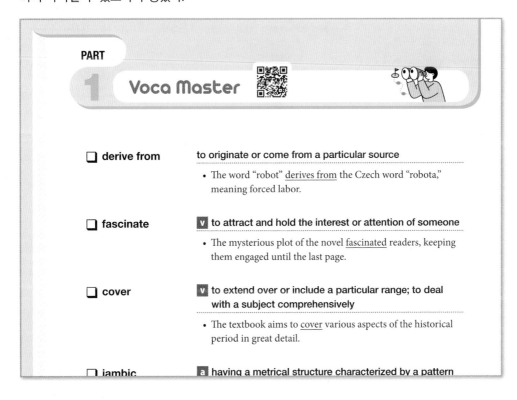

PART 2 Text Reading

PART 2는 본문 읽기로 문단별 또는 주제별로 각 페이지를 구성하고, 특히 문제를 통해서 지문에 대한 이해도를 평가할 수 있도록 했다. 필요시, 각 문단에 중요한 개념을 묻는 문제도 실었다. 또한, 〈어구 및 표현 연구〉를 두어 본문에 대한 꼼꼼한 구문분석을 제공했다.

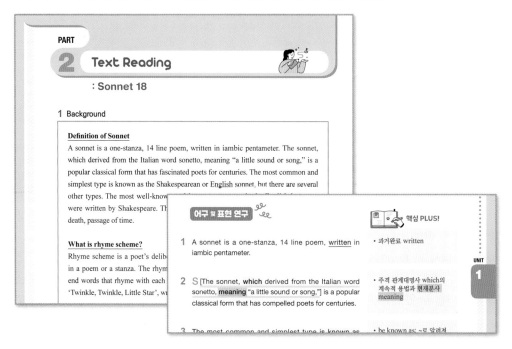

PART 3 Voca Check

PART 3에서 PART 1을 통해 학습한 본문의 어휘를 문맥 속에서 활용할 수 있는 빈칸 채우기 문제를 담았다.

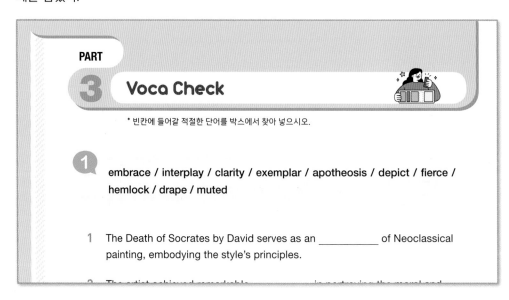

PART 4 Reading Comprehension

PART 4에서는 외고와 자사고에서 접하게 되는 실전유형의 독해 문제가 담겨 있다.

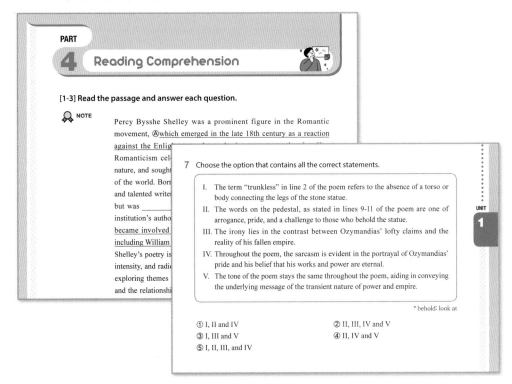

PART 5 Sentence Completion

PART 5에서 어휘의 활용과 글의 논리적 이해, 즉 문해력을 높여주는 문장완성 문제를 담았다.

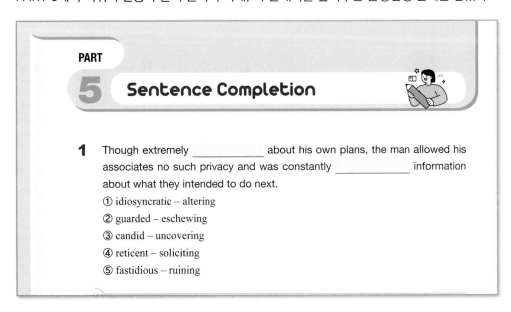

목차

머리말 4

이 책의 구성과 특징 5

UNIT 1

문학_시

Sonnet 18 by William Shakespeare

PART 1 Voca Master 12

PART 2 Text Reading 26

PART 3 Voca Check 50

PART 4 Reading Comprehension 59

PART 5 Sentence Completion 64

UNIT 2

문학_단편소설

Harrison Bergeron by Kurt Vonnegut

PART 1 Voca Master 70

PART 2 Text Reading 88

PART 3 Voca Check 123

PART 4 Reading Comprehension 131

PART 5 Sentence Completion 155

UNIT 3

비문학_예술

Understanding Art Case Study – The Death of Socrates

PART 1 Voca Master 160

PART 2 Text Reading 172

PART 3 Voca Check 182

PART 4 Reading Comprehension 187

PART 5 Sentence Completion 205

UNIT 4 문학_예술

Shelley and Romanticism and Ozymandias

PART 1 Voca Master ·················· 210
PART 2 Text Reading ·················· 214
PART 3 Voca Check ·················· 220
PART 4 Reading Comprehension ·················· 222
PART 5 Sentence Completion ·················· 228

UNIT 5 비문학_생물학

Why Leaves Turn Color in the Fall

PART 1 Voca Master ·················· 234
PART 2 Text Reading ·················· 254
PART 3 Voca Check ·················· 264
PART 4 Reading Comprehension ·················· 271
PART 5 Sentence Completion ·················· 279

UNIT 6 문학_단편소설

The Tell-Tale Heart by Edgar Allan Poe

PART 1 Voca Master ·················· 284
PART 2 Text Reading ·················· 315
PART 3 Voca Check ·················· 344
PART 4 Reading Comprehension ·················· 355
PART 5 Sentence Completion ·················· 378

문학_시

Sonnet 18

by William Shakespeare

☐ **derive from**   to originate or come from a particular source

- The word "robot" <u>derives from</u> the Czech word "robota," meaning forced labor.

☐ **fascinate**   **v** to attract and hold the interest or attention of someone

- The mysterious plot of the novel <u>fascinated</u> readers, keeping them engaged until the last page.

☐ **cover**   **v** to extend over or include a particular range; to deal with a subject comprehensively

- The textbook aims to <u>cover</u> various aspects of the historical period in great detail.

☐ **iambic**   **a** having a metrical structure characterized by a pattern of unstressed and stressed syllables, like in the word "divide"

- Many sonnets are written in <u>iambic</u> pentameter, with five pairs of unstressed and stressed syllables in each line.

☐ **passage of time**   the flow or progress of time

- The novel beautifully captures the <u>passage of time</u>, portraying the characters' growth and experiences.

☐ **deliberate**   **a** done consciously and intentionally

- The decision to change the company's logo was a <u>deliberate</u> move to modernize its image.

☐ **line**   **n** a single row of words in a poem; often grouped into stanzas

- In a sonnet, each <u>line</u> contributes to the overall structure and meaning of the poem.

☐ **identify**
v to recognize or distinguish something; to confirm the identity of someone or something

- The detective worked hard to <u>identify</u> the perpetrator through forensic evidence.

☐ **take**
to examine or consider something in a particular way

- The scientists decided to <u>take</u> a closer look at the microscopic organisms under the microscope.

☐ **iambic pentameter**
a poetic meter consisting of five iambs per line, commonly used in sonnets

- Shakespeare often wrote in <u>iambic pentameter</u>, creating a rhythmic and melodic flow in his sonnets.

☐ **syllable**
a a unit of sound in a word, usually containing a vowel and one or more consonants

- The word "water" has two <u>syllables</u>: wa-ter.

☐ **alternate**
v to happen or appear in turns or one after the other

- The seasons <u>alternate</u>, with winter followed by spring, and so on.

☐ **stressed**
a having emphasis or force; in linguistics, a syllable that is pronounced with greater force

- In the word "happy," the first syllable is <u>stressed</u>.

☐ **be made up of**
to consist of; to be composed of

- The committee <u>is made up of</u> experts from various fields.

☐ **iamb**
n a metrical foot consisting of one unstressed syllable followed by one stressed syllable

- In the word "today," the first syllable is an <u>iamb</u>.

☐ **metrical**

a related to the arrangement of poetic meter; rhythmic and measured

- The poet carefully considered the <u>metrical</u> structure to create a harmonious flow in the poem.

☐ **foot**

n a basic unit of poetic meter, consisting of one stressed syllable and one or more unstressed syllables

- The most common <u>foot</u> in English poetry is the iamb.

☐ **contain**

v to hold or include within

- The bookshelf will <u>contain</u> a diverse collection of literature, spanning different genres.

☐ **wrestle with**

to struggle or grapple with; to attempt to solve or overcome a difficult problem

- The scientist continues to <u>wrestle with</u> the complexities of the unsolved equation.

☐ **capacity**

the ability or power to do, experience, or understand something

- The human brain has an incredible <u>capacity</u> for learning and adapting to new information.

☐ **represent**

to convey, describe, express in words, depict, or draw

- The artist did an excellent job to <u>represent</u> the beauty of nature in their painting.

☐ **anonymous**

without a known or disclosed identity; unnamed

- The donation was made by an <u>anonymous</u> benefactor who wished to remain unidentified.

☐ **try out**

to test or experiment with something, often on a trial basis

- Before launching the new software, the team decided to <u>try out</u> its features to identify any potential issues.

☐ **clichéd**

a characterized by being overly familiar or commonplace, often containing overused phrases or ideas

- The movie's plot was criticized for being too clichéd, following a predictable and well-worn storyline.

☐ **metaphor**

n a figure of speech in which a word or phrase is applied to an object or action to which it is not literally applicable, creating a symbolic comparison

- "Time is a thief" is a poetic metaphor expressing the idea that time steals moments from our lives.

☐ **simile**

n a figure of speech involving the comparison of one thing with another thing of a different kind, using the words "like" or "as"

- Her laughter was as contagious as a cheerful melody, using a simile to emphasize its infectious nature.

☐ **figure of speech**

n a word or phrase used in a non-literal sense to add rhetorical force to an expression

- "Break a leg" is a common figure of speech used to wish someone good luck in a performance.

☐ **make comparisons**

to examine the similarities and differences between two or more things

- The essay will make comparisons between the economic policies of the two countries.

☐ **differ**

v to be unlike or distinct from something in nature, form, or quality

- Despite being twins, their personalities differ significantly.

☐ **velvet**

n a soft fabric with a short, dense pile, often associated with luxury and elegance

- The royal robe was made of rich, red velvet.

☐ **beloved**

a dearly loved; greatly cherished

- The old book was a <u>beloved</u> possession, passed down through generations.

☐ **susceptible to**

easily influenced or affected by something; prone to

- People with weak immune systems are <u>susceptible to</u> infections.

☐ **undertone**

n a subtle or hidden quality, element, or emotion underlying the main theme or tone

- The conversation had an <u>undertone</u> of tension, though it remained unspoken.

☐ **temperance**

n the practice of moderation, self-restraint, or abstinence, especially regarding alcohol

- Some cultures value the virtue of <u>temperance</u> as an essential part of a balanced life.

☐ **moderation**

n the quality of being moderate, avoiding extremes; the avoidance of excess or extremes

- Leading a life of <u>moderation</u> often contributes to overall well-being.

☐ **refer to**

to mention or allude to; to indicate or signify

- The author chose to <u>refer to</u> historical events to provide context for the novel.

☐ **seize upon**

to quickly and eagerly take advantage of an opportunity or idea

- Businesses often <u>seize upon</u> new trends to stay competitive in the market.

☐ **underscore**

v to emphasize or highlight; to underline for emphasis

- The statistics <u>underscored</u> the importance of addressing environmental issues.

☐ **pleasing**　　　**a** giving a sense of satisfaction or enjoyment; agreeable

- The <u>pleasing</u> melody of the music created a calming atmosphere.

☐ **nature**　　　**n** the inherent or essential qualities of a person, thing, or phenomenon; the characteristic features

- The documentary explored the wild <u>nature</u> of untouched landscapes.

☐ **allotted**　　　allocated or assigned; given as a share or portion

- Each participant was given their <u>allotted</u> time to present their ideas during the meeting.

☐ **legal contract**　　　**n** a formal agreement recognized by law, outlining the rights, responsibilities, and obligations of the parties involved

- Before starting the project, the two companies signed a <u>legal contract</u> to define their partnership.

☐ **span**　　　**n** the duration or length of attention, life, or the time between two dates or events

- The <u>span</u> of the bridge was an engineering marvel, connecting two sides of the river.

☐ **implication**　　　**n** the conclusion that can be drawn from something not expressly stated; a hint or suggestion

- The speaker's words carried an <u>implication</u> that changes were imminent.

☐ **possess**　　　**v** to own or have control over something

- She was known to <u>possess</u> a vast collection of rare books.

☐ **rent**　　　**v** to lease or hire for temporary use

- They decided to <u>rent</u> a beach house for their summer vacation.

☐ **complexion** **n** the natural color, texture, and appearance of the skin, especially on the face

- Her <u>complexion</u> glowed with health after spending a week at the spa.

☐ **personify** **v** to attribute human characteristics to something; to represent or embody as a person

- The artist used symbolism to <u>personify</u> nature in the painting.

☐ **sense** **n** the meaning conveyed by a word or phrase; perception through the senses

- The poet's words carried a deep emotional <u>sense</u> that resonated with the audience.

☐ **the Renaissance** **n** a period of cultural, artistic, and intellectual rebirth in Europe from the 14th to the 17th century

- <u>The Renaissance</u> marked a revival of interest in classical art, literature, and humanism.

☐ **fair** beautiful, attractive, or exhibiting fairness

- The princess had a <u>fair</u> complexion and golden hair.

☐ **exceptionally** **ad** to an unusually high degree; unusually or notably

- The chef's dish was <u>exceptionally</u> flavorful, earning rave reviews from the diners.

☐ **remnant** **n** a small remaining quantity of something; a trace or remainder

- The archeologists discovered <u>remnants</u> of an ancient civilization in the excavation.

☐ **usage** **n** the way in which something is used or the act of using

- A dictionary provides information on the correct <u>usage</u> of words in various contexts.

blond-haired   having light-colored or golden hair; synonymous with fair-haired

- The blond-haired child stood out in the crowd with their distinctive hair color.

stripped of   having something removed or taken away, often referring to qualities or possessions

- Stripped of its leaves in winter, the tree appeared stark and bare.

ornament   **n** a decoration or embellishment, often used to enhance beauty

- The Christmas tree was adorned with colorful lights and festive ornaments.

plain   simple, straightforward, lacking embellishments or adornments

- The plain design of the dress highlighted the elegance of its cut and fabric.

contraction   **n** the shortening of a word or phrase by omitting one or more sounds or letters

- "Can't" is a contraction of "cannot."

address   **v** to speak or write to someone; to direct efforts or attention towards something

- The CEO decided to address the company's concerns during the town hall meeting.

assert that S V   state or declare that something is true or factual

- The scientist asserted that the experiment results were consistent with their hypothesis.

moderate   mild, gentle, or restrained in quality; not extreme

- Her moderate approach to problem-solving contributed to effective collaboration.

□ damage　　**v** to harm or cause injury to something

- The storm <u>damaged</u> several houses and uprooted trees in the neighborhood.

□ delicate　　finely crafted, sensitive, or easily broken; requiring careful handling

- The artist used a <u>delicate</u> brush to create intricate details in the painting.

□ short-lived　　having a brief duration; not lasting for an extended period

- Despite its beauty, the flower's bloom was <u>short-lived</u>, lasting only a day.

□ fade　　to gradually lose brightness, color, or clarity

- The memories of that summer seemed to <u>fade</u> with each passing year.

□ golden　　having the color or quality of gold; often used metaphorically to signify excellence or richness

- The artist captured the <u>golden</u> hues of the sunset in the landscape painting.

□ dim　　**v** to make something less bright or clear; to become less intense

- As the evening approached, the sunlight began to <u>dim</u> over the horizon.

□ acknowledge　　**v** to admit or recognize the truth, existence, or rights of something

- The student was quick to <u>acknowledge</u> the help received from the teacher.

□ decline　　**v** to decrease or diminish in quality, quantity, or importance

- The economy showed signs of <u>decline</u> due to various external factors.

☐ **chance**
  n luck or fortune; an opportunity that arises without planning

  • Winning the lottery is often considered a stroke of chance rather than skill.

☐ **contrast A with B**
  v to compare and highlight the differences between A and B

  • He proved us wrong by contrasting the fast-paced urban lifestyle of New York City with the tranquil countryside of Vermont.

☐ **claim**
  v to assert ownership or right to something; to demand as a right

  • The explorer decided to claim the newly discovered island for his country.

☐ **preserve**
  v to protect or maintain something in its original or existing state

  • Efforts were made to preserve the historical artifacts for future generations.

☐ **through time**
  enduring or lasting over time; existing beyond the constraints of time

  • The timeless beauty of classical art transcends trends and remains relevant through time.

☐ **admiration**
  n a feeling of respect, approval, or wonder towards someone or something

  • The audience's admiration for the talented performer was evident in their applause.

☐ **immortalize**
  v to make someone or something immortal or everlasting in memory or fame

  • The poet sought to immortalize the beauty of the landscape through his verses.

☐ **object**

n a person or thing to which an action or feeling is directed; a target

- The painting served as the object of the artist's emotional expression.

☐ **affection**

n a feeling of fondness, warmth, or love towards someone or something

- The dog showed its affection by wagging its tail and licking its owner.

☐ **straightforward**

uncomplicated, direct, or clear; without ambiguity

- The instructions for assembling the furniture were straightforward and easy to follow.

☐ **appropriate**

suitable, fitting, or proper for a particular purpose or situation

- Wearing formal attire is appropriate for a job interview.

☐ **beloved**

a person who is dearly loved or cherished

- She was my beloved, and her memory will always hold a special place in my heart.

☐ **darling**

n a term of endearment for someone dearly loved

- "Goodnight, my darling," he whispered before she fell asleep.

☐ **reflect**

v to show or express; to give evidence of

- The artist's paintings reflect her emotions and experiences.

☐ **work**

v (of a drug or remedy) to produce the desired effect

- The pain medication took some time to work, but eventually, it provided relief.

☐ **inevitable**

certain to happen; unavoidable

- Change is inevitable, and we must learn to adapt to it.

☐ **decline and death**   the process of deteriorating and ultimately passing away

- The elderly patient faced a gradual <u>decline and death</u> as her health worsened.

☐ **document**   **v** to record or report in detail

- The journalist sought to <u>document</u> the events of the protest with accuracy.

☐ **capture**   **v** to take into one's possession; to record or express in a medium

- The photographer aimed to <u>capture</u> the beauty of the landscape in a single shot.

☐ **preserve**   **v** to maintain or keep in its original state

- The museum works to <u>preserve</u> historical artifacts for future generations.

☐ **means**   **n** a method, instrument, or resource used to achieve a goal

- Education is a powerful <u>means</u> of empowering individuals and communities.

☐ **unfold**   **v** ① to open up; to spread out
② to reveal or disclose gradually

- As the events of the story <u>unfolded</u>, the mystery became clearer.

☐ **maturity**   **n** the state or quality of being fully developed or grown

- Achieving financial <u>maturity</u> involves responsible budgeting and investment.

☐ **followed by**   coming after or succeeding in order

- The intense training was <u>followed by</u> a period of rest for the athletes.

☐ **decay**

n the process of gradual deterioration or decline

- The old building showed signs of decay with crumbling walls and peeling paint.

☐ **as such**

ad in the usual or normal sense; typically

- The product, as such, met the industry standards for quality.

☐ **represent**

v to symbolize, depict, or stand for something

- The national flag represents the unity and identity of the country.

☐ **resurrection**

n the act of rising again; revival or renewal

- The resurrection of interest in traditional crafts led to a renaissance in artisanal skills.

☐ **reference**

n a relation or connection between things; to cite or quote as a source

- The author made a reference to historical events to support her argument.

☐ **implicitly**

n without being expressly stated; understood or implied

- By following the rules, participants implicitly agree to abide by the terms of the competition.

☐ **on the grounds that**

based on the reason that

- He was denied entry on the grounds that he did not have a valid visa.

☐ **strained**

unnatural or forced; showing signs of tension or discomfort

- The conversation felt strained as they tried to avoid discussing the sensitive topic.

☐ **inappropriate** — not suitable or proper for a particular occasion, context, or person

- Wearing casual attire to a formal event would be considered <u>inappropriate</u>.

☐ **interpretative** — involving or providing an explanation or understanding; related to interpretation

- The museum offered an <u>interpretative</u> tour to help visitors understand the historical context of the artifacts.

☐ **reject** — **v** to refuse to accept, consider, or use; to dismiss

- The committee decided to <u>reject</u> the proposal due to budget constraints.

☐ **rival** — **v** to compete with or be in competition with someone or something

- The two companies constantly <u>rival</u> each other for market share.

☐ **divinity** — **n** a god or goddess; the state or quality of being divine

- In ancient mythology, each culture had its own pantheon of <u>divinities</u>.

☐ **in terms of** — concerning, with respect to, or from the perspective of

- The report will analyze the company's performance <u>in terms of</u> revenue and market share.

☐ **component** — **n** a part or element of a larger whole; one of the parts that make up a system or machine

- The electronic device has various <u>components</u> that work together to ensure its functionality.

: **Sonnet 18**

1 Background

Definition of Sonnet

A sonnet is a one-stanza, 14 line poem, written in iambic pentameter. The sonnet, which derived from the Italian word sonetto, meaning "a little sound or song," is a popular classical form that has fascinated poets for centuries. The most common and simplest type is known as the Shakespearean or English sonnet, but there are several other types. The most well-known and important sonnets in the English language were written by Shakespeare. These sonnets cover such themes as love, jealousy, death, passage of time.

What is rhyme scheme?

Rhyme scheme is a poet's deliberate pattern of lines that rhyme with other lines in a poem or a stanza. The rhyme scheme, or pattern, can be identified by giving end words that rhyme with each other the same letter. For instance, take the poem 'Twinkle, Twinkle, Little Star', written by Jane Taylor in 1806.

Twinkle, twinkle, little st**ar**	a
How I wonder what you **are**	a
Up above the world so hi**gh**	b
Like a diamond in the sk**y**	b
Twinkle, twinkle, little st**ar**	a
How I wonder what you **are**	a

어구 및 표현 연구

 핵심 PLUS!

1 A sonnet is a one-stanza, 14 line poem, <u>written</u> in iambic pentameter.

- 과거완료 written

2 S [The sonnet, **which** derived from the Italian word sonetto, **meaning** "a little sound or song,"] is a popular classical form that has compelled poets for centuries.

- 주격 관계대명사 which의 계속적 용법과 현재분사 meaning

3 The most common and simplest type <u>is known as</u> the Shakespearean or English sonnet, but there are several other types.

- be known as: ~로 알려져 있다

4 Rhyme scheme is a poet's deliberate pattern of lines (**that** rhyme with other lines in a poem or a stanza).

- 주격 관계대명사 that

5 The rhyme scheme, or pattern, can <u>be identified by</u> giving end words (**that** rhyme with each other the same letter).

- 수동태 be identified by와 주격 관계대명사 that

6 For instance, **take** the poem 'Twinkle, Twinkle, Little Star', written by Jane Taylor in 1806.

- take an example of를 줄여서 take만 종종 사용됨.

 Quick Quiz

1 This is part of "A Psalm of Life" by Henry Wadsworth Longfellow. Identify the rhyme scheme.

> Tell me not, in mournful numbers,
> Life is but an empty dream!
> For the soul is dead that slumbers,
> And things are not what they seem.

What is **Iambic pentameter**?

Iambic pentameter is a rhythmic pattern of ten syllables per line in poetry. The syllables alternate between stressed and unstressed. The pattern sounds like this: da-DUM da-DUM da-DUM da-DUM da-DUM. Iambic pentameter is made up of five iambs. An iamb is a metrical foot that contains an unstressed syllable followed by a stressed one. For example, the words "amuse" (a-MUSE), "portray" (por-TRAY), "delight" (de-LIGHT), and "return" (re-TURN) are all iambs.

ex) "Shall – **I** / com – **pare** / thee – **to** / a – **summ** / er's – **day**"

약 - 강 / 약 - 강 / 약 - 강 / 약 - 강 / 약 - 강
　　1　　　　2　　　　3　　　　4　　　　5

Sonnet 18 by William Shakespeare

"Sonnet 18" is a sonnet written by English poet and playwright William Shakespeare. The poem was likely written in the 1590s, though it was not published until 1609. Like many of Shakespeare's sonnets, the poem wrestles with the nature of beauty and with the capacity of poetry to represent that beauty. Praising an anonymous person (usually believed to be a young man), the poem tries out a number of clichéd metaphors and similes, and finds each of them wanting. It then develops a highly original and unusual simile: the young man's beauty can be best expressed by comparing him to the poem itself.

 어구 및 표현 연구

📖 핵심 PLUS!

1 An iamb is a metrical foot [**that** contains an unstressed syllable (**followed** by a stressed one)].

• 주격 관계대명사 that과 과거분사 followed

2 "Sonnet 18" is a sonnet (**written** by English poet and playwright William Shakespeare).

• 과거분사 written

3 The poem was likely written in the 1590s, [though it was **not** published **until** 1609].

• not A until B: B하고서야 A하는

4 (Like many of Shakespeare's sonnets), the poem wrestles |with the nature of beauty| and |with the capacity of poetry to represent that beauty|.

- wrestle에 걸리는 with가 이끄는 전치사구 병치구조와 capacity를 수식하는 to부정사의 형용사 용법

5 [**Praising** an anonymous person (usually believed to be a young man)], the poem |tries| out a number of clichéd metaphors and similes, and |finds| each of them wanting.

- 분사구문: As it praises~
- 본동사 병치: S tries ~ and finds ~

6 It then develops a highly original and unusual simile: the young man's beauty can **be** best **expressed by** comparing him **to** the poem itself.

- 수동태 be expressed by
- compare A to B

Quick Quiz

2 밑줄 친 표현을 바꾸어 쓰기에 문맥상 어색한 것은?

"Sonnet 18" is a sonnet Ⓐwritten by English poet and playwright William Shakespeare. The poem was likely written in the 1590s, though it was not published until 1609. Like many of Shakespeare's sonnets, the poem Ⓑwrestles with the nature of beauty and with the capacity of poetry to Ⓒrepresent that beauty. Praising an anonymous person (usually believed to be a young man), the poem tries out a number of clichéd metaphors and similes, and Ⓓfinds each of them wanting. It then develops a highly original and unusual simile: the young man's beauty can be best expressed by Ⓔcomparing him to the poem itself.

① Ⓐ penned by
② Ⓑ grapples with
③ Ⓒ capture and convey
④ Ⓓ deems
⑤ Ⓔ contrasts

Metaphor vs Simile

Metaphors and similes are both figures of speech used to make comparisons between two things that are not usually considered to be similar. However, they differ in how the comparison is made.

A simile compares two things using the words "like" or "as." For example, "He was as fast as a cheetah" or "Her voice was like velvet." In these examples, the speaker is using the words "like" and "as" to create a direct comparison between two things.
* A be like B 또는 A is as ~ as B와 같이 like나 as를 사용하여 연결.

On the other hand, a metaphor makes a comparison between two things without using "like" or "as". For example, "He was a cheetah on the track" or "Her voice was velvet." In these examples, the speaker is saying that the person's speed is like that of a cheetah or that the person's voice is smooth and luxurious like velvet, but they are not directly using the words "like" or "as" to make the comparison.
* A be B와 같이 보통 linking verb라고 하는 be동사로 바로 연결.

 Quick Quiz

3 아래 각 문장이 Metaphor인지 Simile인지 구별하시오.

① You are my alarm clock. (   )

② We always fight like cats and dogs; we cannot live without each other either. (   )

③ Your skin looks like glass. (   )

④ Riya's father and mother walking her down the aisle was the icing on the cake. (   )

⑤ Drea is an early bird. (   )

⑥ The teacher was like a lighthouse to her students. (   )

⑦ Music is food to my soul. (   )

⑧ Parvin is like a lion on the football field; he establishes his territory. (   )

⑨ The officers at the bank are as slow as sloths. (   )

⑩ The smoke from the forest fire was spread like a blanket. (   )

핵심 PLUS!

1 Metaphors and similes are both figures of speech [**used** to make comparisons between two things (**that** are not usually considered to be similar)].

- 과거분사 used
- 주격 관계대명사 that

2 However, they differ in (**how** the comparison is made).

- 의문사가 이끄는 명사절

3 A simile compares two things **using** the words "like" or "as."

- 분사구문 using
  전치사 by 삽입 가능: (by) using the words "like" or "as."

4 In these examples, the speaker is using the words "like" and "as" <u>to create</u> a direct comparison between two things.

- to부정사의 부사적 용법

5 In these examples, the speaker is saying [(that the person's speed is like **that** of a cheetah) or (that the person's voice is smooth and luxurious like velvet)], but **they** are not directly using the words "like" or "as" to make the comparison.

- saying에 걸리는 명사절 that의 병치
- that = speed
- they는 앞의 두 문장을 뜻함(He was a cheetah on the track. Her voice was velvet.)

 Quick Quiz

4 Which of the following is <u>NOT</u> an example sentence of simile?
① The night was as dark as coal.
② Her smile was like sunshine on a rainy day.
③ The wind howled like a pack of wolves.
④ The water sparkled like diamonds in the sunlight.
⑤ Love is a battlefield.

· Temperate

Temperate as used in line 2 means that the speaker's beloved is not susceptible to extremes. The word often carries moral undertones and is closely related to the word "temperance," which suggests moderation and self-control. Yet "temperate" can also refer to pleasant weather that is neither too hot nor too cold. Shakespeare seizes upon the word's ability to reference both to emotionality and weather to underscore his beloved's mild, pleasing nature.

· Lease

Lease in line 4 means, essentially, allotted time. Though the word often refers to a legal contract—for example, an agreement to rent an apartment—Shakespeare uses it here to refer simply to a limited span of time. It is used in combination with the word "ow'st." The implication is that summer does not possess its beauty; it simply rents it for a little while.

· Complexion

Complexion refers to the natural appearance of the skin, especially the skin of the face. In the poem, the speaker personifies the sun, giving it skin, in order to compare it to the young man's own complexion.

Quick Quiz

5   밑줄 친 단어의 쓰임이 중 문맥상 어색한 것은?

In line 4 of the poem, "lease" Ⓐconveys the concept of an Ⓑallocated period, essentially denoting a limited time frame. While typically Ⓒassociated with legal contracts, such as renting an apartment, Shakespeare employs it in this context to signify a finite Ⓓduration. The coupling with the word "ow'st" suggests that summer doesn't inherently own its beauty; instead, it Ⓔpermanently holds or borrows it for a brief period.

1 Temperate <u>as used</u> in line 2 means that the speaker's beloved <u>is</u> not <u>susceptible to</u> extremes.

- as used: 사용된 것처럼
- be susceptible to: ~에 취약하다 (to는 전치사)

2 The word often `carries` moral undertones and `is` closely `related` `to` the word "temperance," (**which** suggests moderation and self-control).

- 일반동사 carry와 be related to의 서술부 병치
- 주격 관계대명사의 계속적 용법

3 Yet "temperate" can also refer to pleasant weather (**that** is **neither** too hot **nor** too cold).

- 주격 관계대명사 that
- neither A nor B: A도 아니고 B도 아닌

4 Shakespeare seizes upon the word's ability to <u>reference</u> both to emotionality and weather to underscore his beloved's mild, pleasing nature.

- reference는 여기서 "관련, 관계"의 의미로 쓰이고 있음.

5 The implication is <u>that</u> summer does not possess its beauty; ①<u>it</u> simply rents ②<u>it</u> for a little while.

- 명사절 접속사 that
- ① it = summer ② it = beauty

6 Complexion refers to the natural appearance of the skin, especially the skin of the face. In the poem, the speaker personifies the sun, **giving** it skin, in order to compare it to the young man's own complexion.

- 동격의 코마
- 분사구문 giving은 아래와 같이 분사구문 또는 전치사구를 활용한 표현으로 바꿀 수 있음.
  = In the poem, the speaker personifies the sun **as he gives** it skin, in order to compare it to the young man's own complexion.
  = In the poem, the speaker personifies the sun **by giving** it skin, in order to compare it to the young man's own complexion.

· Fair

Shakespeare uses the word in a different sense. Here it refers to physical beauty. In the Renaissance, to call a man fair was to suggest that he was exceptionally beautiful. There are some remnants of this usage that survive in modern speech: for instance, one might refer to a blond-haired person as "fair-haired."

· Untrimmed

"Untrimm'd" means stripped of ornament or plain.

· Possession

To own or control something. The young man's beauty is his property, something he controls forever.

· Ow'st

The word is a contraction of the verb "own," meaning to possess something.

Quick Quiz

6 Which of the following best explains the contextual meaning of the underlined word "extremes"?

> In line 2, "temperate" signifies that the speaker's beloved is not prone to extremes. This term often carries moral connotations, closely linked to "temperance," which implies moderation and self-control. However, "temperate" can also describe pleasant weather that is neither excessively hot nor cold. Shakespeare exploits the word's dual ability to reference both emotional temperament and weather, emphasizing his beloved's gentle and pleasing nature.

① The speaker's beloved is prone to moral extremes.
② The speaker's beloved experiences extreme weather conditions.
③ The speaker's beloved possesses extreme emotional temperament.
④ The speaker's beloved avoids both moral and weather extremes.
⑤ The speaker's beloved prefers extremely hot weather.

7 In the context, what does the underlined term "ow'st" most likely mean?

> In line 4, "lease" essentially means a limited span of time. While the word commonly refers to a legal contract, such as a rental agreement for an apartment, Shakespeare uses it here to denote a finite duration. Paired with "ow'st," the implication is that summer does not inherently possess its beauty; it merely leases it for a brief period.

① owes   ② owns
③ observes   ④ oaths
⑤ omits

8 What is the purpose of mentioning the underlined "fair-haired" in the passage?

> In a departure from its modern usage, Shakespeare employs "fair" to denote physical beauty. During the Renaissance, calling a man fair suggested exceptional beauty. Some remnants of this usage persist in modern language, such as referring to a blond-haired person as "fair-haired."

① To emphasize the Renaissance's definition of fair as exceptionally beautiful.
② To criticize the outdated usage of the term "fair."
③ To highlight the ambiguity of the term "fair" in the Renaissance.
④ To suggest that calling someone "fair" is irrelevant in modern language.
⑤ To connect the term "fair" to its modern usage.

3 Sonnet 18

Sonnet 18: Shall I compare **thee** to a summer's day?

<RS>

Shall I compare thee to a summer's d**ay**?	a
Thou art more lovely and more temper**ate**:	b
Rough winds do shake the darling buds of M**ay**,	a
And summer's lease hath all too short a d**ate**;	b
Sometime too hot the eye of heaven sh**ines**,	c
And often is his gold complexion d**imm'd**;	d
And every fair from fair sometime dec**lines**,	c
By chance or nature's changing course untr**imm'd**;	d
But thy eternal summer shall not f**ade**,	e
Nor lose possession of that fair thou **ow'st**;	f
Nor shall death brag thou wander'st in his sh**ade**,	e
When in eternal lines to time thou gr**ow'st**:	f
So long as men can breathe or eyes can s**ee**,	g
So long lives this, and this gives life to th**ee**.	g

1. 현대어 번역

Should I compare you to a summer's day?
You are lovelier and more mild.
In May rough winds shake the delicate flower buds,
And the duration of summer is always too short.
Sometimes the Sun, the eye of heaven, is too hot,
And his(= the sun) golden face is often dimmed;
And beauty falls away from beautiful people,
Stripped by chance or nature's changing course.
But your eternal summer will not fade,
Nor will you lose possession of the beauty you own,
Nor will death be able to boast that you wander in his shade,
When you live in eternal lines, set apart from time.
As long as men breathe or have eyes to see,
As long as this sonnet lives, it will give life to you.

어구 및 표현 연구 🎀

2. Line별 분석

📖✎ **핵심 PLUS!**

· Shall I compare thee to a summer's day?

The speaker poses a rhetorical question, asking if they should compare the person they are addressing to a summer's day.

- 화자는 대상(the person)을 여름날에 비유해야 하는지 수사학적 질문을 던짐.

· Thou art more lovely and more temperate:

The speaker immediately answers the question by asserting that the person is more beautiful and moderate than a summer's day.

- 화자는 그 사람이 여름날보다 더 아름답고 온건하다고 단언함으로써 질문에 즉각 대답함.

· Rough winds do shake the darling buds of May,

The speaker describes how the rough winds of spring can shake and damage the delicate flower buds of May.

- 화자는 봄의 거센 바람이 5월의 여린 꽃봉오리를 어떻게 흔들고 손상시킬 수 있는지를 설명함.

· And summer's lease hath all too short a date;

The speaker asserts that summer is too short-lived, and its beauty fades quickly.

- 화자는 여름이 너무 짧고, 그 아름다움이 빨리 사라진다고 주장함.

· Sometime too hot the eye of heaven shines,

The speaker describes how sometimes the sun shines too hotly in the summer.

- 화자는 때때로 여름에 태양이 너무 뜨겁게 비친다고 설명함.

· And often is his gold complexion dimm'd;

The speaker suggests that even the sun's bright and golden appearance can become dimmed and faded.

- 화자는 태양의 밝고 금빛인 모습도 흐려지고 희미해질 수 있다고 암시함.

· And every fair from fair sometime declines,

The speaker acknowledges that all beautiful things eventually fade and decline.

- 화자는 모든 아름다운 것은 결국 퇴색하고 쇠퇴한다는 것을 인정함.

· By chance or nature's changing course untrimm'd;

The speaker suggests that this fading can happen due to chance or natural changes that are beyond anyone's control.

· 화자는 이러한 퇴색은 운(명) 또는 누구도 통제할 수 없는 자연스러운 변화로 인해 발생한다고 함.

· But thy eternal summer shall not fade,

The speaker contrasts the fading of beauty in the natural world with the eternal nature of the beauty possessed by the person they are addressing.

· 화자는 자연계의 아름다움의 퇴색과 언급하고 있는 사람이 지닌 영원한 아름다움을 대조함.

· Nor lose possession of that fair thou ow'st;

The speaker asserts that the person will never lose their beauty, which they rightfully possess.

· 화자는 그 사람이 정당하게 소유하고 있는 아름다움을 결코 잃지 않을 것이라고 주장함.

· Nor shall death brag thou wander'st in his shade,

The speaker suggests that even death cannot claim the person's beauty.

· 화자는 죽음조차도 그 사람의 아름다움을 빼앗을 수 없다고 함.

  » claim: 요구하다, 빼앗다

· When in eternal lines to time thou grow'st:

"When in eternal lines to time thou grow'st" means that the beauty of the subject of the poem will be preserved forever in the "eternal lines" of the poem, which will exist through time. The speaker is essentially saying that even though all beautiful things eventually fade and die, the beauty of the subject will live on forever in the poem.

· So long as men can breathe or eyes can see,

So long lives this, and this gives life to thee.

The speaker declares that as long as there are people alive who can breathe and see, the beauty of the person they are addressing will live on forever in the poem. The speaker believes that the poem is so powerful and timeless that it will give life to the beauty of the person, even after they have died. Essentially, the speaker is saying that their love and admiration for the person will be immortalized in the poem and will continue to exist as long as there are people to read it.

4 Theme of the poem – Art and Immortality

Sonnet 18 is essentially a love poem, though the object of its affection is not as straightforward as it may first seem. The speaker initially tries to find an appropriate metaphor to describe his beloved (traditionally believed to be a young man), suggesting that he might be compared to a summer's day, the sun, or "the darling buds of May."

화자는 처음에 그의 사랑하는 사람(전통적으로 청년으로 여겨짐)을 설명하기 위한 적절한 은유를 찾으려고 함. 그는 그가 여름날, 태양 또는 "사랑스러운 5월의 꽃봉오리"에 비유될 수 있다고 제안함.

Yet as the speaker searches for a metaphor that will adequately reflect his beloved's beauty, he realizes that none will work because all imply inevitable decline and death.

그러나 화자는 사랑하는 사람의 아름다움을 적절하게 반영할 은유를 찾으면서 모든 것이 피할 수 없는 쇠퇴와 죽음을 암시하기 때문에 아무것도 통하지 않을 것임을 깨달음.

Where the first eight lines of the poem document the failure of poetry's traditional resources to capture the young man's beauty, the final six lines argue that the young man's eternal beauty is best compared to the poem itself. It is this very sonnet that both reflects and preserves the young man's beauty. Sonnet 18 can thus be read as honoring not simply to the speaker's beloved but also to the power of poetry itself, which, the speaker argues, is a means to eternal life.

청년의 영원한 아름다움은 시 자체에 가장 잘 비유가 됨. 젊은 이의 아름다움을 반영하고 보존하는 것은 바로 이 소네트임. 따라서 소네트 18은 화자의 사랑하는 사람뿐만 아니라 화자가 주장하는 시 자체의 힘에 경의를 표하는 것으로 읽을 수 있음.

핵심 PLUS!

1 The speaker initially tries to find an appropriate metaphor to describe his beloved (traditionally believed to be a young man), **suggesting** that he might be compared to a summer's day, the sun, or "the darling buds of May."

- 분사구문 suggesting (여기서 suggest는 "~을 드러내다"의 뜻으로 쓰임.)

2 Yet [as the speaker searches for a metaphor (**that** will adequately reflect his beloved's beauty)], he realizes that none will work (because all imply inevitable decline and death).

- 주격 관계대명사 that
- because절에 걸리는 절의 주어는 all임.

3 [Where the first eight lines of the poem / document / the failure of poetry's traditional resources / to capture the young man's beauty], the final six lines argue [that the young man's eternal beauty is best compared to the poem itself].

- Where = Whereas

4 **It** is this very sonnet **that** both reflects and preserves the young man's beauty.

- it ~ that 강조용법

5 Sonnet 18 can thus be read as honoring [not simply to the speaker's beloved but also to the power of poetry itself, **which**, (the speaker argues), is a means to eternal life].

- not simply(only) to V ~ but also to V 병치
- 주격 관계대명사의 계속적 용법과 관계대명사와 동사 사이 삽입구(the speaker argues)

Quick Quiz

9 각 진술이 옳으면 True, 틀리면 False를 고르시오.

① The speaker successfully finds a metaphor in the poem that adequately reflects his beloved's beauty. (True/False)

② The first eight lines of the poem emphasize the success of traditional resources in capturing the young man's beauty. (True/False)

③ The final six lines of the poem argue that the young man's eternal beauty is best compared to nature's timeless elements. (True/False)

④ The speaker suggests that poetry has the power to reflect and preserve the beloved's beauty. (True/False)

⑤ Sonnet 18 primarily honors the speaker's beloved, overlooking the significance of poetry itself in preserving eternal life. (True/False)

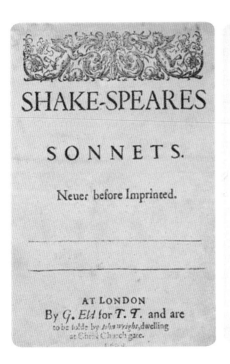

5 Symbols and Literary Device

· **Seasons**

In Western culture, the seasons unfold like a story: birth followed by maturity, maturity followed by decay and death. As such, the seasons are often used in poetry as metaphors for the progress of a human life from youth to old age. And, in a Christian context, the return of spring after the winter often serves to represent the possibility of resurrection.

"Sonnet 18" references this tradition at several key points in the poem. The poem opens by asking whether the speaker should compare the young man to a "summer's day." In line three, he refuses, implicitly, to compare the young man to the "darling buds of May." In line five, he returns to summer as a symbol—and again refuses it, this time on the grounds that summer doesn't last long enough to represent the young man's "eternal summer."

The poem thus has a strained relationship with the tradition of using the seasons as a symbol for human life. It invokes that tradition only to refuse it. Because the symbol implies narrative—change, transformation, aging, decay—the speaker finds it inappropriate for his purposes. This raises interesting interpretative questions: one might wonder, for instance, if the poem also rejects a Christian model of resurrection (which requires death) in favor of its own, poetic form of eternal life.

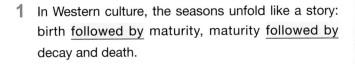

1   In Western culture, the seasons unfold like a story: birth <u>followed by</u> maturity, maturity <u>followed by</u> decay and death.

• A followed by B: A 이후에 B가 따르다

2   As such, the seasons <u>are</u> often <u>used</u> (in poetry) <u>as</u> metaphors [for the progress of a human life (from youth to old age)].

• A is used as B: A가 B로 사용되다

3   The poem opens [by <u>asking</u> (whether the speaker should compare the young man to a "summer's day.")]

• "~인지 아닌지"의 의미를 가진 명사절 whether이 asking의 목적어 자리에 위치.

4   In line three, he refuses, implicitly, to <u>compare</u> the young man <u>to</u> the "darling buds of May."

• compare A to B: A를 B와 비유하다(유사성 비교)

5   In line five, he returns to summer as a symbol— and again refuses it, (this time) <u>on the grounds</u> that summer doesn't last long enough to represent the young man's "eternal summer."

• on the grounds that S V : ~라는 근거에서
• 동격의 명사절 that

6   Because the symbol implies narrative—change, transformation, aging, decay—the speaker <u>finds</u> / <u>it</u> / inappropriate for his purposes.

• 5형식 동사 find
• it = narrative

7   This raises interesting interpretative questions: one might <u>wonder</u>, (for instance), [<u>if</u> the poem also rejects a Christian model of resurrection (which requires death) in favor of its own, poetic form of eternal life].

• if절은 타동사 wonder에 걸리는 명사절임.

[10-12] Sonnet 18의 시를 참고하여 다음을 읽고, 물음에 답하시오.

[A] In Western cultural context, the progression of seasons unfolds akin to a narrative—commencing with birth, advancing through maturity, and Ⓐculminating in decay and death. Consequently, these seasonal transitions often serve as metaphors in poetry to symbolize the journey of human life from youth to old age. In a Christian framework, the resurgence of spring post-winter frequently symbolizes the prospect of Ⓑresurrection.

[B] "Sonnet 18" makes multiple mentions of <u>this convention</u> throughout the poem. It begins by questioning whether the speaker should draw a comparison between the young man and a "summer's day." By the third line, the speaker declines, without explicitly stating, to liken the young man to the "darling buds of May." In the fifth line, the speaker revisits the theme of summer as a symbol but rejects it, this time arguing that summer's Ⓒbrevity does not adequately capture the concept of the young man's "eternal summer."

[C] The poem exhibits a tense connection with the conventional use of seasons as metaphors for human existence. It engages with this tradition but ultimately rejects it. Since the symbol carries connotations of a narrative—encompassing change, transformation, aging, and decay—the speaker deems it Ⓓsuitable for his intentions. This invites intriguing questions for interpretation, such as whether the poem also Ⓔdismisses a Christian concept of resurrection (which involves death) in favor of its unique poetic expression of eternal life.

10 Which of the following refers to the underlined "this convention" in paragraph [B]?

① The rejection of summer's brevity as a symbol
② The speaker's refusal to compare the young man to a "summer's day"
③ The engagement with the tradition of using seasons as metaphors
④ The questioning of whether the speaker should compare the young man to a "summer's day"
⑤ The dismissal of a Christian concept of resurrection in the poem

11 밑줄 친 단어의 쓰임이 <u>어색한</u> 것은?

① Ⓐ culminating
② Ⓑ resurrection
③ Ⓒ brevity
④ Ⓓ suitable
⑤ Ⓔ dismisses

12 Which of the following is the best title for the passage?

① The Symbolic Representation of Seasons in Poetry
② Sonnet 18's Rejection of Traditional Seasonal Metaphors
③ The Cultural Significance of Seasonal Progression
④ Exploring Seasonal Symbolism in Western and Christian Contexts
⑤ The Tension Between Tradition and Innovation in Poetic Symbolism

· The Sun

In Renaissance love poetry, the sun is often used as a symbol for physical or personal beauty. Because the sun is the source of all light and life, comparing someone or something to the sun suggests that they are unusually, even exceptionally beautiful.

In "Sonnet 18," the speaker considers comparing the young man to the sun, but rejects the comparison, noting that the sun's beauty is often dimmed by clouds. To reject this metaphor—to say that the young man is more beautiful than the sun because his beauty is more eternal—raises questions about the poem's relationship to Christianity. The speaker might suggest here that the young man's beauty and importance rival that of the divinity.

· Personification

The speaker occasionally personifies the natural world in the poem. For example, in line 5, he compares the sun to a part of the human body, an "eye."

"Sometime too hot the eye of heaven shines,"

The speaker is comfortable thinking about the natural world in terms of the physical (and psychic) components of a human being. Yet the speaker also clearly resists personification at certain points. The poem's opening rhetorical question might be understood as a moment where the speaker pauses to consider whether he should personify a summer's day. "Is there actually a meaningful resemblance between the summer's day and the young man," he wonders. The heart of the poem lies in the speaker's refusal to accept that there is.

어구 및 표현 연구

핵심 PLUS!

1 In Renaissance love poetry, the sun <u>is</u> (often) <u>used as</u> a symbol for physical or personal beauty.

- A is used as B: A가 B로 사용되다

UNIT 1

2 (Because the sun is the source of all light and life), S [comparing someone or something to the <u>sun</u>] suggests / that they are unusually, even exceptionally beautiful.

- 동명사가 이끄는 주어 파악.

3 In "Sonnet 18," the speaker considers [comparing the young man <u>to</u> the sun], but rejects the comparison, (**noting** that the sun's beauty is often dimmed by clouds).

- consider v-ing: ~하는 것을 고려하다 cf. consider that S V
- compare A to B: A와 B의 (유사점을) 고려하다
- consider와 reject의 서술부 병치
- 분사구문 noting (=~ **as he notes** that the sun's beauty is often dimmed by clouds)

4 [**To reject** this metaphor—to say that the young man is more beautiful than the sun because his beauty is more eternal—] raises questions about the poem's relationship to Christianity.

- to부정사가 이끄는 주어
- 주부에 동격 부연의 dash(-).

5 The speaker might suggest here that the young man's beauty and importance / rival / <u>that</u> of the divinity.

- rival "~와 경쟁하다"라는 뜻의 타동사
- that = beauty and importance

6 The poem's opening rhetorical question might be understood as a <u>moment</u> [<u>where</u> the speaker pauses to consider (<u>whether</u> he should personify a summer's day)].

- a moment는 관계부사 where의 상황 선행사.
- whether는 타동사 consider에 걸리는 명사절.

[13-15] 다음을 읽고, 물음에 답하시오.

> In Renaissance love poetry, the sun is often used as a symbol for physical or personal beauty. Because the sun is the source of all light and life, comparing someone or something to the sun suggests that they are unusually, even exceptionally beautiful.
>
> In "Sonnet 18," the speaker considers comparing the young man to the sun, but rejects the comparison, noting that the sun's beauty is often dimmed by clouds. To reject this metaphor—to say that the young man is more beautiful than the sun because his beauty is more eternal—raises questions about the poem's relationship to Christianity. The speaker might suggest here that the young man's beauty and importance rival that of the divinity.

13 Which of the followings can <u>NOT</u> replace the underlined word "<u>dimmed</u>" in the passage?

① veiled
② eclipsed
③ illuminated
④ faded
⑤ obscured

14 Based on the passage, what does "<u>the sun</u>" symbolize in Christianity?

① Physical or personal beauty
② The source of all light and life
③ Exceptional beauty
④ Impermanence of natural beauty
⑤ Celestial beauty and importance

15 Which of the pairs best fills in the blanks Ⓐ and Ⓑ in the passage?

The speaker occasionally Ⓐ_____ the natural world in the poem. For example, in line 5, he compares the sun to a part of the human body, an "eye."

"Sometime too hot the eye of heaven shines,"

The speaker is comfortable thinking about the natural world in terms of the physical (and psychic) components of a human being. At the same time, the speaker also clearly Ⓑ_____ personification at certain points. The poem's opening rhetorical question might be understood as a moment where the speaker pauses to consider whether he should personify a summer's day. "Is there actually a meaningful resemblance between the summer's day and the young man," he wonders. The heart of the poem lies in the speaker's refusal to accept that there is.

	Ⓐ	Ⓑ
①	personifies	rejects
②	describes	embraces
③	personifies	accepts
④	excludes	invokes
⑤	imagines	contests

1

cover / alternate / capacity / iambic pentameter / passage of time / line / identify / take / syllables / iambic / stressed / be made up of / iamb / metrical / derive from / foot / contain / wrestle with / fascinate / deliberate

1 The verb "유래하다" in Korean means to _____ a particular source.

2 The mysterious storyline managed to _____ the readers with its twists and turns.

3 The forest will _____ a vast area, providing a habitat for various species.

4 The poem follows an _____ structure, a type of metric line used in traditional English poetry and verse drama.

5 Reflecting on the _____, the author pondered the changes that occurred over the years.

6 The decision to postpone the event was a _____ choice made after careful consideration.

7 In poetry, a collection of verses is called a stanza, while a single line is referred to as a _____.

8 It is important to accurately _____ the characteristics that define each species in a scientific study.

9 Scientists often _____ a closer look at microscopic organisms to understand their behavior.

10 Shakespearean sonnets often follow the pattern of _____ consisting of five iambs.

11 A haiku typically consists of three lines with a specific number of _____ in each.

12 The students were instructed to _____ reading paragraphs with their classmates during the activity.

13 In poetry, a _____ syllable typically receives more emphasis or stress than an unstressed one.

14 The committee decided that the committee report would _____ various perspectives on the issue.

15 An _____ is a metrical unit in poetry that consists of one unstressed syllable followed by one stressed syllable.

16 The _____ analysis of the poem revealed a consistent pattern in its rhythmic structure.

17 In poetic meter, a _____ is a basic unit of measurement, usually consisting of stressed and unstressed syllables.

18 The library's collection will _____ a diverse range of literary works from different genres.

19 The author had to _____ complex emotions and ideas while writing the challenging novel.

20 The human brain has an incredible _____ to adapt and learn new information.

2

refer to / try out / make comparisons / underscore / figure of speech / temperance / pleasing / simile / velvet / represent / beloved / susceptible to / undertone / clichéd / moderation / seize upon / metaphor / anonymous / nature / differ

1 The artist aimed to _____ the beauty of nature through intricate brushstrokes.

2 The author chose to remain _____, allowing the work to speak for itself without revealing their identity.

3 As part of the audition process, the actors were asked to _____ a few scenes to showcase their skills.

4 The movie received criticism for its _____ dialogue, filled with overused and predictable expressions.

5 In poetry, a _____ is a powerful tool for conveying meaning through symbolic language.

6 The author used a _____ to compare the night sky to a blanket of darkness studded with stars.

7 A _____ is a colorful and expressive use of language, often involving metaphors and similes.

8 Writers often _____ various elements in their works to highlight similarities or differences.

9 Despite their similarities, the two paintings subtly _____ in terms of color palette and composition.

10 The gown was made of luxurious _____ fabric, adding a touch of elegance to the evening.

11 The _____ novel became a classic, cherished by readers for generations.

12 Some individuals are more _____ stress, making them prone to health issues.

13 The speaker's words carried an _____ of sadness, hinting at deeper emotions beneath the surface.

14 _____ is the practice of avoiding excess and maintaining self-control, particularly in areas like alcohol consumption.

15 The speaker emphasized the importance of approaching challenges with _____, avoiding extremes.

16 When using a term in a paper, it's essential to clearly _____ what it refers to for the reader's understanding.

17 The marketing team decided to _____ the opportunity to launch the new product during the holiday season.

18 The author wanted to _____ the significance of the theme by repeatedly highlighting it in the narrative.

19 The melody had a _____ quality, leaving the audience with a sense of joy and contentment.

20 Human behavior is often influenced by both _____ and nurture, shaping individual characteristics and traits.

3

remnant / span / contraction / implication / ornament / rent / stripped of / personify / the Renaissance / fair / legal contract / complexion / usage / blond-haired / plain / possess / address / allotted / exceptionally / sense

1 The time _____ for completing the project was not sufficient, leading to delays.

2 Before moving in, tenants are required to sign a _____ that outlines

the terms and conditions of their lease.

3   The _____ of a person's attention often varies depending on factors like interest and fatigue.

4   When making a statement, it's essential to consider the _____ it may have on the audience.

5   Individuals who _____ a strong work ethic are likely to achieve success in their careers.

6   The decision to _____ an apartment rather than buy a house depends on various factors.

7   A healthy diet and proper skincare contribute to a radiant _____ and overall well-being.

8   The artist sought to _____ the virtues of courage and resilience through the character in the painting.

9   The word "love" can have different _____ depending on the context in which it is used.

10 _____ was a period of cultural and artistic rebirth in Europe during the 14th to 16th centuries.

11 The garden was adorned with _____ flowers, creating a picturesque scene.

12 She performed _____ well in the challenging exam, earning praise from her peers.

13 The archaeologists discovered a _____ of an ancient civilization buried beneath the layers of soil.

14 Understanding the correct _____ of a tool is crucial for its effective use.

15 The actor with _____ hair stood out in the crowd with his distinctive appearance.

16 The old building, now _____ its original charm, lacked the grandeur it once had.

17 The Christmas tree was adorned with various _____, adding a festive touch to the room.

18 His _____ explanation left no room for confusion, making it easy for everyone to understand.

19 In casual conversations, people often use _____ to make communication more efficient.

20 During the conference, participants had the opportunity to _____ the speaker with questions and comments.

4

short-lived / claim / object / delicate / acknowledge / fade / affection / straightforward / golden / dim / immortalize / decline / damage / chance / contrast / preserve / through / time / admiration / assert / moderate

1 The speaker sought to _____ their viewpoint with confidence during the debate.

2 A _____ approach to problem-solving often leads to more effective and balanced solutions.

3 Harsh weather conditions can _____ the exterior of buildings over time.

4 The artist's paintings are known for their _____ and intricate details.

5 Despite its promising start, the project turned out to be _____ and did not last long.

6 Colors tend to _____ over time when exposed to direct sunlight.

7   The _____ glow of the sunset painted the sky with warm hues.

8   As the evening approached, the surroundings gradually grew _____.

9   It is essential to _____ the efforts of individuals who contribute to the team's success.

10 The decline of traditional industries has led to the _____ of certain communities.

11 Serendipity plays a significant role in life, often presenting unexpected _____.

12 To highlight the differences between the two characters, the author decided to _____ them in the narrative.

13 The explorer was determined to _____ new lands for his country.

14 Efforts to _____ historical artifacts ensure that future generations can learn from the past.

15 The timeless beauty of the artwork resonates _____, transcending the boundaries of eras.

16 The artist's skillful brushstrokes earned the _____ of critics and viewers alike.

17 Writers often seek to _____ their characters by creating memorable and enduring stories.

18 The microscope allowed scientists to closely examine the smallest _____ in the biological sample.

19 The bond between the two friends was built on years of shared experiences and genuine _____.

20 The instructions were _____, making it easy for anyone to follow the steps without confusion.

5

preserve / beloved / appropriate / reflect / decline and death / unfold / inevitable / document / capture / work / resurrection / as such / maturity / grounds / decay / represent / darling / reference / implicitly / means

1 When sending a formal email, it is crucial to use an _____ tone to maintain professionalism.

2 The letter was addressed to his _____, expressing deep affection and longing.

3 The poet dedicated the verses to his _____, capturing the essence of their bond.

4 The artist's masterpiece seemed to _____ the emotions and struggles of the human experience.

5 Certain medications may _____ their optimal effects if taken with food.

6 The progression of life from birth to death is an _____ part of the human experience.

7 The novel explored the theme of _____, portraying the protagonist's journey from prosperity to demise.

8 Journalists aim to _____ events accurately and comprehensively to inform the public.

9 Photographers often strive to _____ fleeting moments in time through their lenses.

10 It is essential to take measures to _____ historical artifacts for future generations.

11 In scientific research, various _____ are employed to gather data and draw conclusions.

12 The story began to _____ as the characters' backgrounds and motivations were revealed.

13 The _____ of an individual involves personal and emotional growth over time.

14 The decision was made on the _____ of the evidence provided during the investigation.

15 The _____ of a once vibrant city can be a poignant reminder of the passage of time.

16 The concept of beauty varies among cultures and is not universally agreed upon _____.

17 Artists often use symbols to _____ abstract ideas or emotions in their works.

18 The _____ of a classic novel can bring new life and relevance to a timeless story.

19 In academic writing, it is crucial to provide proper _____ to sources when presenting research.

20 The message was _____ conveyed through subtle hints and gestures rather than explicit statements.

[1-3] Read the poem and answer each question.

NOTE

Shall I compare thee to a summer's day?
Thou art more lovely and more temperate:
Rough winds do shake the darling buds of May,
And summer's lease hath all too short a date;
Sometime too hot the eye of heaven shines,
And often is his gold complexion dimm'd;
And every fair from fair sometime declines,
By chance or nature's changing course untrimm'd;
But thy eternal summer shall not fade,
Nor lose possession of that fair thou ow'st;
Nor shall death brag thou wander'st in his shade,
When in eternal lines to time thou grow'st:
   So long as men can breathe or eyes can see,
   So long lives this, and this gives life to thee.

1 Which of the following best describes the structure of the poem?

① An argument that presents evidence for a central thesis

② A narrative that tells a story about the speaker and his friend

③ A series of observations about nature and the passage of time

④ A meditation on the nature of love and beauty

⑤ A description of the speaker's emotional state and thoughts

2 Which of the following best describes the role of the natural world in the poem?

① It serves as a backdrop against which the speaker's friend is compared.

② It is a source of joy and beauty that the speaker celebrates.

③ It is a symbol of the fleeting nature of time and mortality.

④ It represents the power and endurance of nature over human life.

⑤ It is an obstacle that the speaker's friend must overcome to be truly beautiful.

3 Choose the option that contains all the correct statements.

> I. The poem is a sonnet.
>
> II. Poet's young beloved friend is addressed to in the poem 'Shall I compare thee to a summer's day', which is an indirect comparison between the friend and a summer's day.
>
> III. By the phrase "the eye of heaven" in line 5 the poet means the sun. This is the personification of the sun.
>
> IV. From the last two lines, it can be inferred that the poet is boldly stating that it is his eternal lines, his poetry, that will make his friend eternal.
>
> V. The ultimate message of the poem is "death is inevitable, but poetry has the power to transcend time and preserve beauty."

① I, II and V

② I, III, IV and V

③ II and IV

④ II, III, IV and V

⑤ I, II and IV

[4-5] Read the poem and answer each question.

Shall I compare thee to a summer's day?
Thou art more lovely and more temperate:
Rough winds do shake the darling buds of May,
And summer's lease hath all too short a date;
Sometime too hot the eye of heaven shines,
And often is his gold complexion dimm'd;
And every fair from fair sometime declines,
By chance or nature's changing course untrimm'd;
But thy eternal summer shall not fade,
Nor lose possession of that fair thou ow'st;
Nor shall death brag thou wander'st in his shade,
When in eternal lines to time thou grow'st:
    So long as men can breathe or eyes can see,
    So long lives this, and this gives life to thee.

4 In the poem, why is a summer's day not an adequate comparison for the speaker's beloved friend?
① Summer is too hot and uncomfortable.
② The sun can be too intense and damaging.
③ Summer is too short-lived.
④ The natural world is subject to chance and change.
⑤ All of the above.

5 Choose the option that contains all the <u>INCORRECT</u> statements.

> I. The main theme of the poem is the power of poetry to immortalize beauty.
> II. When his beloved friend is compared to 'a summer's day,' he is deemed less beautiful but more enduring.
> III. The phrase "his gold complexion" in line 6 refers to "the color of the sun."
> IV. The significance of the phrase "When in eternal lines to time thou grow'st" in line 12 is that it suggests that the speaker's friend will become immortal through the power of poetry.
> V. The literary device prominently used in the final two lines is allusion.

① I only   ② II only   ③ II and III   ④ IV only   ⑤ II and V

[6-9] Read the poem and answer each question.

 NOTE

Shall I compare thee to a summer's day?
ⓐThou ⓑart more lovely and more temperate:
ⓒRough winds do shake the darling buds of May,
And summer's lease ⓓhath all too short a date;
Sometime too hot ⓔthe eye of heaven shines,
And often is ⓕhis gold complexion dimm'd;
And every ⓖfair from fair sometime declines,
By chance or nature's changing course untrimm'd;
But ⓗthy eternal summer shall not fade,
ⓘNor lose possession of that fair thou ow'st;
ⓙNor shall death brag thou wander'st in his shade,
When in eternal lines to time thou grow'st:
So long as men can breathe or eyes can see,
So long lives this, and this gives life to thee.

6 Which of the following is NOT correct?

① 'His' in ⓕ refers to 'the sun.'

② The word 'fair' in ⓖ is used to describe something beautiful, pleasant, or agreeable.

③ ⓗ refers to 'the sun.'

④ One of the interpretations about the phrase 'thou ow'st' is that it means "you own" or "you possess."

⑤ ⓘ in line 11 shows that 'death' is being personified as a person.

7 Among the underlined ⓐ ~ ⓔ, which of the following is NOT correct?

① ⓐ refers to the speaker's beloved, whom he is addressing in the poem. "Thou" is an archaic English pronoun that means "you."

② ⓑ means "are" and is used to describe the qualities of the speaker's beloved, who is being compared to a summer's day.

③ The phrase "darling buds" may be interpreted as a term of endearment for the flowers, emphasizing their strength and durability.

④ "Hath" in ⓓ is an archaic form of the verb "to have" in the third person singular, present tense.

⑤ The "eye of heaven" in ⓔ is a metaphor for the sun.

8 Which of the following words best describes the overall tone of the poem?

① Melancholic

② Despairing

③ Ironic

④ Romantic

⑤ Philosophical

9 Which of the following is the primary purpose of the rhetorical question in the first line of the poem?

① To compare the speaker's beloved friend to a summer's day

② To introduce the central theme of the poem

③ To express doubt or uncertainty about the comparison being made

④ To emphasize the speaker's love and admiration for his friend

⑤ To set a contemplative tone for the rest of the poem

5 Sentence Completion

1 Americans are always talking about wise use of leisure time. They think that they must find something to do for either pleasure or profit, for to them inactivity is _____.

① a deadly sin   ② culturally important

③ a perfect state   ④ greatly desirable

어휘

always 항상, 언제나 talk about ~에 관해 말하다 wise 현명한 use 사용, 이용 leisure time 여가시간 find ~을 찾다, 발견하다 something to do 할 무언가, 할 것 either A or B A또는 B, A와 B 둘 중 하나 pleasure 기쁨, 즐거움 profit 이익, 수익 for [접속사] 왜냐하면(주로 앞에 comma가 있다) inactivity 활동 없음, 게으름 deadly sin 치명적인 잘못 culturally important 문화적으로 중요한 perfect state 완벽한 상태 greatly desirable 매우 바람직한

2 A _____ statement is an _____ comparison.

① sarcastic – unfair   ② blatant – over

③ sanguine – inherent   ④ metaphorical – implied

⑤ bellicose – ardent

어휘

statement 성명, 진술 comparison 비교 sarcastic 풍자의, 신랄한 unfair 불공평한, 부당한 blatant 뻔뻔한; 소란스러운 over ~위의; 과도히, 아주 sanguine 낙관적인, 쾌활한 inherent 타고난, 선천적인 metaphorical 은유적인 implied 함축된, 암시적인, 내포적인 bellicose 호전적인, 싸움을 좋아하는 ardent 열렬한, 격렬한

3 An individual who is _____ is incapable of _____.

① fettered – flight   ② modest – shame

③ penurious – thought   ④ militant – fear

⑤ ambitious – failure

어휘

individual 개개의, 독특한; 개인 be incapable of ~할 능력이 없다 fetter 족쇄; 속박(구속)하다 flight 날기, 비행 modest 겸손한, 적당한, (양 등이) 그리 많지 않은 shame 창피, 수치 penurious 빈곤한, 인색한 thought 생각, 사고 militant 호전적인, 투쟁적인 fear 두려움, 공포 ambitious 야심 있는 failure 실패

4 Something that is _____ is not _____.

① trite – boring   ② violent – vivid

③ common – a cliche   ④ elastic – resilient

⑤ hackneyed – original

어휘

trite 진부한, 흔해빠진 boring 지루한, 따분한 violent 폭력적인, 맹렬한 vivid 생생한, 발랄한 common 보통의, 흔히 있는 cliche 진부한 표현, 상투적인 문구 elastic 탄력(성)있는, 유연한 resilient 되튀는, 탄력 있는, (감정 등이) 잘 돌아오는 hackneyed 진부한, 흔해빠진 original 독창적인, 최초의

5 To _____ is to try to _____ an individual.

① gainsay – corrupt   ② evacuate – dismiss

③ exhume – bury   ④ proselytize – convert

⑤ inhibit – frighten

어휘

try to ⓡ ~하려고 노력하다 individual 개개의, 독특한; 개인 gainsay ~을 부인(반박)하다 corrupt ~을 타락시키다, 더럽히다; 타락한 evacuate (사람을) 피난시키다, (집 등을) 비우다 dismiss 해산시키다, 해고하다, 기각하다 exhume ~을 발굴하다, 찾아내다 bury ~을 묻다, 매장하다 proselytize ~을 개종시키다 convert ~을 전환하다, 개종시키다 inhibit ~을 방해하다 frighten ~을 두려워하게 하다, 무섭게 하다

6 An example of an illegitimate method of argument is to lump _____ cases together deliberately under the _____ that the same principles apply to each.

① unsuitable – impression

② disputable – stipulation

③ irrelevant – assumption

④ dissimilar – pretense

⑤ indeterminate – rationale

어휘

illegitimate 불법의, 위법의, 적절하지 않은 method 방법, 방식 argument 주장, 논쟁 lump ~을 한 묶음으로 하다; 덩어리, 혹; ~을 참다, 인내하다 case 경우, 사건 deliberately 고의적으로, 일부러 principle 원리, 원칙 apply to ~에 적용시키다 each 각각(의) unsuitable 부적당한, 적합하지 않은 impression 인상, 감명 disputable 논쟁의 여지가 있는 stipulation 규정, 명기, 조건 irrelevant 부적절한, 관계없는 assumption 가정; 인수; 횡령 dissimilar 다른, 닮지 않은 pretense 구실, 겉치레 under(on) the pretense of ~을 구실로, ~으로 가장하여 indeterminate 불확실한, 명확하지 않은 rationale 이론적 설명(근거), 근본적 이유, 원리

7 Since the brain actually begins dying shortly after birth, the brain's
_____ is all the more remarkable.

① deterioration   ② obsolescence

③ recovery   ④ longevity

⑤ plurality

어휘

since ~이래로; ~이기 때문에 brain 뇌 actually 실제로, 실은 begin 시작하다 die 죽다 shortly after ~한 직후 birth 탄생, 출생 all (this, the 등과 더불어 힘줌말로) 훨씬, 엄청난 remarkable 주목할 만한, 현저한, 놀랄 만한 deterioration 퇴화, 악화 obsolescence 노폐(화), 노후(화) recovery 회복, 복구 longevity 장수 plurality 복수, 다수

8 This law was enacted in _____ atmosphere, full of _____.

① an apathetic – zeal   ② a restrained – controversy

③ a charged – recriminations   ④ an enthusiastic – duplicity

⑤ an open – equivocation

어휘

law 법, 법률 enact ~을 법령(법제)화하다 atmosphere 분위기, 대기 full of ~로 가득한 apathetic 냉담한, 무관심한 zeal 열정, 열성 restrained 삼가는, 자제하는, 억제된 controversy 논쟁, 논의 charged (분위기 등이) 긴장된, 일촉즉발의, 논쟁이 일어나기 쉬운 recrimination 비난 enthusiastic 열정적인, 열렬한 duplicity 표리부동, 이중성, 사기 equivocation 애매함, 다의성

9 The many faults of the President's economic policies do not include
_____ ; statements of the need to improve business conditions are
followed by proposals that cause the _____ of dozens of firms daily.

① weakness – demise   ② conceit – distress

③ consistency – bankruptcy   ④ socialism – opening

⑤ clarity – confusion

어휘

fault 과실, 결점, 잘못 economic policy 경제 정책 include ~을 포함하다 statement 성명, 진술 need 필요; 결핍 improve ~을 향상시키다, 개량하다 business condition 사업 환경 follow ~을 따르다 *A be followed by B B가 A를 따르다(A가 먼저) proposal 제안, 신청 cause ~의 원인이 되다, 일으키다, 초래하다 dozen 1다스, 12개 dozens of 수십의, 많은 firm 회사; 굳은, 단단한, 고정된 daily 매일(의), 일상의 weakness 약점, 허약 demise 사망, 소멸 conceit 자만, 자부심 distress 비탄, 고통, 가난, 고난 consistency 일관성, 불변함 bankruptcy 파산 socialism 사회주의 opening 개시, 열기, 취직자리 clarity 명료함, 명확함 confusion 혼동, 혼란

10 His remarks were _____ and _____, indicative of his keen and incisive mind.

① unsentimental – deliberate

② ingenuous – noteworthy

③ impartial – apolitical

④ trenchant – penetrating

⑤ apish – dramatic

어휘

remark 논평, 소견, 비평 indicative of ~을 나타내는, ~의 표시인 keen 날카로운, 예리한 incisive 날카로운, 통렬한, 신랄한 mind 마음, 정신, 견해 unsentimental 감정(감성)적이지 않은 deliberate 계획적인, 고의의; 신중한, 생각이 깊은 ingenuous 순진한, 솔직한 noteworthy 주목할 만한 impartial 공정한, 공평한 apolitical 정치에 관심 없는, 정치적 의의가 없는 trenchant 신랄한, 통렬한 penetrating 예리한, 통찰력이 있는; 침투하는, 관통하는 apish 원숭이 같은, 어리석은 dramatic 극의, 극적인

문학_단편소설

Harrison Bergeron
by Kurt Vonnegut

Voca Master

☐ **every which way**

in every direction; all around

....
- The wind blew the leaves <u>every which way</u>, creating a whirlwind of color.

☐ **be due to N**

attributable to or caused by something; the reason for something

....
- The flight delay <u>was due to</u> adverse weather conditions.

☐ **unceasing**

a never stopping; continuous

....
- The <u>unceasing</u> rain caused flooding in many areas.

☐ **vigilance**

n the action or state of keeping careful watch for possible dangers or difficulties

....
- Airport security operates with constant <u>vigilance</u> to ensure passenger safety.

☐ **clammy**

a unpleasantly damp and sticky; moist

....
- Her hands were <u>clammy</u> from the humidity in the room.

☐ **all right**

satisfactory; acceptable

....
- If everything is <u>all right</u>, we can proceed with the plan.

☐ **in short bursts**

in brief, quick episodes or intervals

....
- The athlete sprinted <u>in short bursts</u> during the race.

☐ **transmitter**

n a device that sends out signals, especially one that broadcasts radio or television signals

....
- The radio tower serves as the main <u>transmitter</u> for the station.

☐ **like bandits from a burglar alarm**	similar to criminals fleeing from a triggered burglar alarm	
	• The children scattered <u>like bandits from a burglar alarm</u> when the school bell rang.	

☐ **sashweight** — **n** a counterbalance, typically a weight, used in windows with sashes to facilitate opening and closing

• The old window's <u>sashweight</u> helped it smoothly glide up and down.

UNIT

2

☐ **birdshot** — **n** small pellets fired from a shotgun, used for hunting birds

• The hunter loaded his shotgun with <u>birdshot</u> for the quail hunt.

☐ **feel/look like something the cat brought/dragged/drug in** — to appear or feel disheveled, tired, or worn-out

• After a long day at work, he <u>looked like something the cat dragged in</u>.

☐ **toy with** — play with or consider an idea or concept casually

• She began to <u>toy with</u> the idea of starting her own business.

☐ **wince** — **v** to flinch or make a slight involuntary grimace, often in response to pain or discomfort

• He couldn't help but <u>wince</u> when he stubbed his toe.

☐ **get very far** — to make significant progress or achieve success

• Without a clear plan, it's challenging to <u>get very far</u> in a project.

☐ **sinister** — **a** giving the impression that something harmful or evil is happening or will happen

• The <u>sinister</u> figure in the shadows raised suspicions among the townspeople.

Voca Master | 71

☐ **afoot**

a in progress or happening; afoot means something is being planned or undertaken

- There are rumors afoot about changes in the company's management.

☐ **attest to**

v to provide evidence or bear witness to the truth of something

- The numerous positive reviews attest to the quality of the product.

☐ **compromise**

v to undermine or harm the reputation, honor, or integrity of someone or something

- Engaging in unethical practices can compromise a company's credibility.

☐ **placate**

v to pacify or appease someone, especially by acceding to their demands

- The manager tried to placate the upset customer by offering a refund.

☐ **bear a resemblance to**

to have a notable similarity in appearance to someone else

- The two sisters bear a resemblance to each other, making it clear they are siblings.

☐ **chime**

n the sound produced by a bell or clock, especially a melody played on chimes

- As the clock struck midnight, the gentle chime echoed through the silent town.

☐ **glimmeringly**

ad in a faint or subtle manner

- In the early morning, the first light glimmeringly illuminated the horizon.

☐ **salute**

n a gesture or movement of the hand or another part of the body to express greeting, respect, or recognition

- The soldiers stood at attention and gave a crisp salute to their commanding officer.

a 21-gun salute   a traditional ceremonial act in which a military installation or personnel fire cannons or artillery as a sign of respect or honor

- The president received a formal welcome with a 21-gun salute during the state visit.

doozy   **n** something outstanding or remarkable; often used to describe a difficult or extraordinary situation

- The final exam was a real doozy, testing our knowledge on the entire semester's content.

white   **a** lacking color; pale or pallid

- After the shock, her face turned white as a sheet.

rim   **n** the outer edge or border of something, especially a circular object

- The silver bowl had an intricate pattern around the rim.

padlock   **n** a detachable lock with a hardened steel shackle, typically passed through an opening to prevent use, theft, vandalism, or harm

- He secured the gate with a sturdy padlock to ensure privacy.

weigh   **v** to measure the heaviness of something

- Before boarding the plane, passengers are required to weigh their luggage to comply with weight restrictions.

canvas bag   **n** a bag made of sturdy fabric material, typically used for carrying items like groceries or personal belongings

- She always brings a reusable canvas bag when shopping to reduce plastic waste.

bargain   **n** a negotiated agreement or deal, especially one that is advantageous

- The customer managed to strike a good bargain with the seller for the antique vase.

get away with — to successfully avoid punishment or negative consequences for an action

- He thought he could <u>get away with</u> cheating on the test, but the teacher caught him.

cheat on — to be unfaithful in a romantic relationship

- It is never acceptable to <u>cheat on</u> your partner; trust is crucial in a relationship.

blankly — **ad** in a manner showing no expression or understanding; with a vacant or empty look

- She stared <u>blankly</u> at the board, trying to comprehend the complex equation.

shallow — **a** having little depth; not deep

- The pond was <u>shallow</u>, making it safe for children to play near the edge.

be subjected to — to experience or undergo something unpleasant or challenging

- The new policy meant that employees would <u>be subjected to</u> additional training sessions.

quell — **v** to suppress or extinguish something, often related to disturbances, emotions, or uprisings

- The police worked to <u>quell</u> the protest and restore order in the city.

dissent — **n** the expression of opinions or beliefs that are contrary to the prevailing or official views

- In a democratic society, citizens have the right to express their <u>dissent</u> without fear of retribution.

attest to

v to provide evidence or bear witness to the truth or validity of something

- The numerous testimonials <u>attest to</u> the effectiveness of the new product.

syndicate

v to sell articles, photographs, or television programs to several newspapers or outlets

- The news agency decided to <u>syndicate</u> the investigative report to reach a wider audience.

unsettling

a causing mental disturbance, making someone feel uneasy, or disrupting peace

- The mysterious sound in the dark alley was quite <u>unsettling</u>, making everyone nervous.

disturbing

a causing disruption, discomfort, or a sense of unease

- The movie had a series of <u>disturbing</u> scenes that left a lasting impact on the audience.

clueless

a extremely ignorant or lacking knowledge; having no understanding

- She felt <u>clueless</u> about the advanced mathematical concepts discussed in the lecture.

comforting

a providing encouragement, boosting spirits, or offering solace

- His <u>comforting</u> words reassured her during a difficult time.

ignorant

a lacking knowledge, awareness, or education; uninformed

- It is crucial to educate people to prevent them from remaining <u>ignorant</u> about important issues.

☐ **reassuring**　　　**a** alleviating doubts or fears; providing comfort or confidence

- The doctor's <u>reassuring</u> words helped ease the patient's anxiety about the upcoming surgery.

☐ **naive**　　　**a** showing a lack of experience, sophistication, or worldliness

- His <u>naive</u> perspective on politics revealed his limited understanding of the complexities involved.

☐ **pleasing**　　　**a** enjoyable, likable, or creating a positive impression

- The garden had a <u>pleasing</u> arrangement of flowers and colors.

☐ **brainless**　　　**a** lacking intelligence or common sense; foolish

- Making such a <u>brainless</u> decision without considering the consequences led to disaster.

☐ **all-peen hammer**　　　**n** a hammer with a rounded head, used for shaping and bending metal

- The blacksmith used an <u>all-peen hammer</u> to craft intricate designs in the iron.

☐ **interrupt**　　　**v** to disturb or hinder a process, conversation, or activity

- Please do not <u>interrupt</u> the speaker while they are addressing the audience.

☐ **bulletin**　　　**n** ① an official announcement or statement
② a brief news report or update

- The company issued a <u>bulletin</u> regarding the changes in the upcoming schedule.

☐ **as to**　　　in regard to or concerning; about

- She provided clear instructions <u>as to</u> how the project should be completed.

speech impediment   **n** a condition that hinders a person's ability to speak clearly; a speech disorder

- Despite his <u>speech impediment</u>, he was an eloquent speaker and inspired many.

quell   **v** to suppress or pacify; to bring something under control

- The police worked quickly to <u>quell</u> the riot and restore order in the city.

crush   **v** to press or squeeze something forcefully, causing it to become deformed or broken

- The heavy machinery accidentally <u>crushed</u> the fragile boxes during the unloading process.

suppress   **v** to prevent the development or expression of something; to quash or extinguish

- The government sought to <u>suppress</u> dissenting voices by limiting freedom of speech.

hideous   **a** extremely unpleasant, shocking, or ugly

- The abandoned building had a <u>hideous</u> appearance, with broken windows and crumbling walls.

apologize   **v** to express regret, remorse, or saying sorry for an offense or mistake

- Realizing the error, she decided to <u>apologize</u> to her friend for the misunderstanding.

luminous   **a** emitting light, shining; (of a room, etc.) brightly lit; pertaining to the visual perception of brightness due to the stimulation of the sense of sight by radiant energy

- The <u>luminous</u> moon cast a soft glow over the landscape.

☐ **timeless**

a having no beginning or end; eternal; not restricted to a specific time; existing beyond or above time; not affected by the passage of time

- Classic works of literature often possess a <u>timeless</u> quality that resonates with readers across generations.

☐ **grackle**

n a type of blackbird known for its loud, harsh calls

- The garden was filled with the distinctive calls of the <u>grackles</u>.

☐ **squawk**

v to make a loud, harsh cry or noise, often resembling a bird's call

- The parrot would <u>squawk</u> loudly whenever someone approached its cage.

☐ **suspicion**

n a feeling or belief that someone is guilty of an offense or wrongdoing without specific evidence

- The detective had a <u>suspicion</u> that the witness was hiding something.

☐ **plot**

n a secret plan or scheme, especially one that involves a conspiracy or deceit

- The novel's intricate <u>plot</u> kept readers guessing until the very end.

☐ **overthrow**

v to overturn or defeat, especially in a physical or political sense; to remove from power

- The revolution aimed to <u>overthrow</u> the oppressive regime.

☐ **flash**

v to project or cast light; to appear suddenly and briefly

- The lightning would <u>flash</u> across the sky during the storm.

☐ **calibrate**

v to adjust or standardize (measuring instruments) to a specific scale; to correlate or match precisely

- It is essential to <u>calibrate</u> the equipment before conducting the experiment for accurate results.

☐ **flash**　　　　**v** to pass by quickly; to move swiftly and briefly

- The car would <u>flash</u> past, leaving a trail of dust behind.

☐ **Halloween and hardware**　　a phrase possibly indicating a combination of spooky costumes associated with Halloween and various tools or equipment

- The workshop was filled with an eerie combination of <u>Halloween and hardware</u> items.

☐ **whang**　　　　**v** to produce a loud, resonant sound; to strike forcefully

- The blacksmith would <u>whang</u> the metal with a hammer to shape it.

☐ **scrap metal**　　**n** discarded metal parts or pieces, often collected for recycling

- The junkyard was filled with piles of <u>scrap metal</u> waiting to be recycled.

☐ **hang (-hung-hung)**　　**v** to suspend or attach from above; past tense and past participle forms of the verb

- She decided to <u>hang</u> the painting on the living room wall.

☐ **issue**　　　　**v** to publish or release; to bring out into the open

- The magazine will <u>issue</u> a special edition to commemorate the anniversary.

☐ **junkyard**　　　**n** a place where old or discarded items, especially vehicles and machinery, are collected and stored

- The old car was taken to the <u>junkyard</u> after years of use.

☐ **snaggle-tooth**　　**n** a term describing someone with irregular or uneven teeth

- The cartoon character had a distinctive charm with its endearing <u>snaggle-tooth</u> smile.

reason with — to persuade or discuss with the goal of reaching a logical understanding

- She tried to reason with her friend, explaining the consequences of their actions.

shriek — **n** a sharp, loud cry or scream, often expressing fear, excitement, or pain

- A sudden shriek echoed through the haunted house, startling the visitors.

hinge — **n** a jointed or flexible device that connects two parts and allows them to swing or pivot

- The door swung open smoothly on its well-oiled hinges.

symmetry — **n** the quality of being made up of exactly similar parts facing each other or around an axis; balance or proportion

- The building's architectural design emphasized symmetry, with identical wings on either side.

neatness — **n** the quality of being tidy, orderly, and well-organized

- Her desk was a model of neatness, with everything in its proper place.

offset — **v** to counterbalance or compensate for something; to set off or balance by creating an equal force

- The increased cost of materials was offset by higher efficiency in production.

shave off — **v** to remove hair or a thin layer from the surface by cutting with a razor or sharp tool

- He decided to shave off his beard for a change in appearance.

consternation — **n** a sudden, alarming amazement or dread that results in confusion; dismay

- The unexpected announcement caused consternation among the employees.

☐ **in consternation** — in a state of confusion or dismay

- The sudden change in plans left them in consternation about what to do next.

☐ **throw a person into consternation** — to surprise or shock someone to the point of confusion or dismay

- The sudden appearance of the celebrity threw the crowd into consternation.

☐ **crashing** — a colliding or smashing forcefully

- The crashing waves against the rocks created a mesmerizing sound.

☐ **Many's the time (that) S V** — an expression indicating numerous occurrences of a particular situation

- Many's the time I've walked along this beach and enjoyed the sunset.

☐ **blast** — v ① to explode or blow up
② to criticize or denounce vehemently

- The construction crew had to blast through the rock to create a tunnel.

☐ **breathing** — a ① actively inhaling and exhaling air
② having the appearance of being alive

- The breathing exercises helped him relax and focus.

☐ **clanking** — a making a loud, metallic noise, often repetitive

- The old machinery in the factory could be heard clanking throughout the building.

☐ **clownish** — a resembling or characteristic of a clown; awkward or humorous in a clumsy way

- His clownish antics brought laughter to the audience.

☐ **knob**	**n** a rounded handle or projection, often used for opening a door or drawer
	• She turned the <u>knob</u> and opened the door to the attic.
☐ **uprooted**	**a** having had the roots pulled out of the ground, often referring to plants or trees
	• The storm <u>uprooted</u> several trees in the neighborhood.
☐ **cower**	**v** to crouch or shrink away in fear or timidity
	• The frightened dog would <u>cower</u> in the corner during thunderstorms.
☐ **stamp**	**v** to step forcefully or heavily on a surface
	• He tried to <u>stamp</u> out the embers of the campfire.
☐ **bellow**	**v** to shout loudly, often in a deep or resonant voice
	• The angry bull would <u>bellow</u> as it charged towards the intruders.
☐ **hobble**	**v** to walk unsteadily or with difficulty, often due to injury or physical limitation
	• After the accident, he had to <u>hobble</u> around on crutches for several weeks.
☐ **sicken**	**v** ① To cause nausea or disgust in someone ② To become physically or emotionally affected by illness or distress
	• The gruesome scene in the horror movie made some viewers <u>sicken</u>.
	• The constant exposure to pollution could <u>sicken</u> the residents of the area.

☐ **trap**

n / **v** ① A device, often consisting of a leather strap, used for catching or restraining animals ② To catch or ensnare someone or something

- The hunter set up a snare, a simple type of <u>trap</u>, to catch wild game.
- The spider deftly spun its web, hoping to <u>trap</u> unsuspecting insects.

☐ **harness**

n / **v** ① Equipment or gear used for a specific purpose, often associated with work or transportation ② To utilize or control a source of power for a specific purpose

- The farmer used a horse and <u>harness</u> to plow the fields.
- Engineers strive to <u>harness</u> renewable energy to meet growing demands.

☐ **scrap-iron**

n Pieces of iron or metal that are discarded, often considered as junk or waste

- The blacksmith collected various bits of <u>scrap-iron</u> to forge into new tools.

☐ **crash**

v ① To collapse or break with a loud, resounding noise ② An instance of violent collision or impact

- The old building began to <u>crash</u> to the ground as the demolition crew worked.
- The car accident resulted in a loud <u>crash</u>.

☐ **padlock**

n A sturdy lock that consists of a detachable U-shaped bar hinged at one end, which is passed through the staple of a hasp or a link in a chain

- He secured the shed with a heavy-duty <u>padlock</u>.

UNIT

2

secure [v] ① To fasten or lock something tightly to prevent movement or access ② To obtain or achieve something with certainty or confidence

- Before leaving, she made sure to secure all the windows and doors.
- The team worked hard to secure a victory in the championship game.

snap [v] ① To make a sudden, sharp sound ② To close or fasten with a quick, sharp motion

- The twig snapped as he walked through the forest.
- She snapped her briefcase shut and headed for the door.

celery [n] A type of vegetable with crisp, pale green stalks and leaves, commonly used in salads or as a snack

- A refreshing celery stick can be a healthy and crunchy snack.

smash [v] ① To break or shatter into pieces forcefully ② To hit or collide with great force

- He accidentally dropped the glass, causing it to smash on the floor.
- The two cars smashed into each other at the intersection.

fling [v] ① To throw or hurl something with force ② To move oneself forcefully or recklessly

- In a fit of anger, she flung the book across the room.
- He flung open the door and stormed out of the room.

awe [n] A feeling of reverential respect mixed with fear or wonder

- The majestic mountain peaks inspired a sense of awe in the hikers.

cowering Bending or huddling down in fear or timidity

- The small animal was cowering in the corner, frightened by the loud noise.

willow

n A type of deciduous tree or shrub with narrow leaves and flexible branches

- The gentle swaying of the weeping <u>willow</u> branches created a serene atmosphere.

snap off

v To break off abruptly or with a quick, sharp motion

- He accidentally <u>snapped off</u> the end of the pencil while deep in thought.

delicacy

n The quality of being delicate, intricate, or refined

- The <u>delicacy</u> of the artwork's details impressed the art critics.

last of all

Finally, after everything else

- After a long day of meetings and errands, he saved the best task for <u>last of all</u>.

blinding

a Overwhelmingly bright or intense, causing temporary blindness or extreme discomfort

- The <u>blinding</u> sunshine made it difficult to see without sunglasses.

scramble

v To move or climb quickly and with difficulty, often in a disorderly or hurried manner

- Hikers had to <u>scramble</u> up the rocky terrain to reach the mountain's summit.

strip A of B

To remove or deprive something or someone (A) of a particular attribute or possession (B)

- The storm <u>stripped</u> the trees <u>of</u> their leaves, leaving them bare.

barons and dukes and earls

Members of the nobility or aristocracy, including barons, dukes, and earls

- The grand ballroom was filled with nobility, from <u>barons and dukes</u> to <u>earls</u>, all dressed in their finest attire.

☐ snatch

v To grab or seize something quickly and forcefully

- She snatched the document from his hand before he could react.

☐ slam

v To close or put down with force, producing a loud noise

- Frustrated, he slammed the door shut behind him.

☐ gravely

ad In a serious or solemn manner

- The doctor gravely delivered the news to the patient.

☐ synchronize A with B

To coordinate or align the timing of A with B, ensuring they occur simultaneously

- The dancers practiced to synchronize their movements with the music.

☐ shift

v To move or transfer from one place or position to another

- The workers had to shift heavy boxes to the storage area.

☐ explosion

n A sudden release of energy, resulting in a violent burst

- The loud explosion shook the entire building.

☐ reel

v To stagger or move unsteadily, often as a result of dizziness or disorientation

- After the intense spinning, she felt as if the room were reeling.

☐ whirl

v To spin or rotate rapidly

- The leaves were caught in a gust of wind and began to whirl around.

☐ swivel

v To turn or pivot around a point, typically horizontally

- The chair was designed to swivel 360 degrees for added flexibility.

flounce   **v** To move with exaggerated or bouncy motions, often with an air of annoyance or impatience

- She <u>flounced</u> out of the room after the argument.

caper   **v** To skip or dance playfully

- The children laughed and <u>capered</u> around the meadow.

gambol   **v** To frolic or playfully run and jump

- Lambs are known to <u>gambol</u> in the field during spring.

spin   **v** To rotate rapidly around an axis

- The figure skater began to <u>spin</u> gracefully on the ice.

neutralize   **v** To counteract or make ineffective

- The antidote was administered to <u>neutralize</u> the effects of the poison.

pure   **a** Free from contamination or impurities; untainted

- The mountain spring provided <u>pure</u> and refreshing water.

suspended   **a** Hanging or dangling in a way that is temporarily attached or unsupported

- The chandelier was <u>suspended</u> from the ceiling.

blackout   **n** A sudden loss of electric power resulting in darkness

- The storm caused a complete <u>blackout</u> in the city.

wince   **v** To flinch or show a slight involuntary reaction, often due to pain or discomfort

- She <u>winced</u> as the doctor administered the injection.

rivet   **v** To fasten or fix firmly in place with rivets or similar devices

- The metal plates were <u>riveted</u> together to create a sturdy structure.

Text Reading

: Harrison Bergeron

〈인물도〉

Diana Moon Glampers

* representing the oppressive government and enforcing its handicapping policies

George Bergeron

* Harrison's father and Hazel's husband
* very smart and sensitive
→ handicapped artificially by the government

Harrison Bergeron

* Fourteen years old
* seven feet tall
* most advanced model

Hazel Bergeron

* Harrison's mother and George's wife
* described as perfectly average intelligence

The Ballerina

* a beautiful dancer who was burdened with an especially ugly mask and excessive weights

* **Harrison Bergeron** is a genius who is also absurdly strong, a dancer who can also break out of prison, and a self-proclaimed emperor. Harrison's assassination on live television means that the last, best hope of Americans has failed and there is no longer any chance of escaping the laws of equality. To counteract his physical strength, George Bergeron must wear weights around his neck. George, an intelligent man, must also wear a radio that prohibits him from thinking deeply.

* **The Handicapper General**'s agents enforce the equality laws, forcing citizens to wear "handicaps": masks for those who are too beautiful, loud radios that disrupt thoughts inside the ears of intelligent people, and heavy weights for the strong or athletic.

The year was 2081, and everybody was finally equal. They weren't only equal before God and the law. They were equal every which way. Nobody was smarter than anybody else.

Nobody was better looking than anybody else. Nobody was stronger or quicker than anybody else. All this equality was due to the 211th, 212th, and 213th Amendments to the Constitution, and to the unceasing vigilance of agents of the United States Handicapper General.

Some things about living still weren't quite right, though. April, for instance, still drove people crazy by not being springtime. And it was in that clammy month that the H-G men took George and Hazel Bergeron's fourteen-year-old son, Harrison, away.

It was tragic, all right, but George and Hazel couldn't think about it very hard. Hazel had a perfectly average intelligence, which meant she couldn't think about anything except in short bursts. And George, while his intelligence was way above normal, had a little mental handicap radio in his ear. He was required by law to wear it at all times. It was tuned to a government transmitter. Every twenty seconds or so, the transmitter would send out some sharp noise to keep people like George from taking unfair advantage of their brains.

George and Hazel were watching television. There were tears on Hazel's cheeks, but she'd forgotten for the moment what they were about.

Quick Quiz

[1-3] 본문의 내용에 비추어 다음 빈칸에 들어갈 가장 적절한 표현을 본문에서 찾아 문장 내 빈칸의 자리에 맞게 써넣으시오.

1   By official edict of the United States Handicapper General, under the authority of the 211th, 212th and 213th amendments to the U.S. Constitution, Harrison must be h_____ to bring him on par with the rest of society.

2 Through this handicapping system, the government attempts to distress each citizen as necessary to achieve unmitigated s_____ e_____, normalizing everyone to the lowest commoner.

» unmitigated 누그러지지 않은, 경감되지 않은; 순전한, 완전한 commoner 일반인

3 The handicapper general (HG) of the United States is in charge of dumbing down and disabling those who are a_____ a_____.

 어구 및 표현 연구 핵심 PLUS!

1 All this equality was <u>due to</u> the 211th, 212th, and 213th <u>Amendments to the Constitution</u>

- due to: ~ 때문에
- Amendments to the Constitution: 헌법 수정안

2 Nobody was smarter than anybody else.

- 평등을 추구하기 위해 모두가 바보가 되는 것과 같은 모순적 논리.

3 And **it** was in that clammy month **that** the H-G men took George and Hazel Bergeron's fourteen-year-old son, Harrison, away.

- It ~ that 강조구문

4 And George, while his <u>intelligence was way above normal</u>, had a little mental handicap radio in his ear. He was required by law to wear it at all times.

- handicap radio를 쓰게 하는 목적: to make George "equal" to the rest
- 1번 문장에서 언급한 "평등"의 모순을 드러내는 문장.

[4-5] 다음은 본문에 대한 분석이다. 물음에 답하시오.

> In the opening of the story, Vonnegut presents an idealistic reality in which all citizens are equal. This might seem fantastic, but there's a hint that something sinister is Ⓐafoot: the mention of handicapping, coupled with the word "vigilance" and the focus on government interference makes this world seem, perhaps, (A)_____.
> Harrison's imprisonment, alongside George's diligent use of state-issued handicaps, Ⓑattest to the authoritarian nature of the government. Meanwhile, the Ⓒcompromised state of George's strength and cognition reveals the price of equality in Vonnegut's dystopia. It's worth noting, too, that George and Hazel are introduced in the context of media Ⓓdistracting them from the loss of their son. They watch TV together, and George's thoughts are interrupted by a radio. Media, then, is shown to be a major way of Ⓔplacating them.

4 본문의 빈칸 (A)에 들어갈 단어로 가장 적절한 것은?

① authoritarian   ② utopian
③ democratic   ④ harmonious
⑤ chaotic

5 밑줄 친 Ⓐ~Ⓔ를 바꾸어 쓰기에 문맥적으로 <u>어색한</u> 것은?

① Ⓐ afoot: in progress
② Ⓑ attest to: confirm
③ Ⓒ compromised: intact
④ Ⓓ distracting: diverting
⑤ Ⓔ placating: appeasing

George and Hazel were watching television. There were tears on Hazel's cheeks, but she'd forgotten for the moment what they were about.

On the television screen were ballerinas.

A buzzer sounded in George's head. His thoughts fled in panic, like bandits from a burglar alarm.

"That was a real pretty dance, that dance they just did," said Hazel.

"Huh" said George.

"That dance—it was nice," said Hazel.

"Yup," said George. He tried to think a little about the ballerinas. They weren't really very good—no better than anybody else would have been, anyway. They were burdened with sashweights and bags of birdshot, and their faces were masked, so that no one, seeing a free and graceful gesture or a pretty face, would fccl like something the cat drug in.

George was toying with the vague notion that maybe dancers shouldn't be handicapped.

But he didn't get very far with it before another noise in his ear radio scattered his thoughts.

George winced. So did two out of the eight ballerinas.

어구 및 표현 연구

핵심 PLUS!

1 There were tears on Hazel's cheeks, but she'd forgotten (for the moment) <u>what they were about.</u>

• 의문사 what이 이끄는 명사절

2 His thoughts fled in panic, **like** bandits from a burglar alarm.

• The literary device found in the sentence "His thoughts fled in panic, like bandits from a burglar alarm" is **a simile**. The author is using "like" to create a vivid comparison between the thoughts fleeing in panic and bandits fleeing from a burglar alarm.

3 They(the ballerinas) weren't really very good—<u>no better than</u> anybody else would have been, anyway.

• no better than: ~보다 나을 것이 없는
no better than anybody else would have been, anyway: 어쨌든 다른 누구보다 나을 것도 없는

4 They <u>were burdened with</u> sashweights and bags of birdshot, and their faces <u>were masked</u>, **so that** no one, (<u>seeing a free and graceful gesture or a pretty face</u>), would feel like something the cat drug in.

- 수동표현 be burdened (with), be masked
- 결과/목적의 부사절 so that (so that S V: S V ~ 하도록)
- 부사구문 seeing a free and graceful gesture or a pretty face (= when **he or she saw** a free and graceful gesture or a pretty face)

UNIT

2

5 George was toying with the vague notion **that** maybe dancers shouldn't be handicapped. But he didn't <u>get</u> very <u>far</u> with it before another noise in his ear radio scattered his thoughts.

- 동격의 that
- get far는 여기서 "(사태가) 발전하다"의 의미로 쓰이고 있음.

6 George winced. <u>So did two out of the eight ballerinas</u>.

- 귀에 들리는 handicaps로 인해 조지가 주춤한 것과 같이 8명의 발레리나 중 2명이 그랬다는 것은 조지와 같이 "think hard"하는 above average의 지능을 가진 사람들이란 의미임.

 Quick Quiz

[6-7] 본문에서 발췌한 문장을 통해서 추론할 수 있는 내용을 작성하려고 한다. 빈칸에 들어갈 단어를 적으시오. (단, 제시된 철자로 시작하는 단어를 쓰시오)

6 "George was toying with the vague notion that maybe dancers shouldn't be handicapped."

> The sentence implies the great i_____ of George, but the fact that he's got the "brain" is at odds with the law that everyone should be "e_____."

7 "George winced. So did two out of the eight ballerinas."

> The fact that 2 out of 8 ballerinas winced just as George did imply that these two had the same or similar thoughts as George. This also indicates that they are i_____.

Hazel saw him wince. Having no mental handicap herself, she had to ask George what the latest sound had been.

"Sounded like somebody hitting a milk bottle with a ball peen hammer," said George.

"I'd think it would be real interesting, hearing all the different sounds," said Hazel a little envious. "All the things they think up."

"Um," said George.

"Only, if I was Handicapper General, you know what I would do?" said Hazel. Hazel, as a matter of fact, bore a strong resemblance to the Handicapper General, a woman named Diana Moon Glampers. "If I was Diana Moon Glampers," said Hazel, "I'd have chimes on Sunday—just chimes. Kind of in honor of religion."

"I could think, if it was just chimes," said George.

"Well—maybe make 'em real loud," said Hazel. "I think I'd make a good Handicapper General."

"Good as anybody else," said George.

"Who knows better than I do what normal is?" said Hazel.

"Right," said George. He began to think glimmeringly about his abnormal son who was now in jail, about Harrison, but a twenty-one-gun salute in his head stopped that.

"Boy!" said Hazel, "that was a doozy, wasn't it?"

It was such a doozy that George was white and trembling, and tears stood on the rims of his red eyes. Two of the eight ballerinas had collapsed to the studio floor, were holding their temples.

그림 김민영

핵심 PLUS!

1 <u>Having no mental handicap herself</u>, she had to ask George what the latest sound had been.

- 분사구문 Having no mental handicap herself (= Since she had no mental handicap herself)

2 "(It) Sounded like somebody hitting a milk bottle with a ball peen hammer," said George.

- 문장의 주어인 It이 생략된 형태 (It = the latest sound)
- 직유법(simile)을 활용한 비유

3 Hazel, as a matter of fact, <u>bore</u> a strong <u>resemblance to</u> the Handicapper General, a woman named Diana Moon Glampers.

- bear resemblance to: ~을 닮다
- 동격의 코마

4 "**If** I **was** Diana Moon Glampers," said Hazel, "I'**d** have chimes on Sunday—just chimes. Kind of in honor of religion."

- 가정법 과거로 was → were로 고치는 것이 문법적으론 옳은 표현임.

5 "Who knows better than I do <u>what normal is</u>?" said Hazel.

- 간접의문문의 어순: 의문사 + 주어 + 동사

6 He began to think glimmeringly about his abnormal son (**who** was now in jail), about Harrison, but a twenty-one-gun salute in his head stopped <u>that</u>.

- 코마를 중심으로 전치사구의 병치
- who가 이끄는 주격 관계대명사절
- that = the act of thinking or contemplating about his abnormal son, Harrison, who is now in jail

8 아래 본문에 대한 분석이다. 빈칸에 들어갈 단어로 가장 적절한 것은?

> Hazel saw him wince. Having no mental handicap herself, she had to ask George what the latest sound had been.
>
> "Sounded like somebody hitting a milk bottle with a ball peen hammer," said George.
>
> "I'd think it would be real interesting, hearing all the different sounds," said Hazel a little envious. "All the things they think up."
>
> "Um," said George.

Hazel, "a little envious," says she thinks hearing the sounds in his ear radio would be "real interesting." No laws or handicaps can eliminate envy, which Vonnegut associates with _____ impulses given the reaction of George.

① instinctual   ② benevolent
③ altruistic   ④ sadistic
⑤ harmonious

9 본문의 내용에 비추어 빈칸에 들어갈 표현을 적으시오.

> Harrison Bergeron is a story set in the future where the government has tried to create the "truest form of e_____" among men and women, by creating h_____ for those who weren't already or who were born naturally "talented, gifted" in some way (inclusive of physical attractiveness), and those who were considered "o_____" or already handicapped by society's measures were left alone. It was all done to try to put everyone on being e_____. No one was allowed to be "better than" anyone else in any way. People who were "e_____" in some way were then forced to suppress whatever it was about them that made them e_____.

10 아래 본문의 발췌본을 바탕으로 작성한 비평이다. 빈칸에 들어갈 단어로 가장 적절한 것은?

> "Well–maybe make 'em real loud," said Hazel. "I think I'd make a good Handicapper General."
> "Good as anybody else," said George.
> "Who knows better than I do what normal is?" said Hazel.

Hazel's similarity to Diana Moon Glampers is _____ because it means that the country is being run by people just as _____ as Hazel.

① unsettling – conscious ② disturbing – clueless
③ comforting – ignorant ④ reassuring – naive
⑤ pleasing – brainless

그림 김민영

"All of a sudden you look so tired," said Hazel. "Why don't you stretch out on the sofa, so you can rest your handicap bag on the pillows, honeybunch." She was referring to the forty-seven pounds of birdshot in a canvas bag, which was padlocked around George's neck. "Go on and rest the bag for a little while," she said. "I don't care if you're not equal to me for a while."

George weighed the bag with his hands. "I don't mind it," he said. "I don't notice it any more. It's just a part of me."

그림 김민영

[11-12] 다음 본문을 읽고, 물음에 답하시오.

> "All of a sudden you look so tired," said Hazel. "Why don't you stretch out on the sofa, so you can rest your handicap bag on the pillows, honeybunch." She was referring to <u>the forty-seven pounds of birdshot in a canvas bag</u>, which was padlocked around George's neck. "Go on and rest the bag for a little while," she said. "I don't care if you're not equal to me for a while."
>
> George weighed the bag with his hands. "I don't mind it," he said. "I don't notice it any more. It's just a part of me."

11 다음은 위 본문에 대한 분석이다. 단어의 쓰임이 <u>어색한</u> 것은?

In "Harrison Bergeron," the ①<u>irony</u> of Hazel's statement that she does not mind George not being equal to her for a while is that their society has made it ②<u>pitiable</u> for someone to have any ③<u>inferior</u> abilities. Hazel, who is very low in intelligence as well as lacking any other gifts, feels sorry for George because his handicaps make him ④<u>uncomfortable</u>. This demonstrates that the two of them are not equal and suggests that absolute equality is ⑤<u>impossible</u>.

12 다음은 본문의 밑줄 친 "<u>the forty-seven pounds of birdshot in a canvas bag</u>" 에 대한 분석이다. 문맥상 빈칸에 들어갈 단어로 가장 적절한 것은?

While he is not being literally shot for his strength, he wears a reminder of _____ in his handicap: "forty-seven pounds of birdshot in a canvas bag, which was padlocked around George's neck."

① prosperity　　　　　② superiority
③ prowess　　　　　　④ violence
⑤ ineptitude

"You been so tired lately—kind of wore out," said Hazel. "If there was just some way we could make a little hole in the bottom of the bag, and just take out a few of them lead balls. Just a few."

"Two years in prison and two thousand dollars fine for every ball I took out," said George.

"I don't call that a bargain."

"If you could just take a few out when you came home from work," said Hazel. "I mean—you don't compete with anybody around here. You just sit around."

"If I tried to get away with it," said George, "then other people'd get away with it—and pretty soon we'd be right back to the dark ages again, with everybody competing against everybody else. You wouldn't like that, would you?"

"I'd hate it," said Hazel.

"There you are," said George. "The minute people start cheating on laws, what do you think happens to society?"

If Hazel hadn't been able to come up with an answer to this question, George couldn't have supplied one. A siren was going off in his head.

"Reckon it'd fall all apart," said Hazel.

"What would?" said George blankly.

"Society," said Hazel uncertainly. "Wasn't that what you just said?"

"Who knows?" said George.

 어구 및 표현 연구

 핵심 PLUS!

1 "Two years in prison and two thousand dollars fine for every ball I took out," said George.

- 문장 앞에 There would be가 생략된 가정의 상황.

  → **There would be** two years in prison and two thousand dollars fine for every ball I took out,

2 "**If** you **could** just take a few out when you came home from work," said Hazel.

- 가정법 과거

3 "If I <u>tried</u> to get away with it," said George, "then other people'**d** get away with it—and pretty soon we'**d** be right back to the dark ages again, (<u>with</u> everybody <u>competing</u> against everybody else).

- 가정법 과거
- [with + N + v-ing]의 부대구문

4 "(<u>The minute</u> people start cheating on laws), what do you think happens to society?"

- 부사절 접속사 the minute (The minute S V, S V: ~하자마자)

5 <u>If</u> Hazel <u>hadn't been</u> able to come up with an answer to this question, George <u>couldn't have supplied</u> one.

- 가정법 과거완료

Quick Quiz

13 Which statement best explains how <u>irony</u> is used in the passage?

"If you could just take a few out when you came home from work," said Hazel. "I mean–you don't compete with anybody around here. You just sit around."

"If tried to get away with it," said George, "then other people'd get away with it– and pretty soon we'd be right back to the dark ages again, with everybody competing against everybody else. You wouldn't like that, would you?"

① George is unable to use his reasoning skills because the government handicapped him.

② George, who has a superior intelligence prefers a society with limits rather than one that allows him to compete.

③ George refers to the year 2081 as the dark ages because people are unable to use their talents.

④ Hazel tries to persuade her husband to break a strictly enforced law.

⑤ George thinks of going back to the dark ages as a way to improve the society.

14 다음은 George와 Hazel 간의 대화를 분석한 내용이다. 밑줄 친 단어의 쓰임이 어색한 것은?

"There you are," said George. "The minute people start cheating on laws, what do you think happens to society?"

If Hazel hadn't been able to come up with an answer to this question, George couldn't have supplied one. A siren was going off in his head.

"Reckon it'd fall all apart," said Hazel.

"What would?" said George blankly.

"Society," said Hazel uncertainly. "Wasn't that what you just said?"

"Who knows?" said George.

Because he is smart, George is able to formulate an idea that society would disintegrate if people ①disregarded the laws and to pose that idea as a ②hypothetical question. But because his thinking is interrupted by one of the innumerable noises the government broadcasts over his radio, he ③loses track of the conversation completely. Even though Hazel is able to follow his reasoning, he can't remember what he was talking about moments before, and she isn't bright enough to get him back on track. If George were able to think in peace for a few hours, he might come to believe that the laws he defends are ④absurd. However, these laws, which he would likely ⑤ comply with if he could, are the ones that prevent him from thinking for more than a few seconds at a stretch.

» in peace 편안히, 안심하여

[15-16] Read the passage below and answer each question.

"You been so tired lately—kind of wore out," said Hazel. "If there was just some way we could make a little hole in the bottom of the bag, and just take out a few of them lead balls. Just a few."

"Two years in prison and two thousand dollars fine for every ball I took out," said George.

"I don't call that a bargain."

"If you could just take a few out when you came home from work," said Hazel. "I mean—you don't compete with anybody around here. You just sit around."

"All of a sudden you look so tired," said Hazel. "Why don't you stretch out on the sofa, so you can rest your handicap bag on the pillows, honeybunch." She was referring to the forty-seven pounds of birdshot in a canvas bag, which was padlocked around George's neck. "Go on and rest the bag for a little while," she said. "I don't care if you're not equal to me for a while."

George weighed the bag with his hands. "I don't mind it," he said. "I don't notice it any more. It's just a part of me."

15 Choose one that is not a proper understanding about George.

① George is described as not rebel.

② George seems to believe in obeying the law.

③ George doesn't want to get into trouble by breaking the law.

④ George seems to be a "good" citizen by doing his duty by standing the burden of wearing his handicaps.

⑤ George is not smart enough to notice the burden of handicap bags weighing him down.

» stand the burden of ~의 짐을 견디다

16 본문을 통해 파악할 수 있는 Hazel의 성품을 적으려고 한다. 빈칸에 들어갈 단어를 적으시오.

She is a well-intentioned character, a loving wife and mother, who tries to c_____ her husband by suggesting he r_____ his handicap weights.

» well-intentioned (결과는 여하간에) 선의의, 선의에서 나온, 선의로 행한

The television program was suddenly interrupted for a news bulletin. It wasn't clear at first as to what the bulletin was about, since the announcer, like all announcers, had a serious speech impediment. For about half a minute, and in a state of high excitement, the announcer tried to say, "Ladies and Gentlemen—" He finally gave up, handed the bulletin to a ballerina to read.

"That's all right—" Hazel said of the announcer, "he tried. That's the big thing. He tried to do the best he could with what God gave him. He should get a nice raise for trying so hard."

어구 및 표현 연구

 핵심 PLUS!

1 The television program <u>was</u> suddenly <u>interrupted</u> for a news bulletin.

- 수동태 파악: be interrupted

2 It wasn't clear at first <u>as to</u> (<u>what</u> the bulletin was about), (since the announcer, like all announcers, had a serious speech impediment).

- as to = about
- 의문사 what이 이끄는 명사절

3 He tried to do the best he could with (**what** God gave him).

- 관계대명사 what이 이끄는 명사절로 2번의 의문사 what이 이끄는 명사절과 구별할 것.

Quick Quiz

17 밑줄 친 내용에 주목하면서 추론한 내용이다. 빈칸에 들어갈 단어를 써넣으시오.

> The television program was suddenly interrupted for a news bulletin. It wasn't clear at first as to what the bulletin was about, since the announcer, like all announcers, had a serious speech impediment. For about half a minute, and in a state of high excitement, the announcer tried to say, "Ladies and Gentlemen—" He finally gave up, handed the bulletin to a ballerina to read.
>
> "That's all right—" Hazel said of the announcer, "he tried. That's the big thing. He tried to do the best he could with what God gave him. <u>He should get a nice raise for trying so hard.</u>"

> The announcer is not performing his role properly. But, in Hazel's words, who argue that they should rather get a raise for "not standing out", the government tries every possible way to _____ whatever it is about them that makes them _____.

① quell – inferior
② crush – ordinary
③ suppress – exceptional
④ support – special
⑤ encourage – remarkable

"Ladies and Gentlemen—," said the ballerina, reading the bulletin. She must have been extraordinarily beautiful, because the mask she wore was hideous. And it was easy to see that she was the strongest and most graceful of all the dancers, for her handicap bags were as big as those worn by two-hundred pound men.

And she had to apologize at once for her voice, which was a very unfair voice for a woman to use. Her voice was a warm, luminous, timeless melody. "Excuse me—" she said, and she began again, making her voice absolutely uncompetitive.

"Harrison Bergeron, age fourteen," she said in a grackle squawk, "has just escaped from jail, where he was held on suspicion of plotting to overthrow the government. He is a genius and an athlete, is under-handicapped, and should be regarded as extremely dangerous."

A police photograph of Harrison Bergeron was flashed on the screen—upside down, then sideways, upside down again, then right side up. The picture showed the full length of Harrison against a background calibrated in feet and inches. He was exactly seven feet tall.

 핵심 PLUS!

1 "Ladies and Gentlemen—," said the ballerina, **reading** the bulletin.

- 분사구문: as she was reading ~

2 She **must have been** extraordinarily beautiful, because S[the mask (**that**) she wore] was hideous.

- must have p.p: ~임에 틀림이 없었다
- 목적격 관계대명사 생략: the mask (**that** 또는 **which**) she wore

3 And **it** was easy **to see** that she was the strongest and most graceful of all the dancers, **for** her handicap bags were as big as **those** (**worn** by two-hundred pound men).

- 가주어 it – 진주어 to V
- "왜냐하면"의 해석인 등위접속사 for
- those = handicap bags
- those를 뒤에서 수식하는 과거분사 worn의 형용사구

4 And she had to **apologize** (at once) **for** her voice, **which** was a very unfair voice [(for a woman) **to use**].

- apologize for: ~때문에 용서를 구하다
- 계속적 용법의 관계대명사 which (선행사는 her voice)
- to부정사의 형용사 용법 및 의미상의 주어

5 "Harrison Bergeron, age fourteen," she said in a grackle squawk, "has just escaped from jail, (**where** he was held **on suspicion of** plotting to overthrow the government).

- 장소관계부사 where
- 전치사구 on suspicion of: ~한 혐의로

6 The picture showed the full **length** (of Harrison against a background) **calibrated** in feet and inches.

- 과거분사 calibrated가 length를 수식.

UNIT
2

18 밑줄 내용을 통해서 파악할 수 있는 내용을 작성하려고 한다. 빈칸에 들어갈 단어로 적절한 것은?

> "Ladies and Gentlemen—," said the ballerina, reading the bulletin. She must have been extraordinarily beautiful, because the mask she wore was hideous. And it was easy to see that she was the strongest and most graceful of all the dancers, for her handicap bags were as big as those worn by two-hundred pound men.
> And she had to apologize at once for her voice, which was a very unfair voice for a woman to use. Her voice was a warm, luminous, timeless melody. "Excuse me—" she said, and she began again, making her voice absolutely uncompetitive.

▼

> The act of apologizing by the ballerina represent the _____ of controlling the society by forcing everyone to be _____.

① zeal – ill-mannered
② compliance – uncivil
③ negativities – equal
④ antagonism – polite
⑤ suspicion – impolite

19 글 전체의 내용으로 볼 때 빈칸에 들어갈 단어를 써넣으시오.

> "Harrison Bergeron, age fourteen," she said in a grackle squawk, "has just escaped from jail, where he was held on suspicion of plotting to overthrow the government. He is a genius and an athlete, is under-handicapped, and should be regarded as extremely _____."

20 What literary device is found from the underlined sentence in the following?

And she had to apologize at once for her voice, which was a very unfair voice for a woman to use. Her voice was a warm, luminous, timeless melody. "Excuse me—" she said, and she began again, making her voice absolutely uncompetitive.

① simile
② metaphor
③ personification
④ hyperbole
⑤ alliteration

21 아래 지문의 ㉠과 ㉡을 통해서 the ballerina의 외적 모습을 파악하고, ㉢의 내용을 통해 추론할 수 내용을 우리말로 적으시오.

> "Ladies and Gentlemen—," said the ballerina, reading the bulletin. She must have been extraordinarily beautiful, because ㉠the mask she wore was hideous. And it was easy to see that she was the strongest and most graceful of all the dancers, for ㉡her handicap bags were as big as those worn by two-hundred pound men.
> And she had to apologize at once for her voice, which was a very unfair voice for a woman to use. ㉢Her voice was a warm, luminous, timeless melody. "Excuse me—" she said, and she began again, making her voice absolutely uncompetitive.
> "Harrison Bergeron, age fourteen," she said in a grackle squawk, "has just escaped from jail, where he was held on suspicion of plotting to overthrow the government. He is a genius and an athlete, is under-handicapped, and should be regarded as extremely dangerous."
> A police photograph of Harrison Bergeron was flashed on the screen—upside down, then sideways, upside down again, then right side up. The picture showed the full length of Harrison against a background calibrated in feet and inches. He was exactly seven feet tall.

추론: _____

_____

The rest of Harrison's appearance was Halloween and hardware. Nobody had ever born heavier handicaps. He had outgrown hindrances faster than the H-G men could think them up. Instead of a little ear radio for a mental handicap, he wore a tremendous pair of earphones, and spectacles with thick wavy lenses. The spectacles were intended to make him not only half blind, but to give him whanging headaches besides.

Scrap metal was hung all over him. Ordinarily, there was a certain symmetry, a military neatness to the handicaps issued to strong people, but Harrison looked like a walking junkyard. In the race of life, Harrison carried three hundred pounds. And to offset his good looks, the H-G men required that he wear at all times a red rubber ball for a nose, keep his eyebrows shaved off, and cover his even white teeth with black caps at snaggle-tooth random.

"If you see this boy," said the ballerina, "do not—I repeat, do not—try to reason with him."

그림 김민영

1 <u>No</u>body had ever born heavi<u>er</u> handicaps.

- born은 bear의 과거분사로 "지니다, 가지고 있다"의 뜻과 "지탱하다, 견디다"의 뜻으로 해석이 모두 가능하다. 부정어 주어와 함께 비교급이 활용된 최상급 문장이다.

2 He had outgrown hindrances fast<u>er</u> <u>than</u> the H-G men could think them up.

- hindrance는 "방해, 장애"라는 추상명사이지만, 셀 수 있는 보통명사화 되어 "장애물, 방해물" 같이 해석한다. think up은 "~을 생각해 내다"는 뜻의 이어동사로 대명사가 두 단어 사이에 위치한다.

3 (Instead of a little ear radio / for a mental handicap), he <u>wore</u> a tremendous pair of earphones, and spectacles with thick wavy lenses.

- 여기서 little은 "작은"이라는 뜻의 형용사로 쓰이고 있음.
- wear의 공통 목적어의 병치

4 The spectacles <u>were intended to</u> make him <u>not only</u> half blind, <u>but</u> (also intended) to give him whanging headaches <u>besides</u>.

- be intended to + 동사원형: ~할 의도다
- not only A but also B 구문에서 also intended가 생략된 형태
- besides는 as well과 같은 의미의 부사로 쓰이고 있음.

5 Ordinarily, there was a certain symmetry, a military neatness to the handicaps (issued to strong people), but Harrison looked like a walking junkyard.

- 동격의 코마(,): a certain symmetry에 대한 부연진술
- issued가 이끄는 과거분사구는 앞의 handicaps를 수식하는 형용사구

6 And (to offset his good looks), the H-G men **required** that he (should) wear at all times a red rubber ball for a nose, keep his eyebrows shaved off, and cover his even white teeth with black caps at snaggle-tooth random.

- 제안(suggest), 요구(demand), 명령(order), 주장(insist), 충고(advise) 등의 동사 뒤 that절 내 should가 생략됨.
- 생략된 should에 걸리는 wear ~, keep ~, and cover의 서술부 병치

22 How does the author use a description of technology to create satire in this passage?

> The rest of Harrison's appearance was Halloween and hardware. Nobody had ever borne heavier handicaps. He had outgrown hindrances faster than the H-G men could think them up. Instead of a little ear radio for a mental handicap, he wore a tremendous pair of earphones, and spectacles with thick wavy lenses. The spectacles were intended to make him not only half blind, but to give him whanging headaches besides.

① To show the extremes a society would need to engage in to create equality

② To make fun of people who use earphones all the time

③ To create a humorous view of people who are dedicated to enhancing technology

④ To contrast advanced future technologies with the primitive technologies known to the audience

23 아래 내용에서 묘사되는 Harrison의 특징을 분석한 내용이다. 빈칸에 들어갈 표현이 바르게 짝지어진 것은?

> Scrap metal was hung all over him. Ordinarily, there was a certain symmetry, a military neatness to the handicaps issued to strong people, but Harrison looked like a walking junkyard. In the race of life, Harrison carried three hundred pounds. And to offset his good looks, the H-G men required that he wear at all times a red rubber ball for a nose, keep his eyebrows shaved off, and cover his even white teeth with black caps at snaggle-tooth random.

▼

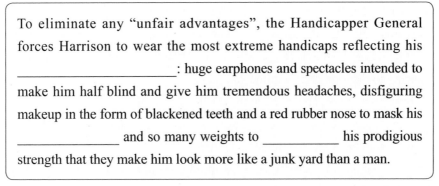

To eliminate any "unfair advantages", the Handicapper General forces Harrison to wear the most extreme handicaps reflecting his _____: huge earphones and spectacles intended to make him half blind and give him tremendous headaches, disfiguring makeup in the form of blackened teeth and a red rubber nose to mask his _____ and so many weights to _____ his prodigious strength that they make him look more like a junk yard than a man.

* disfiguring 추하게 보이는 mask 가리다 prodigious 비범한, 이상한, 놀라운

① unusual natural abilities – extraordinary intelligence – compensate
② extraordinary attributes – extraordinary looks – calibrate
③ run-of-the-mill characteristics – extraordinary personalities – compensate
④ unique qualities – extraordinary personalities – celebrate

24 아래는 본문에서 발췌한 문장이다. 해당 문장에서 발견되는 literary device와 문맥적 설명으로 가장 적절한 것은?

"Scrap metal was hung all over him."

① Simile: He was adorned with scrap metal like a piece of art.
② Hyperbole: He carried the weight of his handicaps like a coat of scrap metal.
③ Personification: Scrap metal clung to him as if it had a will of its own.
④ Metaphor: He was covered in scrap metal, exaggerating the severity of his appearance.
⑤ Alliteration: Scrap metal was strategically suspended, creating a chaotic consonance.

There was the shriek of a door being torn from its hinges.

Screams and barking cries of consternation came from the television set. The photograph of Harrison Bergeron on the screen jumped again and again, as though dancing to the tune of an earthquake.

George Bergeron correctly identified the earthquake, and well he might have—for many was the time his own home had danced to the same crashing tune. "My God—" said George, "that must be Harrison!"

The realization was blasted from his mind instantly by the sound of an automobile collision in his head.

When George could open his eyes again, the photograph of Harrison was gone. A living, breathing Harrison filled the screen.

Clanking, clownish, and huge, Harrison stood in the center of the studio. The knob of the uprooted studio door was still in his hand. Ballerinas, technicians, musicians, and announcers cowered on their knees before him, expecting to die.

"I am the Emperor!" cried Harrison. "Do you hear? I am the Emperor! Everybody must do what I say at once!" He stamped his foot and the studio shook.

"Even as I stand here—" he bellowed, "crippled, hobbled, sickened—I am a greater ruler than any man who ever lived! Now watch me become what I can become!"

어구 및 표현 연구

핵심 PLUS!

1 There was the shriek of a door <u>being torn</u> from its hinges.

- "문이 경첩에서 **찢겨 나오는** 비명소리"
- "사람의 비명소리"에 비유하는 점에서 personification으로 볼 수 있음.

2 The photograph of Harrison Bergeron on the screen jumped again and again, **as though dancing to the tune of an earthquake**.

- 양보절을 이끄는 as though의 분사구문
  as though dancing to the tune of an earthquake
  = as though **it were** dancing to the tune of an earthquake

3 George Bergeron correctly identified the earthquake, and well **he might have**—<u>for</u> <u>many was the time</u> his own home had danced <u>to</u> the same crashing tune.

- he might have 뒤에 이어지는 내용을 바탕으로 he might have **identified and said, "that must be Harrison."**과 같이 말한 내용.
- 등위접속사 for
- many is the time S V: 많은 경우 S V이다
- 전치사 to: ~에 맞춰

4 The realization was blasted from his mind instantly by the sound of an automobile collision in his head.

- "인식이 폭발했다"는 뜻은 아들에 대한 인식이 귀에 장치된 라디오의 자동차 충돌 소리로 인해서 그런 깨달음을 "잊었다, 사라졌다"는 의미로 해석할 수 있다.

5 Ballerinas, technicians, musicians, and announcers <u>cowered</u> on their knees before him, <u>expecting</u> to die.

- cower: (겁을 먹고) 움츠리다
- 분사구문: **as they expected** to die

6 "I am a great**er** ruler **than any** man who ever lived!"

- 비교급을 활용한 최상급 표현

UNIT

2

Harrison tore the straps of his handicap harness like wet tissue paper, tore straps guaranteed to support five thousand pounds.

Harrison's scrap-iron handicaps crashed to the floor.

Harrison thrust his thumbs under the bar of the padlock that secured his head harness. The bar snapped like celery. Harrison smashed his headphones and spectacles against the wall.

He flung away his rubber-ball nose, revealed a man that would have awed Thor, the god of thunder.

"I shall now select my Empress!" he said, looking down on the cowering people. "Let the first woman who dares rise to her feet claim her mate and her throne!"

A moment passed, and then a ballerina arose, swaying like a willow.

Harrison plucked the mental handicap from her ear, snapped off her physical handicaps with marvelous delicacy. Last of all he removed her mask.

Quick Quiz

25 Which of the following is <u>NOT</u> appropriate in explaining the literary devices used in the passage?

① The use of simile in describing Harrison's actions
② The metaphorical comparison of Harrison to Thor, the god of thunder
③ The symbolic act of selecting an Empress
④ The literal description of tearing the straps of the handicap harness
⑤ The comparison of Harrison's strength to wet tissue paper

1 Harrison thrust his thumbs under the bar of the padlock [**that** secured his head harness].

• 주격 관계대명사 that

2 Harrison <u>smashed</u> his headphones and spectacles <u>against</u> the wall.

• smash A against B: (부수기 위해서) A를 B에 부딪히게 하다, 충돌시키다

3 He flung away his rubber-ball nose, revealed a man that <u>would have awed</u> Thor, the god of thunder.

• 가정법 would have p.p: ~도 경외심을 가지게 했을

4 "I shall now select my Empress!" he said, <u>looking down</u> on the cowering people.

• 분사구문: **as he was looking down**

5 "<u>Let</u> [the first woman (<u>who</u> dares rise to her feet)] <u>claim</u> her mate and her throne!"

• 5형식 사역동사 let의 목적보어 claim

6 A moment passed, and then a ballerina arose, <u>swaying</u> like a willow.

• 분사구문: **as she was swaying** like a willow

7 Harrison plucked the mental handicap from her ear, (and) snapped off her physical handicaps with marvelous delicacy.

• 서술부 병치 등위접속사 and의 생략

 Quick Quiz

There was the shriek of a door being torn from its hinges.
Screams and barking cries of consternation came from the television set. The photograph of Harrison Bergeron on the screen jumped again and again, as though dancing to the tune of an earthquake.
George Bergeron correctly identified the earthquake, and well he might have—for <u>many was the time his own home had danced to the same crashing tune</u>. "My God—" said George, "that must be Harrison!"
The realization was blasted from his mind instantly by the sound of an automobile collision in his head.

26 From the underlined sentence, George figured out that the boy in question was none other than his son, Harrison. What figurative language is used in the underlined sentence?

① Simile   ② Personification
③ Paradox   ④ Hyperbole
⑤ Irony

She was blindingly beautiful.

"Now—" said Harrison, taking her hand, "shall we show the people the meaning of the word dance? Music!" he commanded.

The musicians scrambled back into their chairs, and Harrison stripped them of their handicaps, too. "Play your best," he told them, "and I'll make you barons and dukes and earls."

The music began. It was normal at first—cheap, silly, false. But Harrison snatched two musicians from their chairs, waved them like batons as he sang the music as he wanted it played. He slammed them back into their chairs.

The music began again and was much improved.

Harrison and his Empress merely listened to the music for a while—listened gravely, as though synchronizing their heartbeats with it.

They shifted their weights to their toes.

Harrison placed his big hands on the girls' tiny waist, letting her sense the weightlessness that would soon be hers.

And then, in an explosion of joy and grace, into the air they sprang!

Not only were the laws of the land abandoned, but the law of gravity and the laws of motion as well.

They reeled, whirled, swiveled, flounced, capered, gamboled, and spun.

They leaped like deer on the moon.

The studio ceiling was thirty feet high, but each leap brought the dancers nearer to it.

It became their obvious intention to kiss the ceiling. They kissed it.

어구 및 표현 연구

핵심 PLUS!

1 The musicians scrambled back into their chairs, and Harrison <u>stripped</u> them <u>of</u> their handicaps, too.

• strip A of B: A에서 B를 벗겨 내다

2 But Harrison snatched two musicians from their chairs, waved them like batons as he sang the music as he <u>wanted</u> / <u>it</u> / <u>played</u>.

• it = the music.

• 5형식의 목적어 it과 목적보 어 play는 수동의 관계이므로 played로 표현됨.

3 Harrison and his Empress merely listened to the music for a while—listened gravely, **as though synchronizing their heartbeats with it**.

- 분사구문: as though **they synchronized** their heartbeats with it

4 **Not only** were the laws of the land abandoned, **but** the law of gravity and the laws of motion **as well**.

- Not only V S ~ , but S (V) as well 구문

5 The studio ceiling was thirty feet high, but **each leap** / **brought** / the dancers / **nearer** to it.

- 5형식 동사 bring이 활용된 물주구문으로 주어를 부사적으로 해석하고, 목적어를 주어로 해석.

6 **It** became their obvious intention **to kiss** the ceiling.

- 가주어 it/진주어 to V

 Quick Quiz

27 아래 묘사되고 있는 장면에 대한 옳은 진술은 True, 틀린 진술은 False에 표시하시오.

> Harrison placed his big hands on the girls' tiny waist, letting her sense the weightlessness that would soon be hers.
> And then, in an explosion of joy and grace, into the air they sprang!
> Not only were the laws of the land abandoned, but the law of gravity and the laws of motion as well.
> They reeled, whirled, swiveled, flounced, capered, gamboled, and spun.
> They leaped like deer on the moon.
> The studio ceiling was thirty feet high, but each leap brought the dancers nearer to it.
> It became their obvious intention to kiss the ceiling. They kissed it.

① With each leap, the dancers challenge the limitations imposed by the physical environment, suggesting a desire to place boundaries around what seems seemingly out of control. (True / False)

② The simile "They leaped like deer on the moon" further enhances the sense of weightlessness and otherworldliness in their movements. (True / False)

③ The culmination of their leaps is the intention to "kiss the ceiling," an act that symbolizes their rebellion against constraints and a reaching towards the seemingly impossible. (True / False)

And then, neutralizing gravity with love and pure will, they remained suspended in air inches below the ceiling, and they kissed each other for a long, long time.

It was then that Diana Moon Glampers, the Handicapper General, came into the studio with a double-barreled ten-gauge shotgun. She fired twice, and the Emperor and the Empress were dead before they hit the floor.

Diana Moon Glampers loaded the gun again. She aimed it at the musicians and told them they had ten seconds to get their handicaps back on.

It was then that the Bergerons' television tube burned out.

Hazel turned to comment about the blackout to George. But George had gone out into the kitchen for a can of beer.

George came back in with the beer, paused while a handicap signal shook him up. And then he sat down again. "You been crying" he said to Hazel.

"Yup," she said.

"What about?" he said.

"I forget," she said. "Something real sad on television."

"What was it?" he said.

"It's all kind of mixed up in my mind," said Hazel.

"Forget sad things," said George.

"I always do," said Hazel.

"That's my girl," said George. He winced. There was the sound of a rivetting gun in his head.

"Gee—I could tell that one was a doozy," said Hazel.

"You can say that again," said George.

"Gee—" said Hazel, "I could tell that one was a doozy."

 핵심 PLUS!

1 And then, (**neutralizing** gravity with love and pure will), they remained suspended in air inches below the ceiling, and they kissed each other for a long, long time.

- 분사구문: As they neutralized ~

2 It was then that Diana Moon Glampers, the Handicapper General, came into the studio with a double-barreled ten-gauge shotgun. It was then that the Bergerons' television tube burned out.

- 시간의 부사 then을 강조하는 it ~ that 강조구문

3 Hazel turned to comment about the blackout to George. But George **had gone** out into the kitchen for a can of beer.

- 과거보다 한 시제 앞선 과거완료 표현

4 George came back in with the beer, paused while a handicap signal shook him up. And then he sat down again. "**You been crying**" he said to Hazel.

- have 생략: "You have been crying"

5 "I forget," she said. "**Something real sad** on television."

- 형용사 후치: something + 형용사

Quick Quiz

28 George의 답변에 대한 Hazel의 반응을 통해서 파악할 수 있는 Hazel의 특징을 가장 잘 설명한 것은?

> George came back in with the beer, paused while a handicap signal shook him up. And then he sat down again. "You been crying" he said to Hazel.
>
> "Yup," she said.
>
> "What about?" he said.
>
> "I forget," she said.
>
> "Something real sad on television."
>
> "What was it?" he said. "It's all kind of mixed up in my mind," said Hazel.
>
> "Forget sad things," said George.
>
> "I always do," said Hazel.
>
> "That's my girl," said George. He winced. There was the sound of a rivetting gun in his head.
>
> "Gee—I could tell that one was a doozy," said Hazel.
>
> "You can say that again," said George.
>
> "Gee—" said Hazel, "I could tell that one was a doozy."

① Compassionate   ② Annoyed
③ "Average" intelligence   ④ Resilient
⑤ Indifferent

3 Voca Check

* 빈칸에 들어갈 적절한 단어를 박스에서 찾아 넣으시오. (단, 동사의 경우 필요시 문맥에 맞게 형태를 변형할 것)

1

momentum / elusive / unceasing / transmit / afoot / vigilance / bursts /
toy with / breakthroughs / winced / over / relentless / established

1 Albert Einstein, known for his _____ curiosity and intelligence, had a
mind that worked in short _____ of intense creativity. His brilliance was
due to his _____ in exploring ideas from every which way, often
_____ concepts that seemed _____ to others.

2 Einstein's _____ were the result of his _____ pursuit of
knowledge. He _____ at conventional thinking, always ready to challenge
_____ norms. His ideas were _____ to the world like signals
from a visionary transmitter, shaping scientific paradigms.

3 As his theories gained _____, it became clear that Einstein's impact
on science was _____. His revolutionary concepts got very far, reshaping
our understanding of the universe. Even today, the feeling of excitement
persists when exploring the depths of his theories, reminding us that
Einstein's legacy is far from _____.

2 potent / placate / salute / get away with / white / chime / cheat on / attest to / rim / glimmeringly / unsettling / blankly / weigh / compromise / quell / syndicate / unsettling / disturbing / reflect / bear a resemblance to

1 The witness's testimony will _____ the defendant's innocence.

2 His decision to _____ his principles for personal gain was widely criticized.

3 The leader tried to _____ the angry crowd by addressing their concerns.

4 The child's features _____ those of their grandparents.

5 The clock's gentle _____ marked the passing hours.

6 The distant city lights were only _____ visible through the thick fog.

7 Military personnel often give a 21-gun _____ as a sign of respect.

8 The patient's _____ complexion indicated a health issue.

9 The teacup wobbled on the _____ of the saucer.

10 Before making a decision, it's essential to carefully _____ the pros and cons.

11 She managed to _____ a minor reprimand for her actions.

12 The spouse discovered the betrayal when they found evidence of the other's _____.

13 After hearing the news, she stared _____ into space, processing the information.

14 The _____ portrayal of the character in the novel stirred emotions in the readers.

15 The constant noise was _____ to the peaceful atmosphere of the neighborhood.

16 The government's efforts to _____ dissent were met with resistance.

17 The publishing company decided to _____ the latest bestseller to multiple newspapers.

18 The _____ events in the movie left a lasting impact on the audience.

19 The _____ behavior of the suspect made the investigator suspicious.

20 The shallow conversation did not _____ the depth of their relationship.

3

pleasing / comforting / ignorant / naive / timeless / brainless / whang / interrupt / reassuring / quell / hideous / apologize / luminous / impediment / plot / flash / clueless / hang / suspicion / crush

1 The _____ student had no idea about the upcoming surprise party.

2 The _____ words of encouragement from a friend made her feel better.

3 The _____ person had never encountered such a complex problem before.

4 The teacher's _____ words were like a warm embrace during challenging times.

5   It's _____ to assume that everyone understands the intricacies of the topic.

6   The _____ melody of the music created a soothing atmosphere.

7   The _____ comment added nothing valuable to the conversation.

8   Please do not _____ the speaker while they are addressing the audience.

9   A lack of experience can be a significant _____ to success in certain fields.

10 The authorities needed to _____ the riot quickly to prevent further chaos.

11 The reckless driver tried to _____ the evidence of the accident by altering the scene.

12 The _____ appearance of the creature made the onlookers shudder.

13 She felt the need to _____ for her unintentional mistake.

14 The _____ glow of the moon bathed the landscape in soft light.

15 The love story was portrayed as a _____ tale that transcended time.

16 The _____ of guilt hung in the air as the suspect avoided eye contact.

17 The villain's evil _____ to overthrow the government was revealed in the final act.

18 The old film projector began to _____ images on the blank screen.

19 The fast car seemed to _____ as it zoomed past us on the highway.

20 He managed to _____ the hammer against the door to get attention.

4 clownish / harness / symmetry / crash / snap / brainless / snap / cower / delicacy / bellow / hobble / crashing / willow / consternation / neatness / delicate / reason with / clanking / shave off

1 The attempt to _____ the wild horse proved futile as it resisted any form of control.

2 The _____ of the room's design brought a sense of balance and harmony.

3 With _____, she examined the intricate details of the artwork.

4 The sudden noise caused _____ among the guests, who were now confused and alarmed.

5 He decided to _____ the protruding branch with a swift stroke of his axe.

6 The _____ collision between the two cars resulted in extensive damage.

7 The _____ sound of metal echoed through the factory as the machines continued their work.

8 His _____ attempt to fix the broken vase only made the situation worse.

9 The old building began to _____ with a deafening crash, startling everyone nearby.

10 The _____ behavior of the comedian brought laughter to the audience.

11 She hesitated to _____ the delicate flower, fearing it might break.

12 The _____ of the bull echoed through the valley, signaling its dominance.

13 The injured bird tried to _____ away from the approaching predator.

14 The _____ of the gears signaled that the machinery was operating smoothly.

15 The storm _____ the willow trees, leaving them bent and mangled.

16 In the face of danger, she couldn't help but _____ and seek cover.

17 The sudden _____ of the rope caught everyone off guard.

18 The _____ delicacy of the antique vase required careful handling.

19 He decided to _____ the problem by taking a step back and reevaluating the situation.

20 The _____ crash of the waves against the shore created a mesmerizing sound.

5

scramble / reel / swivel / snatch / slam / gravely / flounce / neutralize / barons and dukes and earls / wince / shift / burn out / blinding / strip / synchronize / explosion / spin / gambol

1   The _____ sunlight made it difficult to see anything in the open field.

2   In a desperate attempt to escape, she began to _____ over the obstacles in her path.

3   The thieves decided to _____ the museum of its valuable artifacts under the cover of darkness.

4   The grand ballroom was filled with _____, each adorned in elaborate attire.

5   With a swift _____, he grabbed the document from the table before anyone could react.

6   The loud _____ of the door echoed through the empty hallway.

7   The doctor looked at the patient _____ as he delivered the grim diagnosis.

8   The dancers practiced diligently to _____ their movements with the music.

9   The sudden _____ of colors in the sky marked the beginning of the fireworks display.

10 The unexpected news made her _____ with disbelief and shock.

11 As the helicopter prepared to land, the ground crew worked quickly to _____ its position.

12 The intense heat caused the candle to _____, leaving the room in darkness.

13 The disoriented astronaut began to _____ in the weightlessness of space.

14 The chair was designed to _____, allowing the occupant to turn in any direction.

15 With a dramatic _____, she stormed out of the room in frustration.

16 The playful lambs continued to _____ in the meadow.

17 The figure skater executed a flawless _____, spinning gracefully on the ice.

18 To avoid detection, the spy attempted to _____ his identity by wearing a disguise.

Reading Comprehension 1

1   Among the options, which of the following is <u>THE LEAST</u> persuasive?

 NOTE

The year was 2081, and everybody was finally equal. They weren't only equal before God and the law. They were equal every which way. Nobody was smarter than anybody else.

Nobody was better looking than anybody else. Nobody was stronger or quicker than anybody else. ⓐAll this equality was due to the 211th, 212th, and 213th Amendments to the Constitution, and to the unceasing vigilance of agents of the United States Handicapper General.

Some things about living still weren't quite right, though. ⓑApril, for instance, still drove people crazy by not being springtime. And it was in that clammy month that the H-G men took George and Hazel Bergeron's fourteen-year-old son, Harrison, away.

It was tragic, all right, but George and Hazel couldn't think about it very hard. ⓒHazel had a perfectly average intelligence, which meant she couldn't think about anything except in short bursts. And George, while his intelligence was way above normal, had a little mental handicap radio in his ear. He was required by law to wear it at all times. It was tuned to a government transmitter. ⓓEvery twenty seconds or so, the transmitter would send out some sharp noise to keep people like George from taking unfair advantage of their brains.

George and Hazel were watching television. There were tears on Hazel's cheeks, but she'd forgotten for the moment what they were about.

On the television screen were ballerinas.

ⓔA buzzer sounded in George's head. His thoughts fled in panic, like bandits from a burglar alarm.

"That was a real pretty dance, that dance they just did," said Hazel.

① ㉠ The so-called "perfection" of everyone being equal is a manipulation by a constant government control that has been going on over time.

② ㉡ The fact that the weather makes people "crazy" shows that there are things that the government can't artificially control such as people's emotions. Total equality under control is an illusion.

③ ㉢ People who are considered "perfectly average intelligent" by the government are actually people who are overly intelligent.

④ ㉣ The government's policy of creating people with "equal" brains is ultimately to create a land of cowed, stupid, slow people.

⑤ ㉤ As can be seen from the analogy of the buzzer to a burglar alarm, having a freedom of thought is regarded as a forbidden area.

2 Below is an explanation of ㉠~㉣ in the text. Correctly match the explanations in ① ~④ with ㉠~㉣ in the text.

① Perhaps Hazel is one of the least handicapped among people in that she has a perfectly average intelligence. _____

② The graceful must wear weights to make their performance look "equal" and must hideous masks to disfigure themselves so that their beautiful faces could be neutralized for the so-called total equality. _____

③ The intelligent must listen to earsplitting noises that impede their ability to think. _____

④ Two out of the eight ballerinas are as intelligent as George. _____

On the television screen were ballerinas.

㉠A buzzer sounded in George's head. His thoughts fled in panic, like bandits from a burglar alarm.

"That was a real pretty dance, that dance they just did," said Hazel.

"Huh" said George.

"That dance—it was nice," said Hazel.

"Yup," said George. He tried to think a little about the ballerinas. ㉡They weren't really very good—no better than anybody else would have been, anyway. They were burdened with sashweights and bags of birdshot, and their faces were masked, so that no one, seeing a free and graceful gesture or a pretty face, would feel like something the cat drug in.

George was toying with the vague notion that maybe dancers shouldn't be handicapped.

But he didn't get very far with it before another noise in his ear radio scattered his thoughts.

George winced. ©So did two out of the eight ballerinas.

Hazel saw him wince. ⓔHaving no mental handicap herself, she had to ask George what the latest sound had been.

"Sounded like somebody hitting a milk bottle with a ball peen hammer," said George.

"I'd think it would be real interesting, hearing all the different sounds," said Hazel a little envious. "All the things they think up."

"Um," said George.

[3-4] Read the passage and answer each question.

 NOTE

[가] The year was 2081, and everybody was finally equal. They weren't only equal before God and the law. They were equal ㉮every which way. Nobody was smarter than anybody else. Nobody was better looking than anybody else. Nobody was stronger or quicker than anybody else. ㉠All this equality was due to the 211th, 212th, and 213th Amendments to the Constitution, and to the unceasing vigilance of agents of the United States Handicapper General.

[나] Some things about living still ㉯weren't quite right, though. April, for instance, still drove people crazy by not being springtime. And it was in that clammy month that the H-G men took George and Hazel Bergeron's fourteen-year-old son, Harrison, away.

[다] It was tragic, ㉰all right, but George and Hazel couldn't think about it very hard. Hazel had a ㉱unfairly average intelligence, which meant she couldn't think about anything except in short bursts. And George, while his intelligence was way above normal, had a little mental handicap radio in his ear. He was required by law to wear it at all times. It was tuned to a government transmitter. ㉡Every twenty seconds or so, the transmitter would send out some sharp noise to keep people like George from taking unfair advantage of their brains.

[라] George and Hazel were watching television. There were tears on Hazel's cheeks, but she'd forgotten for the moment what they were about.

On the television screen were ballerinas.

A buzzer sounded in George's head. ㉢His thoughts fled in panic, like bandits from a burglar alarm.

"That was a real pretty dance, that dance they just did," said Hazel.

"Huh" said George.

"That dance—㉲there was something weird about it," said Hazel.

"Yup," said George. ㉣He tried to think a little about the ballerinas. They weren't really very good—no better than anybody else would have been, anyway. ㉤They were burdened with sashweights and bags of birdshot, and their faces were masked, so that no one, seeing a free and graceful gesture or a pretty face, would feel like something the cat drug in.

3 Among ㉮~㉲, find all the options that are <u>AWKWARD</u> in context.

> ㉮ every which way
>
> ㉯ weren't quite right
>
> ㉰ all right
>
> ㉱ unfairly
>
> ㉲ there was something weird about it

① ㉮ and ㉯

② ㉯, ㉰ and ㉱

③ ㉱ and ㉲

④ ㉮ and ㉰

⑤ ㉮, ㉱, and ㉲

4 Choose one of the underlined explanations for ㉠ through ㉣ that is <u>NOT</u> correct.

① ㉠: The ideal of everyone being equal is none other than the by-product of the government's artificial and coercive measures.

② ㉡: The government is in control of the intellectual ability of citizens through sound.

③ ㉢: Freedom of thought is literally a criminal act that goes against the law.

④ ㉣: George's inability to figure out what is going on around him suggests that George was born intellectually inferior.

⑤ ㉤: The government's ploy to make everyone equal is ultimately just a contradictory measure that makes everyone inferior.

* none other than 다름 아닌
* ploy 책, 술책 (=maneuver)

[5-6] Read the passage and answer each question.

 NOTE

"Yup," said George. He tried to think a little about the ballerinas. They weren't really very good—no better than anybody else would have been, anyway. They were burdened with sashweights and bags of birdshot, and their faces were masked, so that no one, seeing a free and graceful gesture or a pretty face, would feel like something the cat drug in.

George was toying with the vague notion that maybe dancers shouldn't be handicapped.

But he didn't get very far with it _____.

George winced. So did two out of the eight ballerinas.

Hazel saw him wince. Having no mental handicap herself, she had to ask George what the latest sound had been.

"Sounded like somebody hitting a milk bottle with a ball peen hammer," said George.

"I'd think it would be real interesting, hearing all the different sounds," said Hazel a little envious. "All the things they think up."

"Um," said George.

[가] "Only, if I was Handicapper General, you know what I would do?" said Hazel. Hazel, as a matter of fact, bore a strong resemblance to the Handicapper General, a woman named Diana Moon Glampers.

"If I was Diana Moon Glampers," said Hazel, "I'd have chimes on Sunday—just chimes. Kind of in honor of religion."

"I could think, if it was just chimes," said George.

"Well—maybe make 'em real loud," said Hazel. "I think I'd make a good Handicapper General."

"Good as anybody else," said George.

"Who knows better than I do what normal is?" said Hazel.

5 Which of the following is the most appropriate expression to fill in the blank based on the context?

① because the ideal that everyone was equal had finally been realized

② as his intellectual ability reached the limit he could

③ because freedom of thought was only allowed by the government

④ because the two ballerina were thinking the same way

⑤ before another ear-piercing radio noise interrupted his thoughts

6 Below is a critique of the underlined part [가]. Which words are correctly paired to fill in the blanks?

> Vonnegut seems to suggest that Hazel's similarity to Diana Moon Glampers is disturbing because it means that the country is being run by people just as _____ as Hazel. When George says that Hazel is as "good as anybody else," we get the idea that she is just as confused and incapable of _____ as every other average American living in the year 2081. Hazel's confidence in her understanding of "normal" is both funny and sinister. Her self-confidence in understanding "normal" is amusing, especially because it comes on the heels of her ludicrous suggestion that the government should _____ thoughts on Sundays with religious-sounding chimes. But it is also a disturbing and subtle reminder that in this futuristic America, the people who run the country are in power not because of their brains or savvy, but because of their _____.

* sinister 불길한《조짐 따위》 * come on the heels of ...의 바로 뒤에 오다

① intelligent – serious thought – interfere with – normalcy

② intelligent – deep thought – interfere with – normalcy

③ clueless – serious thought – interrupt – normalcy

④ clueless – serious thought – interfere with – distinction

⑤ clueless – deep thought – interrupt – distinction

[7-8] Read the passage and answer each question.

"Right," said George. He began to think glimmeringly about his abnormal son who was now in jail, about Harrison, but a twenty-one-gun salute in his head stopped that.

"Boy!" said Hazel, "that was a doozy, wasn't it?"

It was such a doozy that George was white and trembling, and tears stood on the rims of his red eyes. Two of the eight ballerinas had collapsed to the studio floor, were holding their temples.

(가)"All of a sudden you look so tired," said Hazel. "Why don't you stretch out on the sofa, so you can rest your handicap bag on the pillows, honeybunch." She was referring to the forty-seven pounds of birdshot in a canvas bag, which was padlocked around George's neck. "Go on and rest the bag for a little while," she said. "I don't care if you're not equal to me for a while."

George weighed the bag with his hands. "I don't mind it," he said. "I don't notice it any more. It's just a part of me."

"You been so tired lately—kind of wore out," said Hazel. "If there was just some way we could make a little hole in the bottom of the bag, and just take out a few of them lead balls. Just a few."

"Two years in prison and two thousand dollars fine for every ball I took out," said George.

"I don't call that a bargain."

"If you could just take a few out when you came home from work," said Hazel. "I mean—you don't compete with anybody around here. You just sit around."

"If I tried to get away with it," said George, "then other people'd get away with it—and pretty soon we'd be right back to the dark ages again, with everybody competing against everybody else. You wouldn't like that, would you?"

"I'd hate it," said Hazel.

"There you are," said George. "The minute people start cheating on laws, what do you think happens to society?"

If Hazel hadn't been able to come up with an answer to this question, George couldn't have supplied one. A siren was going off in his head.

"Reckon it'd fall all apart," said Hazel.

"What would?" said George blankly.

"Society," said Hazel uncertainly. "Wasn't that what you just said?"

"Who knows?" said George.

7 Choose all the explanations that are persuasive for the underlined (가).

> ㉮ It is ironic that Hazel, who is very low in intelligence as well as lacking any other discernible gifts, says to George that she doesn't care if you're not equal to me for a while.
>
> ㉯ Hazel feels both jealous and pitiable for George because his superior abilities make him wear handicaps, which make them uncomfortable.
>
> ㉰ It shows that George and Hazel are not equal in their ability to think, which suggests that absolute equality is impossible.

① ㉮ and ㉯

② ㉯

③ ㉰

④ ㉯ and ㉰

⑤ ㉮ and ㉰

8 Which of the following statements about George in the text is NOT correct?

① Smart and law-abiding

② Crippled by the government's handicapping program

③ Able to think analytically about society

④ Weaker in physique but smarter than anybody else

⑤ Supportive for the laws of the land

[1-2] Read the passage and answer each question.

 NOTE

"All of a sudden you look so tired," said Hazel. "Why don't you stretch out on the sofa, so you can rest your handicap bag on the pillows, honeybunch." She was referring to ⊙the forty-seven pounds of birdshot in a canvas bag, which was padlocked around George's neck. "Go on and rest the bag for a little while," she said. ⓁNo"I don't care if you're not equal to me for a while."

ⒸGeorge weighed the bag with his hands. "I don't mind it," he said. "I don't notice it any more. It's just a part of me."

"You been so tired lately—kind of wore out," said Hazel. ⓔ"If there was just some way we could make a little hole in the bottom of the bag, and just take out a few of them lead balls. Just a few."

ⓜ"Two years in prison and two thousand dollars fine for every ball I took out," said George.

Ⓗ"I don't call that a bargain."

"If you could just take a few out when you came home from work," said Hazel. "I mean—you don't compete with anybody around here. You just sit around."

Ⓐ"If I tried to get away with it," said George, "then other people'd get away with it—and pretty soon we'd be right back to the dark ages again, with everybody competing against everybody else. You wouldn't like that, would you?"

"I'd hate it," said Hazel.

"There you are," said George. "The minute people start cheating on laws, what do you think happens to society?"

ⓞIf Hazel hadn't been able to come up with an answer to this question, George couldn't have supplied one. A siren was going off in his head.

Ⓧ"Reckon it'd fall all apart," said Hazel.

"What would?" said George blankly.

"Society," said Hazel uncertainly. "Wasn't that what you just said?"

"Who knows?" said George.

1 Which of the following statements about ㉠~㉣ is <u>INCORRECT</u>?

① ㉠: The goal of the bag of birdshot is to make George less athletic and physically capable than others, which shows that he is "unlawfully" superior to others.

② ㉡: It is ironic that Hazel, who is so low in intelligence and physical abilities says to George, "I don't care if you're not equal to me for a while."

③ ㉢ From the sentence, it can be inferred that George is sort of a "static" character because he's just accepted society's rules and does not try to challenge them.

④ ㉢: George is shown to have internalized the system of how the society should be.

⑤ ㉣: Hazel's suggestion of putting down some of the weights George is carrying gives us a glimpse into Hazel's secret scheme to overthrow the government.

UNIT

2

2 ㉤ ~ ㉩에 대한 설명 중 옳은 것을 <u>모두</u> 고르시오.

㉤ Although George has the ability to think rationally, he is not the type of person who actively copes with the absurdity of society.

㉧ In this context, "a bargain" means to pay more than you should.

㉨ George's account of the consequences of law-breaking to Hazel proves that the government attempt of controlling everyone's intelligence is a complete failure.

㉩ The fact that Hazel couldn't answer George's question shows why Hazel isn't physically handicapped unlike George.

㉪ It can be inferred that George loses track of the conversation completely because of the siren.

① ㉤ and ㉪

② ㉤, ㉧ and ㉪

③ ㉨, ㉩ and ㉪

④ ㉤ and ㉪

⑤ ㉤, ㉧ and ㉪

Reading Comprehension | 141

[3-5] Read the passage and answer each question.

 NOTE

The television program was suddenly interrupted for ㉠a news bulletin. It wasn't clear at first as to what the bulletin was about, since the announcer, like all announcers, had a serious speech impediment. For about half a minute, and in a state of high excitement, the announcer tried to say, "Ladies and Gentlemen—" He finally gave up, handed the bulletin to a ballerina to read.

(가)"That's all right—" Hazel said of the announcer, "he tried. That's the big thing. He tried to do the best he could with what God gave him. He should get a nice raise for trying so hard."

"Ladies and Gentlemen—," said the ballerina, reading the bulletin. She must have been extraordinarily beautiful, because the mask she wore was hideous. And it was easy to see that she was the strongest and most graceful of all the dancers, for her handicap bags were as big as those worn by two-hundred pound men.

㉡And she had to apologize at once for her voice, which was a very unfair voice for a woman to use. Her voice was a warm, luminous, timeless melody. "Excuse me—" she said, and she began again, making her voice absolutely uncompetitive.

"Harrison Bergeron, age fourteen," she said in a grackle squawk, "has just escaped from jail, where he was held on suspicion of plotting to overthrow the government. He is a genius and an athlete, is under-handicapped, and should be regarded as extremely dangerous."

A police photograph of Harrison Bergeron was flashed on the screen—upside down, then sideways, upside down again, then right side up. ㉢ The picture showed the full length of Harrison against a background calibrated in feet and inches. He was exactly seven feet tall.

㉣The rest of Harrison's appearance was Halloween and hardware. Nobody had ever born heavier handicaps. He had outgrown hindrances faster than the H-G men could think them up. Instead of a little ear radio for a mental handicap, he wore a tremendous pair of earphones, and spectacles with thick wavy lenses. The spectacles were intended to make him not only half blind, but to give him whanging headaches besides.

NOTE

Scrap metal was hung all over him. Ordinarily, there was a certain symmetry, a military neatness to the handicaps issued to strong people, ©but Harrison looked like a walking junkyard. In the race of life, Harrison carried three hundred pounds. And to offset his good looks, the H-G men required that he wear at all times a red rubber ball for a nose, keep his eyebrows shaved off, and cover his even white teeth with black caps at snaggle-tooth random.

"If you see this boy," said the ballerina, "do not—I repeat, do not—try to reason with him."

3 Select all the appropriate explanations directly derived from the underlined sentences in (가).

> (a) Hazel explicitly illustrates the absurdity of trying to make everyone equal.
> (b) Hazel emphasizes the importance of having compassion for others rather than encouraging being "smarter."
> (c) Hazel has a high regard for putting in one's best effort.
> (d) Hazel fully understands the difficulty in enforcing laws that make everyone equal.

① (a) and (c)
② (a), (b) and (d)
③ (b) and (c)
④ (a), (b) and (c)
⑤ (c) and (d)

UNIT
2

4 Considering the overall story of the novel, choose all that are correct about each underlined sentence. (Two underlined sentences for ㉢)

> ㉠ The news is about Harrison escaping from jail.
>
> ㉡ This illustrates that the insistence on total equality seeps into the citizens, who begin to dumb themselves down or hide their special attributes.
>
> ㉢ By showing Harrison's enormous and hideous appearance, this aims to promote citizens' awareness of how dangerous he is to the public.
>
> ㉣ This reveals that Harrison has the most outstanding ability and the government's control for total equality is not perfect.

① ㉠ and ㉡   ② ㉠ and ㉢
③ ㉠, ㉡ and ㉢   ④ ㉡ and ㉣
⑤ All of them

5 Below is what the author intended through Harrison's photo mentioned in the text. Choose the appropriate expression to fill in the blank.

> The photo is a way of identifying the supposedly dangerous escapee, but it is also a way of _____ television viewers. It gives them a visual example of the handicaps imposed on those who do not _____ their own abilities.

① terrifying – publicize   ② entertaining – stifle
③ enlightening – repress   ④ intimidating – suppress
⑤ terrorizing – soothe

[6-7] Read the passage and answer each question.

There was the shriek of a door being torn from its hinges.

Screams and barking cries of consternation came from the television set. The photograph of Harrison Bergeron on the screen jumped again and again, as though dancing to the tune of an earthquake.

George Bergeron correctly identified the earthquake, and well he might have—for many was the time his own home had danced to the same crashing tune. "My God—" said George, "that must be Harrison!"

The realization was blasted from his mind instantly by the sound of an automobile collision in his head.

When George could open his eyes again, the photograph of Harrison was gone. A living, breathing Harrison filled the screen.

Clanking, clownish, and huge, Harrison stood in the center of the studio. The knob of the uprooted studio door was still in his hand. Ballerinas, technicians, musicians, and announcers cowered on their knees before him, expecting to die.

"I am the Emperor!" cried Harrison. "Do you hear? I am the Emperor! Everybody must do what I say at once!" He stamped his foot and the studio shook.

"Even as I stand here—" he bellowed, "crippled, hobbled, sickened— I am a greater ruler than any man who ever lived! Now watch me become what I can become!"

Harrison tore the straps of his handicap harness like wet tissue paper, tore straps guaranteed to support five thousand pounds.

(가)Harrison's scrap-iron handicaps crashed to the floor.

Harrison thrust his thumbs under the bar of the padlock that secured his head harness. The bar snapped like celery. Harrison smashed his headphones and spectacles against the wall.

He flung away his rubber-ball nose, revealed a man that would have awed Thor, the god of thunder.

"I shall now select my Empress!" he said, looking down on the cowering people. "Let the first woman who dares rise to her feet claim her mate and her throne!"

A moment passed, and then a ballerina arose, swaying like a willow.

(나)Harrison plucked the mental handicap from her ear, snapped off her physical handicaps with marvelous delicacy. Last of all he removed her mask.

She was blindingly beautiful.

"Now—" said Harrison, taking her hand, "shall we show the people the meaning of the word dance? Music!" he commanded.

The musicians scrambled back into their chairs, and Harrison stripped them of their handicaps, too. "Play your best," he told them, "and I'll make you barons and dukes and earls."

The music began. It was normal at first—cheap, silly, false. But Harrison snatched two musicians from their chairs, waved them like batons as he sang the music as he wanted it played. He slammed them back into their chairs.

6 How does Harrison's removal of his handicaps and ballerina's as in the underlined (가) and (나) develop the plot of the story?

① Harrison inspires people to rebel against the government.

② Harrison briefly shows people what is possible without handicaps.

③ Harrison's violent outburst makes the audience believe that handicaps are good.

④ Harrison makes his parents proud that he stood up for what is right.

⑤ Harrison is an exemplary figure representing the ideal of the government.

7 본문을 통해서 파악할 수 있는 내용으로 적절하지 <u>않은</u> 것은?

① Harrison represents the spark of defiance and individuality that still exists in some Americans.

② When George identifies his son, he is interrupted by instantly by the sound of an automobile collision in his head.

③ Harrison shows none of the cowardice and passivity that characterize nearly everyone else in the story.

④ Harrison is depicted as an exaggerated alpha male, a breathtakingly strong man, who is somehow reluctant to strive for power.

⑤ When Harrison rips off his steel restraints and handicaps, the physical strength and beauty he reveals reminds the viewers that underneath their own restraints and handicaps, they too are still talented or lovely.

* defiance 도전; 저항; 반항 alpha male 우두머리 수컷

[1-3] Read the passage and answer each question.

🎗 NOTE

THE YEAR WAS 2081, and everybody was finally equal. They weren't only equal before God and the law. They were equal every which way. Nobody was smarter than anybody else. Nobody was better looking than anybody else. Nobody was stronger or quicker than anybody else. All this equality was due to the 211th, 212th, and 213th Amendments to the Constitution, and to the unceasing vigilance of agents of the United States Handicapper General.

Some things about living still weren't quite right, though. April for instance, still drove people crazy by not being springtime. And it was in that clammy month that the H-G men took George and Hazel Bergeron's fourteen-year-old son, Harrison, away.

1 The narrator's tone can best be described as _____.

① satirical   ② harshly critical

③ wholly frustrated   ④ mildly emotional

⑤ excessively casual

2 The effect of the repetition of the phrase "nobody was" is to _____.

① introduce theme   ② underscore a point

③ instill a sense of loneliness   ④ refute a commonly held assumption

⑤ present three contradictory elements

3 In the first paragraph, the author employs which of the following?

① Internal rhymes

② Mimicry of the speech of the lower class

③ General comparison

④ Parallel construction

⑤ Introduction of the protagonist

[4] Read the passage and answer each question.

 NOTE

THE YEAR WAS 2081, and everybody was finally equal. They weren't only equal before God and the law. They were equal every which way. Nobody was smarter than anybody else. Nobody was better looking than anybody else. Nobody was stronger or quicker than anybody else. All this equality was due to the 211th, 212th, and 213th Amendments to the Constitution, and to the unceasing vigilance of agents of the United States Handicapper General.

Some things about living still weren't quite right, though. ㉠April for instance, still drove people crazy by not being springtime. And it was in that clammy month that the H-G men took George and Hazel Bergeron's fourteen-year-old son, Harrison, away.

It was tragic, all right, but George and Hazel couldn't think about it very hard. Hazel had a perfectly average intelligence, which meant she couldn't think about anything except in short bursts. And George, while his intelligence was way above normal, had a little mental handicap radio in his ear. He was required by law to wear it at all times. It was tuned to a government transmitter. ㉡Every twenty seconds or so, the transmitter would send out some sharp noise to keep people like George from taking unfair advantage of their brains.

George and Hazel were watching television. ㉢There were tears on Hazel's cheeks, but she'd forgotten for the moment what they were about.

On the television screen were ballerinas.

A buzzer sounded in George's head. ㉣His thoughts fled in panic, like bandits from a burglar alarm.

"That was a real pretty dance, that dance they just did," said Hazel.

"Huh" said George.

"That dance-it was nice," said Hazel.

"Yup, " said George. He tried to think a little about the ballerinas. They weren't really very good-no better than anybody else would have been, anyway. They were burdened with sashweights and bags of birdshot, and their faces were masked, so that no one, seeing a free and graceful gesture or a pretty face, would feel like something the cat drug in. ⓓGeorge was toying with the vague notion that maybe dancers shouldn't be handicapped. But he didn't get very far with it before another noise in his ear radio scattered his thoughts.

4 According to the passage above, which of the following statements is <u>INCORRECT</u>?

> I. According to the first paragraph, it is described that the equality in this society could be achieved by the law and the hardworking government agents who watched carefully any case of inequality.
>
> II. According to ⓐ and ⓒ, it is implied that downward leveling made people original and unique.
>
> III. According to ⓑ, it is inferred that the government in this society believes that it only thrives when individuals are able to reach full potential as citizens.
>
> IV. Personification and simile are used in the sentence ⓔ.
>
> V. Through ⓓ, it can be inferred that George is after all no better than Hazel intellectually.

① I and II
② I, II and IV
③ II and III
④ II, III and V
⑤ III, IV and V

[5-6] Read the passage and answer each question.

 NOTE

"All of a sudden you look so tired," said Hazel. "Why don't you stretch out on the sofa, so you can rest your handicap bag on the pillows, honeybunch." She was referring to the forty-seven pounds of birdshot in a canvas bag, which was padlocked around George's neck. "Go on and rest the bag for a little while," she said. "I don't care if you're not equal to me for a while."

George weighed the bag with his hands. "I don't mind it," he said. "I don't notice it any more. It's just a part of me."

"You been so tired lately—kind of wore out," said Hazel. "If there was just some way we could make a little hole in the bottom of the bag, and just take out a few of them lead balls. Just a few."

"Two years in prison and two thousand dollars fine for every ball I took out," said George. "I don't call that a bargain."

"If you could just take a few out when you came home from work," said Hazel. "I mean—you don't compete with anybody around here. You just set around."

"If I tried to get away with it," said George, "then other people'd get away with it—and pretty soon we'd be right back to the dark ages again, with everybody competing against everybody else. You wouldn't like that, would you?"

"I'd hate it," said Hazel.

"There you are," said George. "The minute people start cheating on laws, what do you think happens to society?"

If Hazel hadn't been able to come up with an answer to this question, George couldn't have supplied one. A siren was going off in his head.

"Reckon it'd fall all apart," said Hazel.

"What would?" said George blankly.

"Society," said Hazel uncertainly. "Wasn't that what you just said?"

"Who knows?" said George.

The television program was suddenly interrupted for a news bulletin. It wasn't clear at first as to what the bulletin was about, since the announcer, like all announcers, had a serious speech impediment. For about half a minute, and in a state of high excitement, the announcer tried to say, "Ladies and Gentlemen."

He finally gave up, handed the bulletin to a ballerina to read.

"That's all right—" Hazel said of the announcer, "he tried. That's the big thing. He tried to do the best he could with what God gave him. He should get a nice raise for trying so hard."

"Ladies and Gentlemen," said the ballerina, reading the bulletin. She ㉠must have been extraordinarily beautiful, because the mask she wore was ㉡hideous. And it was easy to see that she was the strongest and most graceful of all the dancers, for her handicap bags were as ㉢ big as those worn by two-hundred pound men.

And she had to apologize at once for her voice, which was a very ㉣ unfair voice for a woman to use. Her voice was a warm, luminous, timeless melody. "Excuse me—" she said, and she began again, making her voice absolutely ㉤competitive.

5 According to the passage above, which of the following statements is <u>CORRECT</u>?

① Hazel tried to overthrow the government by violating the laws.

② George thought of the penalty for taking some lead balls out of the bag as appropriate and reasonable.

③ The world of the passage has entered the era of limitless competition after the age of perfect equality.

④ The fact that the announcer had a serious speech impediment is an example of irony.

⑤ Hazel believed that the announcer should achieve great results to get a raise in his salary.

6 Which of the underlined words ㉠ ~ ㉤ is <u>NOT</u> appropriate in context?

① ㉠ must have been

② ㉡ hideous

③ ㉢ big

④ ㉣ unfair

⑤ ㉤ competitive

[7-8] Read the passage and answer each question.

ⓐA police photograph of Harrison Bergeron was flashed on the screen-upside down, then sideways, upside down again, then right side up. The picture showed the full length of Harrison against a background (A)calibrated in feet and inches. He was exactly seven feet tall.

ⓑThe rest of Harrison's appearance was Halloween and hardware. ⓒ Nobody had ever born heavier handicaps. He had outgrown hindrances faster than the H-G men could think them up. Instead of a little ear radio for a mental handicap, he wore a tremendous pair of earphones, and spectacles with thick wavy lenses. The spectacles were intended to make him not only half blind, but to give him whanging headaches besides.

Scrap metal was hung all over him. Ordinarily, there was a certain symmetry, a military neatness to the handicaps issued to strong people, but Harrison looked like a walking junkyard. In the race of life, Harrison carried three hundred pounds.

And to offset his good looks, the H-G men required that he (B)wore at all times a red rubber ball for a nose, keep his eyebrows (C)shaved off, and cover his even white teeth with black caps at snaggle-tooth random.

"If you see this boy, " said the ballerina, "do not—I repeat, do not— try to reason with him."

ⓓThere was the shriek of a door being torn from its hinges.

Screams and barking cries of consternation came from the television set. The photograph of Harrison Bergeron on the screen jumped again and again, as though dancing to the tune of an earthquake.

George Bergeron correctly identified the earthquake, and well he might have—for many was the time ⓔhis own home had danced to the same crashing tune. "My God—" said George, "that (D)must have been Harrison!"

The realization was blasted from his mind instantly by the sound of an automobile collision in his head.

When George could open his eyes again, the photograph of Harrison was gone. A living, breathing Harrison filled the screen.

Clanking, clownish, and huge, Harrison stood—in the center of the studio. The knob of the uprooted studio door was still in his hand. Ballerinas, technicians, musicians, and announcers cowered on their knees before him, expecting to die.

ⓗ"I am the Emperor!" cried Harrison. "Do you hear? I am the Emperor! Everybody must do what I say at once!" He stamped his foot and the studio shook.

"Even as I stand here" he bellowed, "crippled, hobbled, sickened— I am a greater ruler than any man who ever lived! Now watch me become what I can become!"

Harrison tore the straps of his handicap harness like wet tissue paper, tore straps guaranteed to support five thousand pounds.

Harrison's scrap-iron handicaps crashed to the floor.

Harrison thrust his thumbs under the bar of the padlock that secured his head harness. The bar snapped like celery. Harrison smashed his headphones and spectacles against the wall.

He flung away his rubber-ball nose, revealed a man that (E)would have awed Thor, the god of thunder.

7 According to the passage above, choose one that contains all the person whose statement is <u>CORRECT</u>.

> Jenny: Based on the underlined part ㉠, I can tell that the person in charge of getting the photo up on the screen may be incapable of performing his task properly, similar to the announcers with a stutter in this fiction.
>
> Max: Metaphor and alliteration are used in the underlined sentence ㉡ in order to show how scary and grotesque Harrison Bergeron looks.
>
> Sophia: According to the underlined sentence ㉢, Harrison Bergeron must be one of the most intelligent inventors who design a variety of handicaps.
>
> Micheal: Personification and simile are used in common in the underlined sentences ㉣ and ㉤.
>
> Elizabeth: When Harrison Bergeron yells, like the underlined sentence ㉥, it represents that he is rebelling against authority.
>
> * alliteration: the use, especially in poetry, of the same sound or sounds, especially consonants, at the beginning of several words

① Jenny and Max
② Sophia and Micheal
③ Jenny, Max, and Elizabeth
④ Sophia and Elizabeth
⑤ Michael and Elizabeth

8 How many among (A) ~ (E) is/are grammatically <u>INCORRECT</u>?
① one
② two
③ three
④ four
⑤ five

5 Sentence Completion

1 The credit-card cash advance is becoming as _____ as the automated teller machine.
① fragile
② divergent
③ peripheral
④ ubiquitous

어휘　advance 선대금 automated teller machine ATM fragile 깨지기 쉬운 divergent 분기하는, 벗어난, 다른 peripheral 주변의, 가장자리의 ubiquitous 도처에 깔린

2 For many students, anxiety about tests can be a major _____ to strong performance. If so, you need to set up some strategies for dealing with your anxiety.
① incentive
② impact
③ spur
④ obstacle

어휘　anxiety 근심 anxiety about tests 시험에 대한 근심 strong performance 좋은 성적 set up (전략을) 세우다 deal with 다루다 incentive 동기, 자극 impact 충격, 영향, 반향 spur 충동, 자극, 동기부여 obstacle 장애물

3 Kindness is the most important _____ a public servant can have.
① rule
② question
③ habit
④ effort
⑤ quality

어휘　kindness 친절 public servant 공무원 quality 질, 성질, 속성(attribute), 양질(fineness), 높은 신분, 고급잡지

4 Many people adopt the accepted way of thinking in their group just as easily as they adopt its etiquette. It is easy to find examples of their intellectual _____.

① dependence

② curiosity

③ maturity

④ sophistication

⑤ opinion

5 Criticism that tears down without suggesting areas of improvement is not _____ and should be avoided.

① mandatory

② conciliator

③ reprehensible

④ constructive

6 The orator had completely won over his audience. Eagerly they strained to hear his every word, nodding their heads often to indicate _____.

① affirmation

② disapprobation

③ bewilderment

④ indifference

7 If you _____, you do a job that he/she used to do, and do it as well as he/she did.

① fill someone's shoes

② get through to someone

③ are through with someone

④ make it up to someone

⑤ run around with someone

어휘 fill someone's shoes 남을 대신하다, 남의 책임을 인계받다 get through to ~에 연락이 되다 be through with ~와 관계를 끊다 make it up to ~에게 변상하다 run around with ~와 교제하다, 사귀다

8 Feeling restless and unhappy, he left the house to take a quiet stroll, hoping the tone of the day would not decline further into _____ and uncertainty.

① dissonance

② ardor

③ perversity

④ pretense

⑤ reticence

어휘 restless 불안한, 침착하지 못한 unhappy 불행한, 비참한 leave ~을 떠나다; ~을 남기다 stroll 산책하다 take a stroll 산책하다 quiet 조용한, 고요한 hope ~을 바라다, 기대하다 tone 분위기, 음색 decline 기울다, 쇠하다; ~을 거절하다 further (far의 비교급) 더 멀리, 더 이상 uncertainty 불확실성 dissonance 불화, 부조화 ardor 열정, 열의 perversity 외고집, 심술궂음 pretense 구실, 핑계, 겉치레 reticence 과묵함, 말이 적음

9 Every student is required and expected to observe strict discipline and _____ behavior both inside and outside the campus.

① erratic   ② irksome

③ decorous   ④ surreptitious

어휘 require ~을 요구하다, 필요로 하다 expect ~을 기대하다, 예상하다 be required and expected to Ⓡ ~하기를 요구받고 기대되어지다 observe ~을 지키다, 준수하다; ~을 관찰하다, 주목하다; (명절·축일 따위를) 축하하다, 기념하다 strict 엄한, 엄격한 discipline 규율; 훈련; 학과 behavior 행동 both A and B A와 B 모두 inside ~의 안에 outside ~의 밖에 erratic 별난, 변덕스러운, 상궤를 벗어난 irksome 지루한, 짜증나는 decorous 예의 바른, 점잖은 surreptitious 비밀의, 은밀한

10 The task was _____ and tedious, both mentally and physically.

① arduous

② fun

③ exceptional

④ whimsical

⑤ lonely

UNIT

3

비문학_예술

Understanding Art Case Study – The Death of Socrates

by Jacques-Louis David

☐ **exemplar**

n A typical or representative example

- The old oak tree in the center of the town square is an exemplar of strength and endurance.

☐ **neoclassical**

a Relating to a revival of classical aesthetics and forms, especially in literature, music, or art

- The neoclassical architecture of the government buildings reflects a return to classical design principles.

☐ **bring something to the fore**

To make something noticeable; to bring something to the front

- The new evidence brought to the fore during the trial changed the course of the investigation.

☐ **striking**

a Attracting attention due to being unusual, impressive, or prominent

- Her striking red dress stood out in the crowd of muted colors.

☐ **canvas**

a A strong, durable fabric used for painting on or as a surface for paintings

- The artist stretched the canvas tightly on the wooden frame before starting to paint.

☐ **jump out at**

To be immediately noticeable or prominent

- The bold headline on the front page of the newspaper jumped out at readers.

☐ **right away**

ad Immediately; without delay

- When the fire alarm sounded, everyone evacuated the building right away.

☐ clarity **n** The quality of being clear, coherent, and easily understood

- The professor's explanation provided clarity on the complex scientific concept.

☐ fierce **a** Having a violent or aggressive nature; intense or passionate

- The fierce storm battered the coastal town, causing widespread damage.

☐ gesture **n** A movement or action that expresses an idea, sentiment, or intention

- The speaker used a gesture of open palms to signal honesty and transparency.

☐ interplay **n** The way in which different elements interact or influence each other

- The interplay between light and shadow created a dramatic effect in the artwork.

☐ chalice **n** A large cup or goblet, typically used for religious ceremonies

- The priest raised the chalice during the sacred ritual.

☐ poisoned chalice **n** A thing that seems attractive but is likely to be damaging

- Accepting the leadership role turned out to be a poisoned chalice as it brought unexpected challenges.

☐ drape **v** To arrange or hang cloth gracefully

- She decided to drape the curtains to add a touch of elegance to the room.

☐ depict **v** To represent or portray in art or literature

- The mural on the wall depicted scenes from the town's rich history.

☐ **be sentenced to death**	To receive a punishment of death after a legal trial
	• The notorious criminal <u>was sentenced to death</u> for his heinous crimes.
☐ **hemlock**	**n** A poisonous plant that can be fatal if ingested
	• Socrates famously chose to drink <u>hemlock</u> rather than renounce his philosophical beliefs.
☐ **fear**	**n** An unpleasant emotion caused by the belief that someone or something is dangerous
	• The <u>fear</u> of heights prevented her from enjoying the breathtaking view from the mountaintop.
☐ **embrace**	**v** To hold someone closely in one's arms; to accept or support willingly
	• The friends shared a warm <u>embrace</u> after being reunited.
☐ **apotheosis**	**n** The highest point in the development of something; the elevation of a person to the status of a god
	• The successful entrepreneur's journey was considered the <u>apotheosis</u> of dedication and hard work.
☐ **the moment just as S V**	Refers to a specific instant when a particular action or event occurs
	• <u>The moment just as</u> the sun set, the sky turned vibrant with hues of orange and pink.
☐ **grab for**	To reach out and seize something quickly and eagerly
	• In the crowded market, people would often <u>grab for</u> the discounted items on the shelves.
☐ **poisoned**	**a** Contaminated with a substance that can cause harm or death
	• The <u>poisoned</u> apple had a deadly effect on anyone who took a bite.

□ **draught**

n A current of air, typically coming into a room or space

- She closed the window to prevent the cold <u>draught</u> from entering the room.

□ **at length**

ad After a long period of time or discussion

- The author spoke <u>at length</u> about the inspiration behind their latest novel.

□ **immorality**

n The state of being morally wrong or sinful

- The community condemned the <u>immorality</u> depicted in the controversial film.

□ **implement**

n A tool or instrument used for a particular purpose

- The chef used various kitchen <u>implements</u> to prepare the elaborate meal.

□ **in hand**

Currently being dealt with or managed

- With the new project <u>in hand</u>, the team started planning the necessary steps.

□ **defiant**

Showing open resistance or disobedience

- Despite the warnings, the student remained <u>defiant</u> and refused to follow the rules.

□ **gesture toward**

To make a movement indicating something or someone

- The speaker <u>gestured toward</u> the map to illustrate the upcoming travel route.

□ **afterlife**

n Life after death; the belief in a continuation of existence

- Different cultures have various beliefs regarding what happens in the <u>afterlife</u>.

□ **hasten**

v To hurry or accelerate the occurrence of something

- The dark clouds seemed to <u>hasten</u> the arrival of the impending storm.

☐ **idealize**   **v** To regard or represent something as perfect or ideal

- Some individuals tend to <u>idealize</u> their childhood as a time of innocence and joy.

☐ **muscular**   **a** Relating to or involving the muscles

- Regular exercise helps in building and maintaining a <u>muscular</u> physique.

☐ **rake**   **v** To gather, collect, or move with a tool having teeth or prongs

- The gardener used a <u>rake</u> to gather fallen leaves from the lawn.

☐ **pour**   **v** To cause a liquid to flow in a steady stream

- She carefully <u>poured</u> the hot tea into the cup.

☐ **figure**   **n** A person's bodily shape; a numerical symbol or value

- The artist created a detailed <u>figure</u> in the painting, capturing the subject's posture.

☐ **tableau**   **n** A picturesque grouping or arrangement, often in a still-life format

- The actors posed in a beautiful <u>tableau</u> for the final scene of the play.

☐ **muted**   **a** Subdued in color or tone; not loud or bright

- The <u>muted</u> colors of the sunset created a peaceful and serene atmosphere.

☐ **vivid**   **a** Strikingly bright or intense; producing a clear and distinct impression

- Her <u>vivid</u> descriptions brought the scenes in the novel to life.

☐ **executioner**	**n** A person who carries out the execution of a death sentence
	• In medieval times, the <u>executioner</u> was responsible for carrying out public punishments.

☐ **in red**	Marked or highlighted in the color red
	• She wrote the important points <u>in red</u> to emphasize their significance.

☐ **stoic = stoical**	**a** Enduring pain or hardship without showing emotions or complaining
	• Despite facing adversity, she remained <u>stoic</u> and focused on her goals.

☐ **commitment**	**n** A dedication or obligation to a cause or activity
	• His <u>commitment</u> to the project was evident in the long hours he spent working on it.

☐ **abstract**	**a** Existing in thought or as an idea but not having a physical or concrete existence
	• The concept of justice is often discussed in <u>abstract</u> terms.

☐ **in the face of / in ~ of**	Despite; confronting a difficult situation
	• <u>In the face of</u> adversity, they stood united and faced the challenges together.

☐ **ethical**	**a** Pertaining to or conforming to principles of morality or virtue
	• The company is committed to maintaining high <u>ethical</u> standards in its business practices.

☐ **seek to**	**v** to attempt or aspire to achieve a particular goal
	• The organization <u>seeks to</u> promote education and awareness on environmental issues.

the French Revolution

A period of radical social and political upheaval in France from 1789 to 1799

- The French Revolution had a profound impact on the political landscape of Europe.

monarchy

n A form of government with a monarch (king or queen) as the head

- England has a constitutional monarchy, where the monarch's powers are limited by a constitution.

in decline

Experiencing a gradual decrease or deterioration

- The once-thriving industry is now in decline due to changing market trends.

reformer

n A person who advocates for or works toward positive changes or improvements

- The political reformer campaigned for social justice and equality.

ache to V

Intensely desire or long for something

- She ached to visit her childhood home after many years away.

install

v To set up or place something in position for use

- The technician will install the new software on your computer.

akin to

Similar to or having a family relationship with

- His writing style is akin to that of his favorite author.

Greek antiquity

n The historical period of ancient Greece

- Scholars study Greek antiquity to understand the origins of Western philosophy.

execute

v To carry out or accomplish a task, plan, or order

- The team will execute the project according to the established timeline.

unveil

v To reveal or make something known for the first time

- The company will unveil its new product during the press conference.

the salon

A social gathering or meeting where people engage in intellectual or artistic discussions

- The literary salon was a popular forum for exchanging ideas during the Enlightenment.

commission

n An official order or authorization to do something

- The artist received a commission to paint a portrait for a wealthy patron.

wildly

ad In an uncontrolled or unrestrained manner

- The rumors about the upcoming product spread wildly across social media.

identify

v To recognize or distinguish someone or something

- It is important to identify the key factors contributing to the problem for effective solutions.

Xanthippe

The wife of Socrates, known for her sharp and shrewish temperament

- Xanthippe was often portrayed in literature as a challenging but intriguing figure.

distress

a Experiencing hardship, danger, or suffering

- The ship sent out a distress signal when it encountered rough seas.

☐ **clutch**   **v** to Grasp or hold tightly

- She <u>clutched</u> her bag tightly as she walked through the crowded street.

☐ **signal**   **n** A gesture, action, or sound conveying information or instructions

- The traffic light turned red, <u>signaling</u> drivers to stop.

☐ **strive**   **v** To make great efforts to achieve something

- She <u>strives</u> for excellence in her academic and professional pursuits.

☐ **besides**   **ad** In addition to; moreover

- <u>Besides</u> studying, he enjoys playing musical instruments in his free time.

☐ **altering**   **a** Changing or modifying

- The artist spent hours <u>altering</u> the colors and composition of the painting.

☐ **echo**   **n** A repeated sound caused by the reflection of sound waves

- Her laughter <u>echoed</u> through the empty hallway.

☐ **popularize**   **v** To make something widely known or enjoyed by the public

- The invention of the printing press helped to <u>popularize</u> books among the masses.

☐ **teachings**   **n** Ideas or principles taught by a person or institution

- The professor's <u>teachings</u> on philosophy influenced many students.

☐ **stage**　　　　**n** A raised platform on which performances take place

- The actors rehearsed on the <u>stage</u> before the play's opening night.

☐ **protagonist**　　　**n** The main character in a story, often the central figure in the plot

- In the novel, the <u>protagonist</u> embarks on a journey of self-discovery.

☐ **melt into**　　　Blend or merge into something seamlessly

- The colors of the sunset seemed to <u>melt into</u> the horizon.

☐ **withdrawn**　　　**a** Reserved or introverted; avoiding social interaction

- He became <u>withdrawn</u> after the loss of a close friend.

☐ **explode**　　　**v** To burst or shatter violently due to internal pressure

- The fireworks <u>exploded</u> in a dazzling display of colors.

☐ **re-contextualize**　　**v** To place something in a new or different context

- The artist aimed to <u>re-contextualize</u> historical events through their artwork.

☐ **idealized**　　　**a** Represented or viewed in an ideal form; portraying something in an idealized manner

- The painting <u>idealized</u> the picturesque landscape, emphasizing its beauty.

☐ **position**　　　**n** A place or location; the way in which something is placed

- He carefully adjusted the <u>position</u> of the furniture in the room.

☐ **frozen**　　　**a** Turned into ice or hardened by cold temperatures

- The lake was <u>frozen</u>, and people were ice skating on its surface.

☐ **lateral** **a** Relating to or situated at the side; moving sideways

- The lateral movement of the crab allowed it to navigate the sandy beach.

☐ **give way to** To yield or make room for; allow something new to replace

- The old traditions gave way to modern practices in the evolving society.

☐ **fall out** To have a disagreement or conflict; to lose friendship or cooperation

- The friends fell out over a minor misunderstanding and stopped talking.

☐ **restage** **v** To stage or present (a play, performance, etc.) again

- The director decided to restage the classic play with a modern twist.

☐ **painstakingly** **ad** With great care, thoroughness, and attention to detail

- She painstakingly restored the antique furniture to its original condition.

☐ **serve the needs of** To fulfill or meet the requirements or demands of someone or something

- The new policies aim to serve the needs of the diverse community.

☐ **rigorous** **a** Thorough, accurate, and demanding strict attention to procedures

- The scientific experiment underwent rigorous testing to ensure validity.

☐ **betray** **v** To be disloyal or unfaithful; to reveal or disclose something

- His actions seemed to betray the trust of those who believed in him.

☐ **construction**　　**n** The act or process of building or assembling something

- The <u>construction</u> of the new bridge will begin next month.

☐ **terror**　　**n** Extreme fear, often caused by a perceived threat or danger

- The town lived in <u>terror</u> after the series of mysterious events.

☐ **blunt**　　**a** Having a dull edge or point; straightforward and direct in speech or manner

- The knife was too <u>blunt</u> to cut through the tough meat.

☐ **render**　　**v** To provide, submit, or deliver something; to cause to become or make

- The artist <u>rendered</u> the landscape in vivid colors on the canvas.

2 Text Reading

: Understanding Art Case Study –
The Death of Socrates

Text 1

This is *The Death of Socrates* by Jacques-Louis David. Completed in 1787, it is an exemplar of the Neoclassical period in France which David virtually created and brought to the fore himself. Before I say more, it's important to note just how striking this canvas is, not knowing anything about it.

So much jumps out at me right away: the clarity of the scene; the fierce gesture of the man in the middle; the interplay of the chalice; and the hand that reaches for it; the angles of the light and the men; the soft draping garments; the bare flat stone wall.

As the title suggests, the scene depicts the death of Socrates, told famously by Plato in his dialogue on the soul, *The Phaedo*. Socrates had been convicted in Athenian court of failing to acknowledge the gods of the city and corrupting the city's youth and sentenced to death by drinking hemlocks. As Plato makes clear in another dialogue, *the Crito*, Socrates could have escaped into exile, but instead he chooses to die, taking the opportunity to teach his final lesson, that death is not to be feared by the philosopher, but embraced as an apotheosis of the soul.

핵심 PLUS!

1 (**Completed** in 1787), **it** is an <u>exemplar</u> of the Neoclassical period in France (**which** David virtually created and brought to the fore himself).

- it을 수식하는 과거분사 completed
- it = *The Death of Socrates*
- 선행사 exemplar를 수식하는 생략 가능한 목적격 관계대명사 which
  → an **exemplar** of the Neoclassical period in France (**which**) David virtually created and brought to the fore himself.

2 Before I say more, it's important to note (just) (**how** striking this canvas is), <u>not knowing</u> anything about it.

- 의문부사 how가 이끄는 명사절
- 분사구문 not knowing anything about it은 문맥상 especially when you(or we) don't even know anything about it 또는 even though you(or we) don't know anything about it 정도로 바꾸어 쓸 수 있음.

UNIT

3

3 So <u>much</u> jumps out at me right away.

- 주어인 much가 대명사로 쓰인 문장.

4 As the title suggests, the scene depicts <u>the death</u> of Socrates, (**told** famously by Plato in his dialogue on the soul, *The Phaedo*).

- 과거분사 told가 이끄는 형용사구는 the death를 수식.

5 Socrates had been convicted (in Athenian court) **of** [[failing] to acknowledge the gods of the city) and [corrupting] the city's youth)] and sentenced to death by drinking hemlocks.

- be convicted of: ~로 인해 유죄를 받다
- 전치사 of에 걸리는 동명사 병치: of fail**ing** ~ and corrupt**ing**
- 서술부 생략/병치: had been **convicted** ~ and **sentenced** ~

6 As Plato makes clear in another dialogue, *the Crito*, Socrates <u>could have escaped</u> into exile, but instead he chooses to die, taking the opportunity to teach his final lesson, (**that** death is not to be feared by the philosopher, but embraced as an apotheosis of the soul).

- could have p.p: ~ 할 수 있었다
- 분사구문: ~, and he takes the opportunity to teach his final lesson
- the opportunity = death is not to be feared by the philosopher, but embraced as an apotheosis of the soul
- 동격의 that

David chooses to paint the moment just as Socrates is grabbing for the poisoned draught. He's been discussing at length the immorality of the soul and doesn't even seem to care that he's about to take the implement of his death in hand. On the contrary, Socrates is defiant, gesturing toward the afterlife to which he hastens.

David idealizes him. Socrates would have been 70 at the time and somewhat less muscular and beautiful than painted here. The raking light coming in from the top-left pours onto Socrates, the brightest figure in the tableau. The colors muted at the sides become vivid in the center with the executioner in red and Socrates.

For David, Socrates is a symbol of strength over passion, of stoic commitment to an abstract principle even in the face of death. But this is the ethical message David sought to offer the French, two years before the French Revolution, as the monarchy was in decline and reformers ached to install a democracy akin to that of Socrates' own time in Greek antiquity, or the United States which had just executed its own revolution five years prior. Indeed, Thomas Jefferson himself was present at the unveiling of this painting at the Salon of 1787. The image commissioned by two radical political reformers was wildly popular.

어구 및 표현 연구

 **핵심 PLUS!**

1 David chooses to paint <u>the moment</u> (just <u>as</u> Socrates is grabbing for the poisoned draught).

- 부사구 삽입주의: 타동사 + (부사구) + 목적어
- 접속사 as가 이끄는 부사절이 마치 the moment의 동격절과 같이 해석됨에 주의: "~할 때의 바로 그 순간"

2 He's been <u>discussing</u> (at length) <u>the immorality of the soul</u> and doesn't even seem to <u>care</u> (<u>**that**</u> he's about to take the implement of his death in hand).

- 타동사 discuss의 목적어: the immorality of the soul
- 타동사 care의 목적어 자리에 명사절 that: care **that** S V

3 On the contrary, Socrates is defiant, gesturing toward the afterlife **to which** he hastens.

- [전치사 + 관계대명사]에서 to는 hasten to에서 to가 관계대명사 앞으로 이동한 경우임.
- hasten to (장소): ~로 서두르다

4 Socrates would have been 70 at the time and somewhat less muscular and beautiful than painted here.

- would have p.p: ~이었을 것이다
- be동사 뒤에 걸리는 보어 병치

5 S [The raking light **coming** in from the top-left] pours onto Socrates, the brightest figure in the tableau.

- light를 수식하는 후치수식의 현재분사: N **v-ing** ~
- 동격의 코마: Socrates = the brightest figure

6 S [The colors (**muted** at the sides)] become vivid in the center (with the executioner in red and Socrates).

- 주어 자리에서 명사를 후치하는 과거분사: N v-ed ~

7 For David, Socrates is a symbol (of strength over passion), (of stoic commitment to an abstract principle even in the face of death).

- symbol을 수식하는 of가 이끄는 전치사구 병치: N (of N ~), (of N ~)

8 But this is the ethical message (that) David sought to offer the French, two years before the French Revolution, [**as** the monarchy was in decline and reformers ached to install a democracy (which was) akin to **that** of Socrates' own time in Greek antiquity, or the United States (**which** had just executed its own revolution five years prior)].

- 타동사 seek(sought)의 목적어가 생략된 목적격 관계대명사의 생략
- 부사절을 이끄는 접속사 내 [주격 관계대명사 + be동사]의 생략과 the United States를 수식하는 주격 관계대명사절
- that = democracy

9 [The image [(which was) **commissioned** by two radical political reformers]] was wildly popular.

- [주격 관계대명사 + be동사]의 생략과 과거분사 commissioned의 image 수식

David had already made his names with another severe moralistic canvas, *The Oath of the Horatii*, which effectively invented the neoclassical style. Taking its cues from the stark simplicity of ancient Greece and Rome, from the ancient obsession with anatomy and musculature, from the two-dimensional freezes depicting historical events, Neoclassicism, as rendered by David, made its points strongly and severely. This was in direct opposition to the dominant Rococo style that reflected the ornate and hedonistic lifestyles of the monarchy.

In the *Horatii*, as in *The Death of Socrates*, those dedicated to principle are depicted with angular geometry, while those ruled by passion are curved and weak. In both canvases, the backgrounds are flat, fixing attention on the foreground, where like a freeze the action can be read from side to side.

One way to read *The Death of Socrates* is right to left. The anguish of Socrates followers curling and twisting opens up onto the calm expression of the man himself and flows down through his right arm which hovers over the cup of poison. The space between the hand and the cup, the exact center of the image, is the seat of maximum narrative charge, then it falls back into the pain of the man who delivers the poison, who turns his gaze away from Socrates and finally comes to rest on the man sitting at the foot of the bed, unengaged. More on him in a moment.

어구 및 표현 연구

핵심 PLUS!

1 David had already made his names with another severe moralistic canvas, *The Oath of the Horatii*, **which** effectively invented the neoclassical style.

• 계속적 용법의 관계대명사 which

2 [**Taking** its cues (from the stark simplicity of ancient Greece and Rome), (from the ancient obsession with anatomy and musculature), and (from the two-dimensional freezes **depicting** historical events)], S [Neoclassicism, **as rendered by** David], made its points strongly and severely.

• 분사구문에 걸리는 전치사구의 병치

• freezes를 수식하는 현재분사 depicting

• render는 "표현하다, 묘사하다; 연주[연출]하다" 뜻의 타동사임.
as rendered by: ~에 의해서 표현된 것처럼

3 This was in direct opposition to the dominant Rococo style (**that** reflected the ornate and hedonistic lifestyles of the monarchy).

- 주격 관계대명사 that

4 In the *Horatii*, as in *The Death of Socrates*, [those (which are) dedicated to principle] are depicted with angular geometry, while [those (which are) ruled by passion] are curved and weak.

- [주격 관계대명사 + be동사]의 생략

5 In both canvases, the backgrounds are flat, (**fixing** attention on the foreground), [where (like a freeze) the action can be read from side to side].

- 분사구문의 관계대명사 전환: the backgrounds are flat, which **fixes** attention on the foreground
- where(= whereas)에 걸리는 구조 파악.

6 S [The anguish of Socrates followers (**curling** and **twisting**)] opens up onto the calm expression of the man himself and flows down through his right arm (**which** hovers over the cup of poison).

- 현재분사의 후치수식과 S opens ~ and flows ~의 서술형 병치
- 선행사 his right arm을 수식하는 주격 관계대명사 which

7 S [The space between the hand and the cup, the exact center of the image], is the seat of maximum narrative charge, then (it) **falls** back into the pain of the man (**who** delivers the poison), (**who** **turns** his gaze away from Socrates) and finally **comes** to rest on the man sitting at the foot of the bed, unengaged).

- 동격의 코마 (The space = the exact center of the image)
- 선행사 man을 수식하는 관계대명사 병치: N (who ~, who ~)
- 구조상 it을 생략하고, S V1, V2, and V3로 파악해 볼 것.

David doesn't identify anyone in the painting, but we can infer from accounts of Socrates' actual death that in the background is Socrates' wife, Xanthippe, led away in distress, and clutching Socrates' leg is Crito, his oldest and most faithful student. Under Crito, we can see that David has signed his own name, signaling a feeling of connection with the man. David, weaker than his ideal of moral strength, nonetheless grabs and strives toward him.

Besides altering Socrates' face and physique, David decreases the number of people present at the event from over fifteen to twelve, echoing the number of disciples at Da Vinci's Last Supper. But I think the most significant change is the addition of the character at the foot of the bed.

This is Plato. The man who popularized Socrates' teachings by staging him as the protagonists in over 30 philosophical dialogues. But simply without Plato, there would be no Socrates. The two men melt into each other historically. It's hard to determine where Socrates' philosophy ends and Plato's begins. Not only was Plato absent at the death of Socrates, but he was a young man at the time. Here David has him as old and withdrawn.

어구 및 표현 연구

 핵심 PLUS!

1   David doesn't identify anyone in the painting, but we can <u>infer</u> (from accounts of Socrates' actual death) <u>that in the background</u> is **Socrates' wife**, Xanthippe, <u>led away</u> in distress, and (<u>**clutching**</u> Socrates' leg) is Crito, his oldest and most faithful student.

- infer that S V의 구조

- Socrates' wife, Xanthippe is (in the background)에서 장소방향의 부사 in the background가 문두로 나간 1형식 도치구문임.

- led는 Socrates' wife 수식하는 과거분사

- 동명사 clutching이 이끄는 주어

2   Under Crito, we can see that David has signed his own name, **signaling** a feeling of connection with the man.

- 분사구문의 관계대명사 전환
  David has signed his own name, **signaling** a feeling of connection with the man.
  → David has signed his own name, **which signals** a feeling of connection with the man.

3 [David, (who is) weaker than his ideal of moral strength], nonetheless grabs and strives toward him.

• [주격 관계대명사 + be동사] 생략

4 (Besides altering Socrates' face and physique), David decreases [the number of people (who are) present at the event from over fifteen to twelve], **echoing** the number of disciples at Da Vinci's *Last Supper*.

• 전치사 besides가 이끄는 부사구
• [주격 관계대명사 + be동사] 생략
• 분사구문 echoing: , which echoes ~

5 This is **Plato**. **The man** who popularized Socrates' teachings by staging him as the protagonists in over 30 philosophical dialogues.

• Plato의 동격적 성격으로 명사구가 이어지는 경우.

6 But (simply **without** Plato), there **would** be no Socrates.

• 가정법 과거: without, would
• without은 **but for**, **if it were not for**, **were it not for**로 바꾸어 쓸 수 있음.

7 **It**'s hard [**to determine** (**where** Socrates' philosophy ends and Plato's begins)].

• 가주어 it/진주어 to V
• 진주어 내 to부정사에 걸리는 타동사 determine의 목적어 자리에 **의문사가 이끄는 명사절의 어순**: 의문사 + 주어 + 동사

8 **Not only** was Plato absent at the death of Socrates, but he (**also**) was a young man at the time.

• not only가 문두로 위치하면서 주어와 동사의 도치가 일어남.
• 생략된 also의 위치 확인.

I said earlier that you can read the canvas from right to left, but you can also read it from left to right. The whole scene, it seems to me, appears to explode out of the back of Plato's head, re-contextualizing it as a memory, an idealized memory in which Socrates gestures in the exact same way he does in *Raphael's School of Athens*. Significantly, Plato is positioned apart from the flat background where the frozen lateral moment gives way to the depth of time and reality. It strikes me that this is the way memories often fall out, restaged with smooth edges and perfect light, two-dimensional, idealized, painstakingly arranged to serve the needs of the present. In the character of Plato, the rigorous ethical reality of the scene is betrayed by its own self-awareness as a construction, and in only a few short years, the noble ideals of the French Revolution will be betrayed as well by the terror that is to follow. Maybe this is why almost prophetically David signs his name here a second time. Neoclassicism like this may seem severe and blunts, but so much is happening in David's Death of Socrates, an interplay of historical, personal, political, and aesthetic elements rendered forcefully, subtly, and beautifully. Put another way, it's a work of genius.

어구 및 표현 연구

 핵심 PLUS!

1 The whole scene, (<u>it seems to me</u>), appears to explode out of the back of Plato's head, <u>re-contextualizing</u> it as a memory, an idealized memory (<u>in which</u> Socrates gestures in the exact same way he does in *Raphael's School of Athens*).

- it seems to me that S V에서 it seems to me가 S V 사이에 삽입된 형태.
- 동격의 코마: a memory = an idealized memory
- 분사구문 re-contextualizing
- 완전절을 가지는 [전치사 + 관계대명사]: in which S V (완전절)

2 Significantly, Plato is positioned apart from the flat background (<u>where</u> the frozen lateral moment gives way to the depth of time and reality).

- 선행사 background를 수식하는 관계부사 where: N(장소 선행사) where S V(완전절)

3 **It strikes me that** this is [**the way** memories often fall out, (restaged with smooth edges and perfect light), (two-dimensional), (idealized), (painstakingly arranged to serve the needs of the present)].

- It strikes me that S V: S V가 나에게 떠오르다
- the way (in which) S V
- 밑줄 친 표현은 모두 memories에 대한 부연설명.

4 (In the character of Plato), the rigorous ethical reality of the scene **is betrayed by** its own self-awareness as a construction, and (in only a few short years), the noble ideals of the French Revolution will **be betrayed** (as well) **by** the terror (**that is to** follow).

- be p.p by의 수동태
- 선행사 terror를 수식하는 주격 관계대명사
- be to용법: 예정

5 Maybe this is [**why** almost prophetically David signs his name here a second time].

- 관계부사 why: why S V

6 Neoclassicism like this may seem severe and blunts, but so **much** is happening in David's *Death of Socrates*, (an interplay of historical, personal, political, and aesthetic elements **rendered** forcefully, subtly, and beautifully).

- 주어 자리의 much는 대명사의 역할.
- 코마 이후의 내용은 much에 대한 동격 부연.
- elements를 수식하는 과거분사 rendered

7 **Put another way**, it's a work of genius.

- put은 여기서 "표현하다"의 과거분사로 **If it is** put another way에서 밑줄 친 표현이 생략된 형태임.

Voca Check

* 빈칸에 들어갈 적절한 단어를 박스에서 찾아 넣으시오.

1

embrace / interplay / clarity / exemplar / apotheosis / depict / fierce /
hemlock / drape / muted

1   The Death of Socrates by David serves as an _____ of Neoclassical
painting, embodying the style's principles.

2   The artist achieved remarkable _____ in portraying the moral and
philosophical themes of Socrates' demise.

3   The _____ between light and shadow in the painting adds depth to
the composition, creating a dramatic effect.

4   The tragic scene reaches its _____ as Socrates willingly drinks the
hemlock, symbolizing his chosen path.

5   The way David chose to _____ the figures in classical attire enhances
the timeless quality of the artwork.

6   The color palette is intentionally _____, conveying a somber mood
befitting the gravity of the subject.

7   In his masterpiece, David skillfully _____ the final moments of
Socrates' life, capturing the philosopher's essence.

8   The presence of the _____, a poisonous plant used for execution,
adds a layer of symbolism to the painting.

9   The figures' poses and expressions reflect the profound philosophical
_____ present in Socrates' teachings.

10 The artist's use of strong, _____ brushstrokes adds intensity to the
emotions conveyed in the artwork.

2 muted / monarchy / figure / tableau / executioner / vivid / reformer /
ethical / commitment / stoic

1 The artist skillfully portrays the _____ atmosphere of the scene
   through the use of subdued colors.

2 The _____ of Socrates, draped in classical attire, becomes a central
   element in the composition.

3 The painting serves as a poignant _____ of philosophical sacrifice and
   unwavering dedication to principles.

4 The _____ colors used for Socrates' figure contrast with the darker
   tones, emphasizing his significance.

5 The ominous presence of the _____, ready to carry out the execution,
   adds a sense of impending doom.

6 Socrates' _____ demeanor in the face of death becomes a focal point
   of the Neoclassical masterpiece.

7 The artist captures the unwavering _____ of Socrates, who chooses
   to drink the hemlock willingly.

8 The _____ values upheld by the philosopher were evident in his moral
   teachings.

9 The downfall of the _____ led to a shift towards more democratic
   ideals.

10 The _____ aimed to bring about positive changes in the political and
   social systems.

3 commission / akin / execute / unveil / distress / wildly / install / Xanthippe / antiquity / identify

1 The artist was tasked to _____ a mural on the building's exterior.

2 The new discovery has features _____ to those found in ancient civilizations.

3 The artifact dates back to the _____, showcasing its historical significance.

4 The court decided to _____ the convicted criminal for his heinous crimes.

5 The museum will soon _____ a new exhibit featuring rare artifacts.

6 The government appointed a special committee to _____ a report on the matter.

7 The news of the unexpected event spread _____ throughout the community.

8 It is crucial to _____ the suspect accurately before making any arrests.

9 Historical records _____ as the wife of the renowned philosopher.

10 The villagers were in a state of _____ after the unexpected natural disaster.

4 idealized / teach / re-contextualize / position / popularize / signal / explode / stage / frozen / echo

1 The actor delivered a powerful monologue while standing center

_____.

2 The teacher worked tirelessly to _____ the complex concepts to the students.

3 The author's new book aims to _____ the ideas presented in their previous work.

4 The charismatic speaker sought to _____ their ideas to a broader audience.

5 The explorer used a flare gun to _____ their location in the wilderness.

6 The artist chose to _____ the traditional boundaries of sculpture with their avant-garde piece.

7 The historian sought to _____ historical events by examining them from diverse perspectives.

8 The painting portrayed an _____ version of the cityscape, emphasizing its beauty and perfection.

9 The professor argued for a different _____ on the controversial issue during the debate.

10 The river remained _____ during the harsh winter, with a layer of ice covering its surface.

5

painstakingly / blunt / fell out / terror / gave way to / render / lateral / rigorous / construction / betrayed

1   The _____ movement of the dancer added a unique dimension to the performance.

2   As the old traditions _____ new ideas, the society underwent a significant transformation.

3   The friendship between the two friends began to _____ after a series of misunderstandings.

4   The architect _____ designed every detail of the building, ensuring perfection in its construction.

5   The soldiers faced moments of sheer _____ as they advanced into the heart of the enemy territory.

6   The professor's _____ grading system challenged students to strive for excellence.

7   His actions seemed to _____ the trust that others had placed in him, leaving them disappointed.

8   The _____ of the new bridge was completed ahead of schedule, showcasing the engineering team's expertise.

9   She was known for her _____ honesty, always speaking her mind without sugarcoating the truth.

10 The artist's goal was to _____ the beauty of the landscape through a series of detailed paintings.

Reading Comprehension **1**

[1–2] 다음을 읽고, 물음에 답하시오.

  NOTE

This is *The Death of Socrates* by Jacques-Louis David. Completed in 1787, it is an exemplar of the Neoclassical period in France which David virtually created and ㉠<u>brought to the fore</u> himself. Before I say more, it's important to note just how striking this canvas is, not knowing anything about. So much jumps out at me right away: the clarity of the scene; the fierce gesture of the man in the middle; the interplay of the chalice; and the hand that reaches for it; the angles of the light and the men; the soft draping garments; the bare flat stone wall.

As the title suggests, the scene depicts the death of Socrates, told famously by Plato in his dialogue on the soul, *The Phaedo*. Socrates had been convicted in Athenian court of failing to acknowledge the gods of the city and corrupting the city's youth and sentenced to death by drinking ㉡<u>hemlocks</u>. As Plato makes clear in another dialogue, *the Crito*, Socrates could have escaped into exile, but instead he chooses to die taking the opportunity to teach his final lesson, that death is not to be feared by the philosopher, but embraced as an ㉢<u>apotheosis</u> of the soul.

David chooses to paint the moment just as Socrates is grabbing for the poisoned draught. He's been discussing at length the immorality of the soul and doesn't even seem to care that he's about to take the implement of his death in hand. On the contrary, Socrates is defiant, gesturing toward the afterlife to which he hastens. David idealizes him. Socrates would have been 70 at the time and somewhat less muscular and beautiful than painted here. The raking light coming in from the top-left pours onto Socrates, the brightest figure in the ㉣<u>tableau</u>. The colors muted at the sides become vivid in the center with the executioner in red and Socrates.

For David, Socrates is a symbol of strength over passion, of ⓪stoic commitment to an abstract principle even in the face of death. But this is the ethical message David sought to offer the French, two years before the French Revolution, as the monarchy was in decline and reformers ached to install a democracy akin to that of Socrates' own time in Greek antiquity, or the United States which had just executed its own revolution five years prior. Indeed, Thomas Jefferson himself was present at the unveiling of this painting at the Salon of 1787. The image commissioned by two radical political reformers was wildly popular.

1 본문에서 언급된 내용이 <u>아닌</u> 것은?

① Images that you intuitively recognize when you first encounter the work
② Symbolic meanings of the actions of the protagonist depicted in the piece
③ Detailed description of the piece
④ Messages conveyed through the picture
⑤ Three reasons why Socrates was sentenced to death

2 ㉠~⑩에 대한 설명으로 옳지 <u>않은</u> 것을 하나 고르면?

① ㉠: If something or someone is brought to the fore, they are willing to come forward and face the reality.
② ㉡: Hemlock refers to a poisonous plant.
③ ㉢: If something is the apotheosis of something else, it is an ideal or typical example of it.
④ ㉣: A tableau is a piece of art such as sculpture or painting.
⑤ ⑩: If you say that someone is stoic, you mean that he is determined not to complain or show your feelings, especially when something bad happens to him.

In *the lloratii*, as in *The Death of Socrates*, those dedicated to principle are depicted with angular geometry, while those ruled by passion are curved and weak. In both canvases, the backgrounds are flat, fixing attention on the foreground, where like a freeze the action can be read from side to side.

[가] David doesn't identify anyone in the painting, but we can infer from accounts of Socrates' actual death that in the background is Socrates' wife, Xanthippe, led away in distress, and clutching Socrates' leg is Crito, his oldest and most faithful student. Under Crito, we can see that David has signed his own name, signaling a feeling of connection with the man. David, weaker than his ideal of moral strength, nonetheless grabs and strives toward him.

[나] The man who popularized Socrates' teachings by staging him as the protagonists in over 30 philosophical dialogues. But simply without Plato, there would be no Socrates. The two men melt into each other historically. It's hard to determine where Socrates' philosophy ends and Plato's begins. Not only was Plato absent at the death of Socrates, but he was a young man at the time. Here David has him as old and withdrawn.

[다] One way to read *The Death of Socrates* is right to left. The anguish of Socrates followers curling and twisting opens up onto the calm expression of the man himself and flows down through his right arm which hovers over the cup of poison. The space between the hand and the cup, the exact center of the image, is the seat of maximum narrative charge, that it falls back into the pain of the man who delivers the poison, who turns his gaze away from Socrates and finally comes to rest on the man sitting at the foot of the bed, unengaged. More on him in a moment

[라] Besides altering Socrates' face and physique, David decreases the number of people present at the event from over fifteen to twelve, echoing the number of disciples at Da Vinci's Last Supper. But I think the most significant change is the addition of the character at the foot of the bed. This is Plato.

① (라) – (나) – (가) – (다)
② (나) – (가) – (라) – (다)
③ (가) – (라) – (나) – (다)
④ (다) – (가) – (라) – (나)
⑤ (다) – (라) – (나) – (가)

[4-7] 다음을 읽고, 물음에 답하시오.

 NOTE

David had already ⓐmade his names with another severe moralistic canvas, *The Oath of the Horatii*, which effectively invented the neoclassical style. Taking its cues from the stark simplicity of ancient Greece and Rome, from the ancient obsession with anatomy and musculature, from the two-dimensional freezes depicting historical events, Neoclassicism, as rendered by David, made its points strongly and severely. This was in direct opposition to the dominant Rococo style that reflected the ornate and ⓑhedonistic lifestyles of the monarchy.

In the lloratii, as in *The Death of Socrates*, those dedicated to principle are depicted with angular geometry, while those ruled by passion are curved and weak. In both canvases, the backgrounds are flat, fixing attention on the foreground, where like a freeze the action can be read from side to side.

(가)One way to read The Death of Socrates is right to left. The anguish of Socrates followers curling and twisting opens up onto the calm expression of the man himself and flows down through his right arm which hovers over the cup of poison. The space between the hand and the cup, the exact center of the image, is the seat of maximum narrative charge, that it falls back into the pain of the man who delivers the poison, who turns his gaze away from Socrates and finally comes to rest on the man sitting at the foot of the bed, unengaged. More on him in a moment.

David doesn't identify anyone in the painting, but we can infer from accounts of Socrates' actual death that in the background is Socrates' wife, Xanthippe, led away ⓒin distress, and clutching Socrates' leg is Crito, his oldest and most faithful student. (나)Under Crito, we can see that David has signed his own name, signaling a feeling of connection with the man. David, weaker than his ideal of moral strength, nonetheless grabs and strives toward him.

Besides altering Socrates' face and physique, David decreases the number of people present at the event from over fifteen to twelve, echoing the number of disciples at Da Vinci's Last Supper. But I think the most significant change is the addition of the character at the foot of the bed.

This is Plato. The man who popularized Socrates' teachings by staging him as the protagonists in over 30 philosophical dialogues. But simply without Plato, there would be no Socrates. The two men melt into each other historically. It's hard to determine where Socrates' philosophy ends and Plato's begins. Not only was Plato absent at the death of Socrates, but he was a young man at the time. Here David has him as old and withdrawn.

I said earlier that you can read the canvas from right to left, but you can also read it from left to right. The whole scene, it seems to me, appears to explode out of the back of Plato's head, re-contextualizing it as a memory, an idealized memory in which Socrates' gestures in the exact same way ㉣he does in Raphael's School of Athens. Significantly, Plato is positioned apart from the flat background where the frozen lateral moment gives way to the depth of time and reality. It strikes me that this is the way memories often fall out, restaged with smooth edges and perfect light, two-dimensional, idealized, painstakingly arranged to serve the needs of the present.

In the character of Plato, the rigorous ethical reality of the scene is betrayed by its own self-awareness as a construction and in only a few short years, the noble ideals of the French Revolution will be betrayed as well by the terror that is to follow. Maybe this is why almost prophetically David signs his name here a second time.

Neoclassicism like this may seem severe and blunts, but so much is happening in David's Death of Socrates, an interplay of historical, personal, political, and aesthetic elements ㉤rendered forcefully, subtly, and beautifully. Put another away, it's a work of genius.

4 아래를 그림을 보면서 만약 본문의 밑줄 친 (가)와 달리 <u>왼쪽에서 오른쪽으로</u> 그림을 읽을 때 파악 또는 추론할 수 있는 내용으로 가장 설득력 있는 내용은?

① The first recognized character is Socrates.

② When read from left to right, it can be interpreted as a past recollection of Socrates' death in that Plato appears to be old.

③ Even if you read the picture on the left, you can see that Socrates' death was already fore-ordained by the fact that there is a cup of poison in the center of the picture.

④ The image of an aged Plato sitting away from Socrates seen from the far left, indicates he has abandoned his moral values.

⑤ An old-aged version of Plato sitting with his back turned away from Socrates shows that he was opposed to Socrates' ideas in his last years.

5 밑줄 친 (나)의 내용 추론으로 가장 적절한 것은?

① The painter is too material to pursue ideal values like Socrates.

② The painter is skeptical of Socrates' risking his life to uphold his moral ideals.

③ The painter related most to someone just like Crito who clutches at the morals and values that Socrates represent.

④ The painter would have been more aggressive in curbing Socrates' actions had he been Crito.

⑤ The painter emphasizes that he can practice moral ideals just as much as Socrates did.

UNIT

3

6 본문과 일치하지 <u>않거나</u> 추론할 수 <u>없는</u> 것은?

① Neoclassical art is much more ornamental and theatrical in style compared to Rococo art.

② The paint sighed the piece twice.

③ The number of people who participated in the event was more than the 12 people depicted in the piece.

④ Plato makes an appearance in the piece.

⑤ In Raphael's School of Athens, Plato points his finger towards the sky just like Socrates does in The Death of Socrates.

7 ㉠~㉤의 설명 중 옳지 <u>않은</u> 것은?

① The underlined phrase in ㉠ means to become well-known or famous.

② The opposite of a hedonistic lifestyle as in the underlined ㉡ is asceticism, which is a strong aversion to experiencing physical pleasure.

③ If someone is in distress as in ㉢, he or she is very upset.

④ "he" in ㉣ refers to Socrates.

⑤ The word "render" in ㉤ means to represent something in a work of art or a performance.

[1-3] 다음을 읽고, 물음에 답하시오.

 NOTE

This is *The Death of Socrates* by Jacques-Louis David. Completed in 1787, it is an ㉠exemplar of the Neoclassical period in France which David virtually created and brought to the fore himself. Before I say more, it's important to note just how striking this canvas is, not knowing anything about.

So much jumps out at me right away: the clarity of the scene; the fierce gesture of the man in the middle; the interplay of the chalice; and the hand that reaches for it; the angles of the light and the men; the soft draping garments; the bare flat stone wall.

As the title suggests, the scene depicts the death of Socrates, told famously by Plato in his dialogue on the soul, *The Phaedo*. Socrates had been ㉡convicted in Athenian court of failing to acknowledge the gods of the city and corrupting the city's youth and sentenced to death by drinking hemlocks. (가) As Plato makes clear in another dialogue, the Crito, Socrates could have escaped into exile, but instead he chooses to die taking the opportunity to teach his final lesson, that death is not to be feared by the philosopher, but embraced as an apotheosis of the soul. (나)

David chooses to paint the moment just as Socrates is grabbing for the poisoned draught. He's been discussing at length the immorality of the soul and doesn't even seem to care that he's about to take ㉢

the implement of his death in hand. (다) David idealizes him. Socrates would have been 70 at the time and somewhat less muscular and beautiful than painted here. (라) The raking light coming in from the top-left pours onto Socrates, the brightest figure in the tableau. The colors ㉣muted at the sides become vivid in the center with the executioner in red and Socrates. (마)

For David, Socrates is a symbol of strength over passion, of stoic commitment to an abstract principle even in the face of death. But this is the ethical message David sought to offer the French, two years before the French Revolution, as the monarchy was in decline and reformers ached to install a democracy akin to that of Socrates' own time in Greek antiquity, or the United States which had just executed its own revolution five years prior. Indeed, Thomas Jefferson himself was present at the unveiling of this painting at the Salon of 1787. The image ㉤(commission) by two radical political reformers was wildly popular.

UNIT

3

1   ㉠~㉤에 대한 설명 중 옳지 않은 것은?

① The word "exemplar" in ㉠ means "someone or something that is good enough to imitate."

② The word "convicted" in ㉡ means "having officially been found guilty of a crime in a law court."

③ ㉢ refers to the cup that contains poison hemlock.

④ The word "muted" in ㉣ means "strong in color."

⑤ The correct form of the word in parentheses for ㉤ is "commissioned."

2   (가) ~ (마) 중 아래 문장이 들어가기에 적절한 곳은?

On the contrary, Socrates is defiant, gesturing toward the afterlife to which he hastens.

① (가)   ② (나)   ③ (다)   ④ (라)   ⑤ (마)

3 본문에서 설명하는 The Death of Socrates에 대해 파악 또는 추론할 수 있는 내용으로 <u>가장 거리가 먼</u> 것은?

① David was the leading artist of the Neoclassical period.

② The painting portrays the classical theme of the 'trial and execution of Socrates.'

③ The color of the painting is more softened towards the center and becomes vibrant in the edges.

④ The underlying message of the painting is about resistance against France's unfair ruling authority during those times.

⑤ Thomas Jefferson appreciated this art piece for depicting Socrates, who was ideally the first reformer challenging the unfair political authority.

4 제시문에 이어지는 순서를 바르게 잡은 것은?

> *In the Horatii*, as in *The Death of Socrates*, those dedicated to principle are depicted with angular geometry, while those ruled by passion are curved and weak. In both canvases, the backgrounds are flat, fixing attention on the foreground, where like a freeze the action can be read from side to side.

[가] David doesn't identify anyone in the painting, but we can infer from accounts of Socrates' actual death that in the background is Socrates' wife, Xanthippe, led away in distress, and clutching Socrates' leg is Crito, his oldest and most faithful student. Under Crito, we can see that David has signed his own name, signaling a feeling of connection with the man. David, weaker than his ideal of moral strength, nonetheless grabs and strives toward him.

[나] The man who popularized Socrates' teachings by staging him as the protagonists in over 30 philosophical dialogues. But simply without Plato, there would be no Socrates. The two men melt into each other historically. It's hard to determine where Socrates' philosophy ends and Plato's begins. Not only was Plato absent at the death of Socrates, but he was a young man at the time. Here David has him as old and withdrawn.

[다] One way to read *The Death of Socrates* is right to left. The anguish of Socrates followers curling and twisting opens up onto the calm expression of the man himself and flows down through his right arm which hovers over the cup of poison. The space between the hand and the cup, the exact center of the image, is the seat of maximum narrative charge, that it falls back into the pain of the man who delivers the poison, who turns his gaze away from Socrates and finally comes to rest on the man sitting at the foot of the bed, unengaged. More on him in a moment

[라] Besides altering Socrates' face and physique, David decreases the number of people present at the event from over fifteen to twelve, echoing the number of disciples at Da Vinci's Last Supper. But I think the most significant change is the addition of the character at the foot of the bed. This is Plato.

① (라) – (나) – (가) – (다)　　　　② (나) – (가) – (라) – (다)
③ (가) – (라) – (나) – (다)　　　　④ (다) – (가) – (라) – (나)
⑤ (다) – (라) – (나) – (가)

[5–7] 다음을 읽고, 물음에 답하시오.

NOTE

This is The Death of Socrates by Jacques-Louis David. Completed in 1787, it is an exemplar of the Neoclassical period in France which David virtually created and brought to the fore himself. Before I say more, it's important to note just how striking this canvas is, ㉠not knowing anything about it.

So much jumps out at me right away: the clarity of the scene; the fierce gesture of the man in the middle; the interplay of the chalice; and the hand that reaches for it; the angles of the light and the men; the soft draping garments; the bare flat stone wall.

As the title suggests, the scene depicts the death of Socrates, ㉡told famously by Plato in his dialogue on the soul, *The Phaedo*. Socrates had been convicted in Athenian court of failing to acknowledge the gods of the city and ㉢had corrupted the city's youth and sentenced to death by drinking hemlocks. As Plato makes clear in another dialogue, *the Crito*, Socrates ㉣must've escaped into exile, but instead he chooses to die taking the opportunity to teach his final lesson, that death is not to be feared by the philosopher, but embraced as an apotheosis of the soul.

David chooses to paint the moment just as Socrates is grabbing for the poisoned draught. He's been discussing at length the immorality of the soul and doesn't even seem to care that he's about to take the implement of his death in hand. On the contrary, Socrates is defiant, gesturing toward the afterlife ㉤to which he hastens.

5 다음 〈보기〉 중 윗글을 읽고 바르게 이해한 것의 개수는?

〈보기〉

ⓐ The art of Jacques Louis David embodies the style known as Neoclassicism.

ⓑ Looking at The Death of Socrates even for the first time leaves viewers with vivid impressions of the scene.

ⓒ Plato mentions the death of Socrates in more than one dialogue.

ⓓ Socrates had no certainty about the afterlife, but was not afraid of death.

① 1개   ② 2개   ③ 3개   ④ 4개   ⑤ 없음

6 밑줄 친 부분 중 어법상 틀린 것을 2개 고르면?

① ⓐ not knowing anything about it   ② ⓑ told famously by Plato

③ ⓒ had corrupted   ④ ⓓ must've escaped

⑤ ⓔ to which

7 문맥상 밑줄 친 빈칸에 공통으로 들어가기에 가장 적절한 내용은?

Socrates, otherwise known as the father of philosophy, has been credited with providing humanity with one of its greatest gifts, the Socratic method. Now known as the scientific method, the Socratic method entails that we question everything that we are told, to question until a contradiction has occurred. Socrates sought contradiction as it proved that not one person knows the answer. According to Socrates, "true knowledge exists in knowing that _____."
This belief that knowledge meant that you are aware that _____ stressed to the core of the Socratic method; to question your ideas and others in the pursuit of knowledge, making the individual more aware. Socrates imposed this idea upon his disciples and to others around him so that they may discover their own truth, rather than trusting in the belief of others to be true.

* be credited with ~의 공로자로 인정되다

① the opinions of others are also important

② you must develop your own independent mindset

③ you know nothing at all

④ it is not a good idea to methodically disagree with others

⑤ truth is completed in character

[8] 다음을 읽고, 물음에 답하시오.

NOTE

For David, Socrates is a symbol of strength over passion, of stoic commitment to an abstract principle even in the face of death. But this is the ethical message David sought to offer the French, two years before the French Revolution, as the monarchy was in decline and reformers ached to install a democracy akin to that of Socrates' own time in Greek antiquity, or the United States which had just executed its own revolution five years prior. Indeed, Thomas Jefferson himself was present at the unveiling of this painting at the Salon of 1787. The image commissioned by two radical political reformers was wildly popular.

David had already made his names with another severe moralistic canvas, *The Oath of the Horatii*, which effectively invented the neoclassical style. Taking its cues from the stark simplicity of ancient Greece and Rome, from the ancient obsession with anatomy and musculature, from the two-dimensional freezes depicting historical events, Neoclassicism, as rendered by David, made its points strongly and severely. This was in direct opposition to the dominant Rococo style that reflected the ornate and hedonistic lifestyles of the monarchy.

8 윗글에 대한 이해로 옳은 추론을 <u>모두</u> 고르면?

> ㉠ Socrates used a death to model stoic strength to his students.
> ㉡ Socrates was deeply critical of the Athenian government and was not quiet about his opinions.
> ㉢ Thomas Jefferson himself was at the scene of the event, which inspired him to overthrow the government.
> ㉣ David was a leading figure in creating the neoclassical style.
> ㉤ The French Revolution preceded the American Revolution by several years.

① ㉠ and ㉢
② ㉢ and ㉣
③ ㉡, ㉢ and ㉤
④ ㉠ and ㉤
⑤ ㉠, ㉡ and ㉣

[9] 다음을 읽고, 물음에 답하시오.

Besides altering Socrates' face and physique, David decreases the number of people present at the event from over fifteen to twelve, echoing the number of disciples at Da Vinci's Last Supper. But I think the most significant change is the addition of the character at the foot of the bed.

This is Plato. The man who popularized Socrates' teachings by staging him as the protagonists in over 30 philosophical dialogues. But simply without Plato, there would be no Socrates. The two men melt into each other historically. It's hard to determine where Socrates' philosophy ends and Plato's begins. Not only was Plato absent at the death of Socrates, but he was a young man at the time. Here in this drawing, David has him as old.

9 제시된 그림을 좌측에서 우측으로 분석한다고 할 때 밑줄 친 내용을 통해 작가의 의도를 가장 설득력 있게 추론한 사람은?

① 철수: I suppose that the appearance of old Plato and the energetic Socrates on the outside seem to portray the inner conflict between them in a dramatic way.

② 근명: I think the way the picture portrayed shows Plato's lamenting his reluctance to prevent Socrates from taking the poisoned hemlock.

③ 춘식: I think the reason David placed the old image of Plato on the left is that he wanted viewers to see the events of the time as if they were "recalling" through Plato's point of view.

④ 병석: I think David portrays Plato as an old man to show his guilt derived from his feeble determination not to actively prevent his master from choosing to die.

⑤ 준재: I think the old Plato sitting far away from Socrates shows the ideological confrontation between the two thinkers.

* feeble 박약한, 나약한

10 제시문 1과 2의 내용을 참고하여 제시문 3의 빈칸에 들어갈 표현으로 바르게 짝지어진 것은?

〈제시문 1〉

As the title suggests, the scene depicts the death of Socrates, told famously by Plato in his dialogue on the soul, The Phaedo. Socrates had been convicted in Athenian court of failing to acknowledge the gods of the city and corrupting the city's youth and sentenced to death by drinking hemlocks. As Plato makes clear in another dialogue, *the Crito*, Socrates must've escaped into exile, but instead he chooses to die taking the opportunity to teach his final lesson, that death is not to be feared by the philosopher, but embraced as an apotheosis of the soul.

〈제시문 2 – 외부지문〉

Besides altering Socrates' face and physique, David decreases the number of people present at the event from over fifteen to twelve, echoing the number of disciples at Da Vinci's Last Supper. But I think the most significant change is the addition of the character at the foot of the bed.

This is Plato. The man who popularized Socrates' teachings by staging him as the protagonists in over 30 philosophical dialogues. But simply without Plato, there would be no Socrates. The two men melt into each other historically. It's hard to determine where Socrates' philosophy ends and Plato's begins. Not only was Plato absent at the death of Socrates, but he was a young man at the time. Here David has him as old and withdrawn.

〈제시문 3 – 외부지문〉

The Death of Socrates portrays the real-life execution of Socrates, a Greek philosopher who helped pioneer Western philosophy, in 399 BCE. Using Plato's Phaedo as a reference, David captures the moment that Socrates—who had been sentenced to death by the Athenian courts for "㉠_____" and "corrupting the young"—is given poison hemlock to drink.

As he willingly reaches for the cup, he continues to preach to his young followers, illustrating both his respect for the democratically reached decision and his ㉡ _____ to philosophy. According to Plato, after humbly thanking the Greek god of health for a peaceful death, Socrates "raised the cup to his lips and very cheerfully and quietly drained it."

Though this event actually happened, David took some artistic ㉢_____ when documenting it. This is especially true of the figures he opted to include in the painting.

① misleading – indifference – excellence   ② impiety – dedication – license

③ impiety – reluctance – excellence   ④ impiety – dedication – excellence

⑤ misleading – dedication – license

NOTE

〈제시문 1〉

The Death of Socrates is one of the most well-known works of art to come out of the Neoclassic period. In the 1780s, French artist Jacques-Louis David began producing pieces that showcased an interest in classical themes and (가)aesthetic austerity. He completed The Death of Socrates at the height of this phase in 1787, and submitted it to the Paris salon that year.

〈제시문 2〉

㉠Neoclassical artists approached composition with just as much intention as content. Specifically, they strived to achieve balance in their works, culminating in scenes that almost appear to be set on a stage.

This is particularly apparent in the paintings of David. ㉡In this painting, he opted to arrange the figures in a staged fashion. Though they are shown interacting with one another, their movements are posed and their expressions are stoic. This distinctive approach to placement is due to David's disregard for emotion and preference for balance and detail—a quality that is also present in his draughtsmanship.

㉢David is renowned for his use of bold, strong lines and minimal ornamentation. Though this aspect is illustrated in the completed Death of Socrates painting, it is even more evident in the preliminary sketches that he produced for the piece. ㉣Stripped of all color, tonality, and treatment of light, this drawing accentuates his simplistic approach to his craft—and, ultimately, his general ideas on art. "In the arts," he said, "㉤the way in which an idea is rendered, and the manner in which it is expressed, is much more important than the idea itself."

* tonality 색조

11 제시문 1의 밑줄 친 (가)의 "aesthetic austerity"의 특징을 구체적으로 나타내는 문장을 제시문 2에서 두 개 고르면?

① ㉠   ② ㉡

③ ㉢   ④ ㉣

⑤ ㉤

12 밑줄 친 ⓜ의 문장의 render의 문맥적 의미에 대한 영영풀이는?

① to cause someone or something to be in a particular state

② to change words into a different language

③ to affect something or someone so as to be changed in a completely different shape

④ to put a first layer of plaster or cement on a wall

⑤ to represent something in a work of art or a performance

13 Neoclassicism의 대표적 작품과 함께 본문에서 설명되는 Neoclassicism의 특징을 바탕으로 추론할 수 있는 내용으로 가장 거리가 먼 것은?

> This is The Death of Socrates by Jacques-Louis David. Completed in 1787, it is an exemplar of the Neoclassical period in France which David virtually created and brought to the fore himself. Before I say more, it's important to note just how striking this canvas is, not knowing anything about it.
>
> So much jumps out at me right away: the clarity of the scene; the fierce gesture of the man in the middle; the interplay of the chalice; and the hand that reaches for it; the angles of the light and the men; the soft draping garments; the bare flat stone wall.
>
> David had already made his names with another severe moralistic canvas, The Oath of the Horatii, which effectively invented the neoclassical style. Taking its cues from the stark simplicity of ancient Greece and Rome, from the ancient obsession with anatomy and musculature, from the two-dimensional freezes depicting historical events, Neoclassicism, as rendered by David, made its points strongly and severely. This was in direct opposition to the dominant Rococo style that reflected the ornate and hedonistic lifestyles of the monarchy.
>
> This is particularly apparent in the paintings of David. In this painting, he opted to arrange the figures in a staged fashion. Though they are shown interacting with one another, their movements are posed and their expressions are stoic. This distinctive approach to placement is due to David's disregard for emotion and preference for balance and detail.

① In painting it generally took the form of an emphasis on austere linear design in the depiction of Classical themes and subject matter, using archaeologically correct settings and clothing.

② Neoclassicism in the arts is an aesthetic attitude based on the art of Greece and Rome in antiquity, which invokes harmony, clarity, restraint, universality, and idealism.

③ Neoclassicism is characterized by lightness, elegance, and an exuberant use of curving natural forms in ornamentation.

④ Neoclassicism arose partly as a reaction against the sensuous and decorative Rococo style that had dominated European art from the 1720s on.

⑤ Artists of Neoclassicism tend to prefer somewhat more specific qualities, which include line over colour, straight lines over curves, frontality and closed compositions over diagonal compositions into deep space, and the general over the particular.

1 Man is essentially a _____ animal and tends to _____ others.

① selfish – resent　　　　　　② vicarious – work with

③ maudlin – belittle　　　　　④ preserve – adopt

⑤ gregarious – associate with

> **어휘**　man (단수, 관사 없이 집합적) 인간, 사람, 인류; 남자 essentially 본질적으로, 본래 tend to Ⓡ ~하는 경향이 있다, ~하기 쉽다 selfish 이기적인 resent ~에 분개하다, 화내다 vicarious 대리의, 대신하는 (= acting) work with ~와 함께 일하다, 작업하다 maudlin 감상적인, 특히 취하기만하면 우는 belittle ~을 경시하다, 무시하다 preserve ~을 보존(보호)하다 adopt ~을 채택하다; 양자로 삼다 gregarious 사교적인, 교제를 좋아하는 associate with ~와 교제하다, ~을 연합시키다

2 Bloodhounds are a breed of dog that have an especially keen sense of smell. They have the ability to follow a person by smelling tracks on the ground. They are sometimes used by police to locate lost children, escaped prisoners and _____.

① criminals　　　　　　　　② victims

③ schools　　　　　　　　　④ police dogs

> **어휘**　breed 품종, 종족, 종류 especially 특히 keen 예리한, 날카로운 sense 감각; 의미 smell 후각, 냄새; 냄새를 맡다 ability 능력 follow ~을 따라가다, 따르다 by ~ing ~함으로써 track 흔적, 지나간 자국 ground 지면, 땅; 근거, 이유; 기초; (외출·출장 등을) 금지시키다; 비행을 금지하다 locate ~에 위치시키다; ~의 위치를 알아내다 lost children 미아 escaped 도망친 prisoner 죄수 criminal 범죄자, 범인 victim 희생자 school 학교; 학파 police dog 경찰견

3 Unlike the carefully weighed and _____ compositions of Dante, Goethe's writing have always the sense of _____ and enthusiasm.

① inspired – vigor　　　　　② planned – immediacy

③ laborious – endeavor　　　④ developed – construction

⑤ contrived – languor

> **어휘**　unlike ~와 달리, ~을 닮지 않은 carefully 주의 깊게, 신중히 weigh 숙고하다, 평가하다; ~의 무게를 달다 carefully weighed and planned 신중히 생각되고, 계획된 composition 작문; 작곡; 구성 enthusiasm 열정, 열의 inspired 영감을 받은; 탁월한 vigor 활기, 힘, 정력 immediacy 즉시성 laborious 힘든, 고된, 애쓴 endeavor 노력 developed 발달된, 발전한 construction 건설, 구성, 구조 contrived 부자연스러운, 인위적인 languor 피로, 무기력

4 Not everyone dreams of owning a mansion and a brand-new car. In recent years, there has been a worldwide trend toward _____ and fewer material goods.

① waste
② indebtedness
③ simpler living
④ exemption

> **어휘**
> not everyone ~ 모든 사람들이 ~한 것은 아니다(부분부정) dream of ~을 꿈꾸다 own ~을 소유하다; 인정하다; 자기 자신의, 고유한 mansion 대저택 brand-new 새로운, 신품의 recent 최근의 worldwide 세계적인 trend 경향, 추세 toward ~로 향하여, ~쪽으로 fewer 더 적은 material 물질적인; 중요한; 재료 goods 물건, 상품; 재산 waste 낭비; 쓰레기 indebtedness 부채, 은혜를 입음 simpler living 더 간소한 생활 exemption 면제

5 Christmas gift-giving _____ the wheels of commerce and warms the hearts of givers and recipients.

① crimps
② stop
③ turn
④ greases

> **어휘**
> wheel 바퀴; (자동차의) 핸들 commerce 상업, 거래 warm ~을 따뜻하게 하다 heart 마음, 심장; 중심 giver 주는 사람 recipient 받는 사람 crimp (머리·천 따위를) 곱슬곱슬하게 하다, 지지다 grease ~에 기름을 바르다; ~에게 뇌물을 주다

6 Our department will be connected to the Internet as well as several on-line commercial vendors, thus making us _____ and _____ people across this country.

① much stronger – much happier
② more wanted – in need of
③ more accessible – in touch with
④ more knowledgeable – more agreeable

> **어휘**
> department 부서, 부문 connect 연결하다, 잇다 be connected to ~에 연결되다 B as well as A A뿐만 아니라 B도 several 몇몇의, 여러 가지의 commercial 상업의 vendor 행상인, 상인 thus 따라서, 이렇게 across this country 전국에, 전 세계에 much stronger 훨씬 더 강한 much happier 훨씬 더 행복한 more wanted 더 가난한, 부족한 in need of ~이 부족한, 결핍한 more accessible 더 접근하기 쉬운, 더 이용하기 쉬운 in touch with ~와 접촉(교제)하여 more knowledgeable 더 지식이 있는, 더 총명한 more agreeable 더 기분 좋은, 마음에 드는

7 I can recommend him for this position because I have always found him
_____ and reliable.

① voracious   ② veracious

③ vindictive   ④ valorous

⑤ mendacious

3

8 The literary artist, concerned solely with the creation of a book or story as
close to perfection as his powers will permit, is generally a quiet individual,
contemplative and _____.

① effusive   ② somnolent

③ retiring   ④ poetic

⑤ gregarious

9 He was not _____ and preferred to be alone most of the time.

① antisocial   ② gracious

③ gregarious   ④ cordial

⑤ handsome

10 There has been a large amount of _____ and lack of _____ in the description of such categories as ethnic, and especially racial, groups.

① disagreement – consensus

② bias – prejudice

③ agreement – harmony

④ violence – lawfulness

⑤ indoctrination – malaise

어휘 amount 양; 총계 lack 부족, 결핍 description 기술, 묘사, 서술 such 그러한, 이와 같은 category 범주, 종류 ethnic 민족의 especially 특히 racial 인종의 group 그룹, 집단 disagreement 불일치, 불화 consensus (의견 등의) 일치 bias 편견, 선입관 prejudice 편견, 선입관 agreement 합의, 동의 harmony 조화, 일치 violence 폭력, 격렬함 lawfulness 합법, 타당함 indoctrination (교의·신앙·이론· 원리 따위의) 주입, 가르침 malaise 불안, 불쾌 (= disquiet, uneasiness)

UNIT 4

문학_예술
Shelley and Romanticism and Ozymandias

☐ **prominent**   **a** Well-known, distinguished, or outstanding

- The artist became <u>prominent</u> in the contemporary art scene after winning several prestigious awards.

☐ **emerge**   **v** To come into view or become visible; to appear or arise

- As the fog lifted, the beautiful landscape began to <u>emerge</u>.

☐ **a reaction against**   A response or opposition to something, typically against an idea or situation

- The protest was <u>a reaction against</u> the government's controversial policy.

☐ **rationality**   **n** The quality of being logical, reasonable, or based on sound judgment

- The decision-making process should be guided by <u>rationality</u> rather than emotions.

☐ **celebrate**   **v** To praise, honor, or express admiration for someone or something

- We gathered to <u>celebrate</u> her achievements on her graduation day.

☐ **seek to**   **v** To attempt or strive for; to aim at achieving a particular goal

- The organization <u>seeks to</u> promote environmental sustainability through various initiatives.

☐ **gifted**   **a** Naturally talented or possessing exceptional abilities

- The young pianist was <u>gifted</u> with extraordinary musical talent.

☐ **talented**   **a** Having a natural aptitude or skill in a particular field; gifted

- She is a <u>talented</u> writer, known for her creative storytelling.

☐ **from an early age**   Since a young age; starting at an early point in one's life

- He showed an interest in technology <u>from an early age</u>, building his first computer at ten.

☐ **expel**   **v** To force someone or something to leave, typically from a place or organization

- The school had to <u>expel</u> the student for repeated violations of the code of conduct.

☐ **pamphlet**   **n** A small booklet or printed piece of paper containing information, usually on a single subject

- She distributed <u>pamphlets</u> explaining the benefits of healthy eating in the community.

☐ **lyrical**   **n** Expressing deep personal emotions or feelings, often in a poetic or musical form

- The song's <u>lyrical</u> composition resonated with listeners, conveying a sense of profound emotion.

☐ **sublime**   **a** Of such excellence, grandeur, or beauty as to inspire great admiration or awe

- The view from the mountaintop was <u>sublime</u>, capturing the breathtaking beauty of nature.

☐ **meditation**   **n** The act of engaging in contemplation or deep thought; a mental exercise for relaxation or spiritual growth

- She practiced <u>meditation</u> daily to achieve a sense of inner peace and mindfulness.

☐ **transformative**   **a** Having the power or tendency to bring about significant changes or transformations

- The technological advancements of the past decade have been <u>transformative</u>, reshaping various industries.

☐ **force**

n Strength or energy exerted; a powerful influence or effect

- The hurricane hit with such force that it caused widespread damage to buildings and infrastructure.

☐ **be reflected in**

To be mirrored or manifested in; to be evident or visible in

- The company's commitment to sustainability is reflected in its eco-friendly practices and policies.

☐ **fierce**

a Having a violent or intense nature; showing strong, unrestrained emotion or activity

- The fierce competition among the athletes showcased their determination to win.

☐ **the establishment**

n The existing social, political, or economic order; the dominant or mainstream system

- The candidate promised to bring about change and challenge the norms of the establishment.

☐ **advocate for**

To publicly support or argue in favor of a particular cause, idea, or policy

- She has dedicated her career to advocate for equal rights and social justice.

☐ **call for**

To demand or require something

- The citizens gathered to call for justice and accountability.

☐ **tyranny**

n Unjust use of power or oppressive rule, often characterized by cruelty and harsh control

- The people revolted against the tyranny of the dictator.

☐ **mark**

v To indicate or distinguish a particular feature; to make something noticeable

- The unique architecture marks this building as a historical landmark.

□ suffer from　To experience or endure the effects of something unpleasant or harmful

- She has been suffering from a chronic illness for several years.

□ financial difficulties　Challenges or problems related to money, income, or financial resources

- The company faced financial difficulties due to economic downturns.

□ drown　**v** To die by suffocating in water; to be submerged and unable to breathe

- The swimmer almost drowned in the deep sea but was rescued in time.

□ short-lived　**a** Lasting for a brief period; not enduring for a long time

- The joy of their reunion was short-lived as they had to part ways again.

□ boating　**n** The activity of traveling or recreating on a boat

- They spent the weekend engaged in boating on the lake.

□ activism　**n** The policy or action of using vigorous campaigning to bring about social or political change

- His years of activism focused on environmental conservation.

□ antique　**a** Relating to or belonging to the past; typically, an object or piece of furniture from a bygone era

- The antique shop showcased a collection of vintage items.

□ trunkless　**a** Without a trunk; lacking the main stem or central part

- The statue, now trunkless, once stood as a symbol of strength and endurance.

□ upright　**a** In a vertical position; standing straight without leaning

- The soldier remained upright even during challenging conditions.

UNIT

4

PART

2 Text Reading

: Shelley and Romanticism and Ozymandias

1 Shelley and Romanticism

Percy Bysshe Shelley was a prominent figure in the Romantic movement, which emerged in the late 18th century as a reaction against the Enlightenment's emphasis on reason and rationality. Romanticism celebrated the power of imagination, emotion, and nature, and sought to express the individual's subjective experience of the world. Born in 1792 in Sussex, England, Shelley was a gifted and talented writer from an early age. He attended Oxford University but was expelled after publishing a pamphlet that criticized the institution's authorities. Shelley then moved to London, where he became involved with a group of radical writers and intellectuals, including William Godwin, Mary Wollstonecraft, and Lord Byron.

Shelley's poetry is characterized by its lyrical beauty, emotional intensity, and radical politics. He often wrote about the natural world, exploring themes such as the sublime, the power of the imagination, and the relationship between humanity and nature. One of his most famous works, "Ode to the West Wind," is a meditation on the role of the poet as a transformative force in society. Shelley's political views were also reflected in his poetry. He was a fierce critic of the establishment and advocated for social and political reform. His poem "The Masque of Anarchy," written in response to the Peterloo Massacre of 1819, calls for non-violent resistance to tyranny and injustice.

In spite of his talent and influence, Shelley's life was marked by tragedy. He suffered from depression and financial difficulties, and his first wife Harriet drowned herself in 1816. Shelley later married Mary Wollstonecraft Godwin, the daughter of his mentor, and they had several children together. However, their happiness was short-lived: Shelley died in a boating accident in 1822, at the age of just 29.

In conclusion, Percy Shelley was a key figure in the Romantic movement, known for his poetic genius, political activism, and tragic life. His work continues to inspire and challenge readers today, as it did during his own time.

 핵심 PLUS!

1 Percy Bysshe Shelley was a prominent figure in the Romantic movement, (**which** emerged in the late 18th century as a reaction against the Enlightenment's emphasis on reason and rationality).

• the Romantic movement를 선행사로 하는 계속적 용법의 주격 관계대명사 which

2 (**Born** in 1792 in Sussex, England), <u>Shelley</u> was a gifted and talented writer (from an early age).

• Shelley를 수식하는 과거분사 Born이 이끄는 분사구문

3 He attended Oxford University but <u>was expelled</u> [**after** publishing a pamphlet (**that** criticized the institution's authorities)].

• 수동태 표현: be expelled
• **after**가 있는 전치사구 내 주격 관계대명사

4 Shelley then moved to London, [**where** he became involved with a group of radical writers and intellectuals, (including William Godwin, Mary Wollstonecraft, and Lord Byron)].

• 장소의 선행사(London)를 가지는 관계부사 where

5 He often wrote about the natural world, <u>exploring</u> <u>themes</u> such as the sublime, the power of the imagination, and the relationship between humanity and nature.

• 분사구문 exploring
• themes를 수식하는 전치사구 내 명사구의 병치: Ns such as N, N, and N

6 S [His poem "The Masque of Anarchy," (**written** in response to the Peterloo Massacre of 1819)], calls for non-violent resistance to tyranny and injustice.

• 후치수식의 과거분사 written

7 Shelley later married Mary Wollstonecraft Godwin, the daughter of his mentor, and they had several children together.

• 동격의 코마: Mary Wollstonecraft Godwin = the daughter of his mentor

8 In conclusion, Percy Shelley was a key figure in the Romantic movement, **known for** his poetic genius, political activism, and tragic life.

- figure를 수식하는 과거분사 known
- be known for: ~로 유명하다

9 His work continues to **inspire and challenge readers** today, as it **did** during his own time.

- 대동사 did = inspired and challenged readers

24   **THE EXAMINER.**

ORIGINAL POETRY.

OZYMANDIAS.

I met a Traveller from an antique land,
Who said, " Two vast and trunkless legs of stone
Stand in the desert. Near them, on the sand,
Half sunk, a shattered visage lies, whose frown,
And wrinkled lip, and sneer of cold command,
Tell that its sculptor well those passions read,
Which yet survive, stamped on these lifeless things,
The hand that mocked them, and the heart that fed:
And on the pedestal these words appear:
" My name is Ozymandias, King of Kings."
Look on my works ye Mighty, and despair!
No thing beside remains. Round the decay
Of that Colossal Wreck, boundless and bare,
The lone and level sands stretch far away.

GLIRASTES.

Type: **sonnet**

Rhyme scheme: **ABABACDCEDEFEF**

First published in: 11 January 1818

Shelley's "Ozymandias" is a sonnet, written in loose iambic pentameter, but with an atypical rhyme scheme, which violates the rule that there should be no connection in rhyme between the octave and the sestet. "Ozymandias" refers to Ramses II, also known as Ramesses the Great. He was a pharaoh of ancient Egypt who reigned from 1279 to 1213 BCE. The poem reflects on the fleeting nature of human achievements and power, as evidenced by the ruined statue of Ozymandias (Ramses II) in the desert.

Ozymandias

BY PERCY BYSSHE SHELLEY

I met a traveller from an antique land,
Who said—"Two vast and trunkless legs of stone
Stand in the desert. . . . Near them, on the sand,
Half sunk a shattered visage lies, whose frown,
And wrinkled lip, and sneer of cold command,
Tell that its sculptor well those passions read
Which yet survive, stamped on these lifeless things,
The hand that mocked them, and the heart that fed;
And on the pedestal, these words appear:
'My name is Ozymandias, King of Kings;
Look on my Works, ye Mighty, and despair!'
Nothing beside remains. Round the decay
Of that colossal Wreck, boundless and bare
The lone and level sands stretch far away."

- I met a traveller from an antique land,

  - The speaker of the poem meets a traveller who came from an ancient land.
    * antique = ancient 고대의

- Who said—"Two vast and trunkless legs of stone

  Stand in the desert. . . .

  - The traveller describes two large stone legs of a statue, which lack a torso to connect them and which stand upright in the desert.
    * trunkless (= a statue, which lack a torso) 토르소《머리·손발이 없는 나체 조각상》
    * upright 직립한, 똑바로[곧추]선

- Near them, on the sand,

  Half sunk a shattered visage lies,

  - Near the legs, half-buried in sand, is the broken face of the statue.

- whose frown, And wrinkled lip, and sneer of cold command,

  - The statue's facial expression—a frown and a wrinkled lip—form a commanding, haughty sneer.
    * commanding 위풍 당당한
    * haughty 오만한, 건방진
    * sneer 냉소; 비웃음, 경멸《at》; 남을 깔보는 듯한 표정

- Tell that its sculptor well those passions read

  Which yet survive, stamped on these lifeless things,

  - The expression shows that the sculptor understood the emotions of the person the statue is based on, and now those emotions live on, carved forever on inanimate stone.

- The hand that mocked them, and the heart that fed;

  - In making the face, the sculptor's skilled hands mocked up a perfect recreation of those feelings and of the heart that fed those feelings (and, in the process, so perfectly conveyed the subject's cruelty that the statue itself seems to be mocking its subject).
    * mock up 실물 크기의 모형을 만들다, 임시 변통으로 만들다

- And on the pedestal, these words appear:

- The traveller next describes the words inscribed on the pedestal of the statue, which say:

  * pedestal 축받이대

- 'My name is Ozymandias, King of Kings;

- My name is Ozymandias, the King who rules over even other Kings.

- Look on my Works, ye Mighty, and despair!'

- Behold what I have built, all you who think of yourselves as powerful, and despair at the magnificence and superiority of my accomplishments.

- Nothing beside remains.

- There is nothing else in the area.

- Round the decay

  Of that colossal Wreck, boundless and bare

  The lone and level sands stretch far away."

- Surrounding the remnants of the large statue is a never-ending and barren desert, with empty and flat sands stretching into the distance.

Voca Check

* 빈칸에 들어갈 적절한 단어를 박스에서 찾아 넣으시오.

1

gifted / emerge / rationality / celebrate / a reaction against / antique /
expelled / sublime / lyrical / prominent

1   The _____ architecture of the historic building made it a landmark in
    the city.

2   As the sun began to set, the moon started to _____ in the night sky.

3   The new art movement was seen as _____ the constraints of
    traditional styles.

4   The philosophy emphasized the importance of _____ in decision-
    making rather than relying solely on emotions.

5   The community decided to _____ the achievements of its talented
    members through an annual awards ceremony.

6   The museum displayed a collection of _____ furniture, showcasing
    craftsmanship from the past.

7   The disruptive student was eventually _____ from the school for
    repeated misconduct.

8   The poet's _____ verses captured the essence of love and nature in a
    profound way.

9   The view from the mountaintop was described as _____, evoking a
    sense of awe and beauty.

10 The school identified and supported _____ students, providing them
    with specialized educational programs.

2 call for / boating / advocate / be reflected in / fierce / tyranny / meditation / short-lived / advocate for / transformative

1 The practice of daily _____ allowed her to find inner peace and clarity of mind.

2 The _____ power of the experience made positive changes in his outlook on life.

3 The political activist dedicated his life to _____ change and challenging oppressive systems.

4 The artist's passion for nature and wildlife could often _____ his paintings and sculptures.

5 Despite facing _____ opposition, the social reformer continued to fight for justice and equality.

6 The protestors gathered to _____ an end to corruption and demand political reform.

7 The philosopher warned against the dangers of _____ and emphasized the importance of individual freedom.

8 The rebellion against the oppressive regime was _____ but had a lasting impact on the nation.

9 The environmentalist was a fervent _____ of sustainable practices and conservation efforts.

10 The serene lake provided a perfect setting for an afternoon of peaceful _____.

Reading Comprehension

[1-3] Read the passage and answer each question.

Percy Bysshe Shelley was a prominent figure in the Romantic movement, Ⓐwhich emerged in the late 18th century as a reaction against the Enlightenment's emphasis on reason and rationality. Romanticism celebrated the power of imagination, emotion, and nature, and sought to express the individual's _____ experience of the world. Born in 1792 in Sussex, England, Shelley was a gifted and talented writer from an early age. He attended Oxford University but was _____ after publishing a pamphlet that criticized the institution's authorities. Shelley then moved to London, Ⓑwhere he became involved with a group of radical writers and intellectuals, including William Godwin, Mary Wollstonecraft, and Lord Byron.

Shelley's poetry is _____ _____ its lyrical beauty, emotional intensity, and radical politics. He often wrote about the natural world, exploring themes such as the sublime, the power of the imagination, and the relationship between humanity and nature. ⒸOne of his most famous works, "Ode to the West Wind," is a meditation on the role of the poet as a transformative force in society. Shelley's political views were also _____ in his poetry. He was a fierce critic of the _____ and advocated for social and political reform. ⒹHis poem "The Masque of Anarchy," written in response to the Peterloo Massacre of 1819, calling for non-violent resistance to tyranny and injustice.

In spite of his talent and influence, Shelley's life was marked by tragedy. He suffered from depression and financial difficulties, and his first wife Harriet drowned herself in 1816. Shelley later married Mary Wollstonecraft Godwin, the daughter of his mentor, and they had several children together. However, their happiness was short-lived: Shelley died in a boating accident in 1822, at the age of just 29.

In conclusion, Percy Shelley was a key figure in the Romantic movement, known for his poetic genius, political activism, and tragic life. ⒠His work continues to inspire and challenge readers today, as it was during his own time.

1 밑줄 친 Ⓐ~Ⓔ 중 어법상 <u>어색한</u> 곳을 포함한 것을 <u>두 개</u> 고르면?

① Ⓐ   ② Ⓑ

③ Ⓒ   ④ Ⓓ

⑤ Ⓔ

2 빈칸에 들어갈 단어 또는 표현으로 적절하지 <u>않은</u> 것은?

① objective

② expelled

③ characterized by

④ reflected

⑤ establishment

3 Choose the option that contains all the correct statements.

> I. Through his poetry, Shelley delved into the beauty of nature and the role of the poet as a transformative force. However, underlying these lyrical expressions lay a strong political message.
>
> II. One of Shelley's writings, such as "The Masque of Anarchy," convey his belief in standing up against tyranny and injustice, emphasizing the need for violent reform.
>
> III. Moving to London and associating with radical writers and intellectuals further solidified his role as an activist, encouraging the public to conform to established institutions.

① I only   ② I and II

③ II only   ④ II and III

⑤ III only

UNIT

4

[4-5] Read the poem and answer each question.

 NOTE

Ozymandias
I met a traveller from an antique land
Who said: Ⓐ"Two vast and trunkless legs of stone
Stand in the desert . . . Near them, on the sand,
Half sunk, a shattered Ⓑvisage lies, whose frown,
And wrinkled lip, and sneer of cold command,
ⒸTell that its sculptor well those passions read
Which yet survive, stamped on these lifeless things,
The hand that mocked them, and the heart that fed;
And on the pedestal these words appear:
'My name is Ozymandias, king of kings;
Look on my works, ye Mighty, and despair!'
ⒹNothing beside remains. ⒺRound the decay
Of that colossal wreck, boundless and bare
The lone and level sands stretch far away."

4 Which of the following is NOT true of the poem above? (P.217 내용참고)

① "Ozymandias" is a sonnet written by the English Romantic poet Percy Bysshe Shelley.

② The title "Ozymandias" refers to an alternate name of the ancient Egyptian pharaoh Ramses II.

③ Shelley describes a crumbling statue of Ozymandias as a way to portray the permanence of political power and to praise art's ability to preserve the past.

④ Although the poem is a 14-line sonnet, it breaks from the typical sonnet tradition in both its form and rhyme scheme.

⑤ Shelley's departure from the typical sonnet tradition reflects his interest in challenging conventions, both political and poetic.

5 Among Ⓐ~Ⓔ, which of the interpretation is the most INAPPROPRIATE?

① From Ⓐ, it can be inferred that two large stone legs of a statue described by the traveller lack a torso to connect them and stand upright in the desert.

② Ⓑ refers to "the broken face of the statue."

③ From ⓒ, it can be inferred that the statue symbolizes the power of art in that through the sculptor's skill, the statue captures and preserves the "passions" of its subject by stamping them on "lifeless" rock.

④ ⓓ ironically shows that time has been kind to the statue.

⑤ From ⓔ, it can be inferred that the fact that even the "king of kings" depicted in the poem lies decaying in a distant desert suggests that no amount of power can withstand the merciless and unceasing passage of time.

6 아래 시에 대한 설명으로 옳지 <u>않은</u> 것은?

> I met a traveller from an antique land
> Who said: "Two vast and trunkless legs of stone
> Stand in the desert . . . Near them, on the sand,
> Half sunk, a shattered visage lies, whose frown,
> And wrinkled lip, and sneer of cold command,
> Tell that its sculptor well those passions read
> Which yet survive, stamped on these lifeless things,
> The hand that mocked them, and the heart that fed;
> And on the pedestal these words appear:
> 'My name is Ozymandias, king of kings;
> Look on my works, ye Mighty, and despair!'
> Nothing beside remains. Round the decay
> Of that colossal wreck, boundless and bare
> The lone and level sands stretch far away."

① It presents a powerful and thought-provoking image through the encounter between a narrator and a traveler who describes a crumbling statue in the desert.

② The poem explores themes of the transience of human achievements, the passage of time, and the inevitable decline of power and empire.

③ The sculptor of the statue captured the passions and emotions of the ruler it represents, whose heart and mind are now long gone.

④ The traveler informs the narrator that the statue bears an inscription on its pedestal, though not declaring the identity of the figure.

⑤ The inscription boldly challenges any onlooker to survey the ruler's works and despair at their own insignificance.

[7-8] Read the poem and answer each question.

 NOTE

I met a traveller from an antique land
Who said: "Two vast and trunkless legs of stone
Stand in the desert . . . Near them, on the sand,
Half sunk, a shattered visage lies, whose frown,
And wrinkled lip, and sneer of cold command,
Tell that its sculptor well those passions read
Which yet survive, stamped on these lifeless things,
The hand that mocked them, and the heart that fed;
And on the pedestal these words appear:
'My name is Ozymandias, king of kings;
Look on my works, ye Mighty, and despair!'
Nothing beside remains. Round the decay
Of that colossal wreck, boundless and bare
The lone and level sands stretch far away."

7 Choose the option that contains all the correct statements.

> I. The term "trunkless" in line 2 of the poem refers to the absence of a torso or body connecting the legs of the stone statue.
>
> II. The words on the pedestal, as stated in lines 9-11 of the poem are one of arrogance, pride, and a challenge to those who behold the statue.
>
> III. The irony lies in the contrast between Ozymandias' lofty claims and the reality of his fallen empire.
>
> IV. Throughout the poem, the sarcasm is evident in the portrayal of Ozymandias' pride and his belief that his works and power are eternal.
>
> V. The tone of the poem stays the same throughout the poem, aiding in conveying the underlying message of the transient nature of power and empire.

* behold: look at

① I, II and IV   ② II, III, IV and V

③ I, III and V   ④ II, IV and V

⑤ I, II, III, and IV

8 The poem above is constructed around a single image. Which of the following is NOT correct about the image and the deeper ideas or truths it conveys?

① The single image around which the poem is constructed is that of a crumbling statue in the desert.

② This image of a fallen monument represents the remnants of a once-mighty empire and its ruler, Ozymandias.

③ The deeper ideas and truths conveyed by this image are related to the transience of human achievements, the passage of time, and the inevitable decline of power.

④ The image conveys the idea that nature and time are forces that surpass human power and authority.

⑤ The poem praises the humility of the ruler who believes his empires and achievements will eventually wither away.

5 Sentence Completion

1 Though extremely _____ about his own plans, the man allowed his associates no such privacy and was constantly _____ information about what they intended to do next.

① idiosyncratic – altering

② guarded – eschewing

③ candid – uncovering

④ reticent – soliciting

⑤ fastidious – ruining

어휘
constantly 지속적으로 intend to ~하려고 의도하다 idiosyncratic 특이질의, 특유한, 기이한 alter 바꾸다 eschew 회피하다, 삼가다 (= avoid, forbear, refrain, refuse, shun) candid 솔직한, 즉흥적인 cf. candid shots 몰래 찍는 사진(꾸미지 않은 사진을 담기 위해) reticent 과묵한 solicit 간청하다, 손님을 끌다 fastidious 까다로운, 괴팍스러운

2 Despite her compassionate nature, the new nominee to the Supreme Court was single-minded and _____ in her strict _____ the letter of the law.

① merciful – interpretation of

② uncompromising – adherence to

③ dilatory – affirmation of

④ vindictive – deviation from

⑤ lenient – dismissal of

어휘
compassionate 인정이 많은, 측은히 여기는 nominee 지명된 사람 single-minded 단 하나의 목적을 가진 strict 엄격한 merciful 자비로운 uncompromising 타협하지 않는, 단호한 (= inflexible, obdurate) adherence 고수 dilatory 느린, 더딘 vindictive 복수심이 있는, 악의에 찬, 악심 깊은 deviation 이탈 lenient 관대한 (= easygoing, indulgent, lax) dismissal 해산, 면직

3 The lawyer's goal was to _____ her client and prove him innocent on all charges.

① indict
② prosecute
③ vindicate
④ intimidate

어휘 client 고객 prove 증명하다 innocent 결백한 (= blameless) charge 혐의 indict 기소하다, 나무라다 prosecute 기소하다 vindicate 진실성을 입증하다, ~의 정당함을 입증하다 intimidate 협박하다

4 While he tries to project the image of a _____ and concerned leader, those who know him well speak of a darker side to his character.

① vicious
② languid
③ benevolent
④ treacherous

어휘 concerned 근심하는 dark 어두운 vicious 나쁜, 악의 있는, 악덕의 languid 나른한, 기운이 없는, 불경기의 benevolent 자비로운, 자선을 위한 treacherous 배반하는, 불안정한

5 Thomas Paine had many enemies, and when he died a few tried to simulate grief and other continued to _____ him.

① praise
② defend
③ slander
④ question

어휘 enemy 적 simulate 흉내 내다 grief 슬픔 praise 칭찬하다 defend 옹호하다 slander 중상하다

6 An ancient religion taught that man should observe the good in the world without ignoring the evil. In other words, look for the good, but remember that _____.

① evil is also there
② all is good
③ all is evil
④ it does not exist
⑤ nothing is evil

어휘 the good 선 the evil 악

7 The side aspects of an affair frequently capture our attention more quickly than the major events upon which they are attendant. Similarly, many are the books in which the footnotes are more enjoyable than the _____.

① author   ② index
③ glossary   ④ text
⑤ illustrations

> **어휘**
> side aspect 부수적인 면 capture 사로잡다 major event 주된 사건 be attendant upon ~에 수반되다

8 A human being in perfection ought always to preserve a calm and peaceful mind, and never to allow passion or a transitory desire to disturb his _____.

① anxiety   ② tranquility
③ intensity   ④ honesty
⑤ seriousness

> **어휘**
> tranquility 평온, 평정 preserve 보존하다 disturb 방해하다, 교란하다 transitory 일시적인, 덧없는 anxiety 걱정, 근심 intensity 강도, 강렬함 seriousness 진지함, 중대함

9 For years, it was thought that the United States was and should be a "melting pot" — in other words that people from all over the world come and adopt the American culture as their own. More recently, some people have compared the United States to a mosaic — a picture made of many different pieces. America's strength, they argue, lies in its _____ and the contributions made by people of many different cultures.

① unity   ② diversity
③ variation   ④ discrimination
⑤ history

> **어휘**
> melting pot 용광로 adopt 채택하다, contribution 기여, 공헌 unity 단합 diversity 다양성 variation 변이, 편차 discrimination 차별화

10 Salary alone does not tell how much a man gets from his employer. Many companies offer their employees bonuses, stock, summer vacations at company-owned resorts, and other _____.

① benefits   ② side incomes

③ taxes   ④ salaries

⑤ jobs

어휘 company-owned resorts 회사 소유의 휴양지

비문학_생물학

Why Leaves Turn Color in the Fall

Voca Master

☐ **stealth**

n The action of moving, proceeding, or acting in a covert or secret way

- The spy operated with great <u>stealth</u> to gather sensitive information.

☐ **catch**

v To seize or capture someone or something, often with a sudden or quick motion

- The catcher managed to <u>catch</u> the fast-flying ball with ease.

☐ **unaware**

a Not conscious or cognizant of something; lacking knowledge or awareness

- She remained <u>unaware</u> of the surprise party planned by her friends.

☐ **goldfinch**

n A small songbird characterized by its colorful plumage, often with yellow feathers

- The <u>goldfinch</u> perched on the branch, singing a cheerful melody.

☐ **perch**

v To sit or rest on a raised or elevated place; a place where a bird sits

- The eagle found a high <u>perch</u> to survey the landscape.

☐ **red-winged blackbird**

A type of blackbird with distinctive red patches on its wings

- The marsh echoed with the calls of <u>red-winged blackbirds</u>.

☐ **sugar maple**

n A type of maple tree, known for its sweet sap used in maple syrup production

- The vibrant colors of the <u>sugar maple</u> leaves signaled the arrival of autumn.

☐ **close up shop**   To cease business operations for any length of time

- Due to economic challenges, the small bookstore had to <u>close up shop</u>.

☐ **keen-eyed**   **a** Having sharp or discerning eyesight; observant and perceptive

- The hawk, <u>keen-eyed</u>, spotted its prey from a great distance.

☐ **leopard**   **n** A large, carnivorous feline with a distinctive spotted coat

- The <u>leopard</u> stealthily moved through the jungle in search of prey.

☐ **stand still**   To remain in a stationary position without moving

- The deer sensed danger and chose to <u>stand still</u> in the forest.

☐ **squint**   **v** To partially close one's eyes to see more clearly or to reduce glare

- She had to <u>squint</u> in the bright sunlight to read the small print.

☐ **signs of movement**   Indications or evidence that something has changed or shifted

- Tracks in the snow were <u>signs of movement</u> in the deserted area.

☐ **frost**   **n** A thin layer of ice crystals formed by the freezing of dew or moisture

- The morning <u>frost</u> sparkled on the grass as the sun rose.

☐ **sit on**   To be located or positioned on a particular surface or area

- The ancient castle <u>sits on</u> the hill overlooking the village.

☐ **barbed**   **a** Having sharp points or projections, often designed to cause injury

- The fence was lined with <u>barbed</u> wire to deter trespassers.

UNIT

5

☐ **barbed wire** — Wire with sharp points, used as a barrier or fencing

- The military installation was surrounded by <u>barbed wire</u> for security.

☐ **a string of** — A sequence or series of connected or related things

- He had <u>a string of</u> successful business ventures.

☐ **distant** — **a** Far away in space or time; not near

- The <u>distant</u> mountains were covered with a blanket of snow.

☐ **square** — **n** A four-sided figure with equal sides and right angles; an open area in a town or city

- The town <u>square</u> was a gathering place for community events.

☐ **lighted** — **a** Illuminated; having light

- The <u>lighted</u> candles created a warm and cozy atmosphere.

☐ **dawn on** — To become clear or understood to someone; to realize

- It finally <u>dawned on</u> him that he had forgotten his keys at home.

☐ **baggage** — **n** Collective term for luggage or suitcases

- Passengers gathered their <u>baggage</u> at the carousel after the flight.

☐ **chilly** — **a** Cold, with a slight discomfort caused by low temperatures

- The wind made the evening feel <u>chilly</u>, so she wrapped herself in a warm scarf.

☐ **macabre** — **a** Disturbing and horrifying, often dealing with death or gruesome subjects

- The artist created a <u>macabre</u> painting depicting eerie scenes of a haunted forest.

□ macabre holiday   **n** A holiday or celebration characterized by eerie or disturbing themes

- Some people enjoy participating in <u>macabre holidays</u> like Halloween with elaborate costumes and spooky decorations.

□ spectacular   **a** Impressive, breathtaking, or remarkable in appearance

- The fireworks display on New Year's Eve was truly <u>spectacular</u>.

□ heart-stoppingly   **ad** In a manner that causes a sudden and intense emotional reaction, often fear or excitement

- The magician's dangerous stunt was <u>heart-stoppingly</u> thrilling for the audience.

□ cringe   **v** To recoil or flinch in embarrassment, fear, or discomfort

- She couldn't help but <u>cringe</u> at the awkward moment during the speech.

□ roll up   To arrive, often in a vehicle or on foot

- They watched as the performers <u>rolled up</u> in colorful carnival floats.

□ in clenched fists   With hands tightly closed into a fist

- He stood there, with the contract <u>in clenched fists</u>, contemplating his decision.

□ fall off   To separate and drop from a surface

- The leaves began to <u>fall off</u> the trees as autumn approached.

□ seedpod   **n** The protective casing or container for seeds in a plant

- Children enjoy collecting interesting <u>seedpods</u> during nature walks.

□ rattle   **v** To make a rapid series of noisy sounds

- The loose window pane would <u>rattle</u> whenever the wind blew.

UNIT
5

☐ **tiny**

a Very small in size; minute

- In the palm of her hand, she held a <u>tiny</u>, delicate flower.

☐ **gourd**

n A fleshy, typically large fruit with hard skin, often used for decoration or as a container

- The artisan crafted a decorative bowl from a dried <u>gourd</u>.

☐ **gushing**

a Overflowing or pouring out rapidly and forcefully

- The <u>gushing</u> water fountain added a sense of tranquility to the garden.

☐ **pastel**

a Having a soft, light, and delicate color, often associated with pastel hues

- The nursery was painted in <u>pastel</u> colors to create a soothing environment.

☐ **confetti**

n Small pieces of colored paper thrown during celebrations, especially weddings or parades

- The crowd celebrated by showering the newlyweds with <u>confetti</u>.

☐ **stare at**

To look fixedly and intently at someone or something

- The mysterious painting made everyone stop and <u>stare at</u> its intricate details.

☐ **sunlight**

n The light from the sun; sunlight is the primary source of illumination during the day

- The garden was bathed in warm <u>sunlight</u> as the flowers bloomed.

☐ **rule**

v To govern or manage; to exercise authority over

- The queen <u>ruled</u> the kingdom with wisdom and fairness.

☐ **edict**

n A decree or official order issued by an authority or ruler

- The king issued an <u>edict</u> declaring a day of celebration throughout the kingdom.

shorten — **v** To become shorter or to reduce in length; to make something shorter

- To save time, they decided to <u>shorten</u> the meeting agenda.

summer solstice — **n** The point in time when the sun reaches its highest or northernmost point in the sky, occurring around June 21st in the Northern Hemisphere

- The <u>summer solstice</u> marks the longest day of the year.

reconsider — **v** To think about something again; to review or change one's opinion

- After hearing new evidence, the jury had to <u>reconsider</u> their verdict.

feed — **v** To provide food for someone or something; to eat

- She carefully <u>fed</u> the baby bird with a tiny spoon.

in the dog days of summer — Refers to the hottest and most oppressive period of summer, typically in July and August

- <u>In the dog days of summer</u>, people seek relief from the scorching heat.

pull A back into B — To draw or bring A back into the confines or influence of B

- The coach hoped to <u>pull</u> the team <u>back into</u> contention with a strategic play.

choke off — **v** To obstruct or stop something, often growth or progress

- The economic downturn threatened to <u>choke off</u> funding for many small businesses.

corky — **a** Resembling or related to cork material

- The <u>corky</u> texture of the tree bark provided insulation against extreme weather.

☐ **slender** **a** Thin and delicate in appearance; gracefully slim

- The ballet dancer had a slender figure and moved with incredible grace.

☐ **petiole** **n** The stalk that attaches a leaf to a stem; leafstalk

- Botanists study the characteristics of the petiole to understand plant structures.

☐ **scar** **n** A mark left on the skin after a wound or injury has healed

- The old soldier bore a scar on his cheek from a battle long ago.

☐ **undernourished** **a** Not receiving adequate nutrition; malnourished

- Children in impoverished regions may appear undernourished due to a lack of proper food.

☐ **shocking** **a** used when describing something very surprising, intense, or startling, often because it is unexpected or vivid

- Her sudden and shocking announcement left everyone in the room speechless, unable to comprehend the unexpected news.

☐ **photosynthesis** **n** The process by which green plants and some other organisms use sunlight to synthesize foods with the help of chlorophyll

- Photosynthesis is crucial for the production of oxygen in the atmosphere.

☐ **cease** **v** To stop or discontinue an action; to come to an end

- The rain finally ceased, and the sun emerged from behind the clouds.

☐ **migrate** **v** To move from one region or habitat to another, often with the change of seasons

- Birds often migrate south for the winter in search of warmer climates.

| □ hibernate | **v** To spend the winter in a dormant or inactive state |
| | • Bears <u>hibernate</u> in caves during the cold winter months. |

| □ drop | **v** To let fall or allow to fall by gravity |
| | • A single tear <u>drop</u> fell from her eye as she listened to the sad news. |

| □ fragile | **a** Easily broken or delicate |
| | • Handle the glassware with care; it's very <u>fragile</u>. |

| □ a few fragile threads (of) | Some delicate or easily breakable strands |
| | • The spider's web hung in the corner, consisting of <u>a few fragile threads</u>. |

| □ fluid-carrying | **a** Capable of transporting liquids |
| | • The xylem is a <u>fluid-carrying</u> tissue in plants responsible for water transport. |

| □ stem | **n** The main structural part of a plant above ground that supports leaves, flowers, and fruits |
| | • The rose has a thorny <u>stem</u>. |

| □ xylem | **n** The tissue in plants responsible for carrying water and nutrients from the roots to other parts of the plant |
| | • The <u>xylem</u> plays a crucial role in the upward movement of water in plants. |

| □ stay | **v** To remain in a particular state or condition |
| | • The temperature needs to <u>stay</u> consistent for the experiment to yield accurate results. |

| □ reveal | **v** To make something known or disclose information |
| | • The detective <u>revealed</u> the identity of the mysterious culprit. |

UNIT

5

☐ **splotch**

n A mark or spot, often discolored

- A <u>splotch</u> of paint on the canvas added an interesting touch to the artwork.

☐ **chlorophyll**

n The green pigment in plants that plays a key role in photosynthesis

- <u>Chlorophyll</u> absorbs sunlight and converts it into energy for the plant.

☐ **break down**

To decompose or separate into smaller components

- Microorganisms help <u>break down</u> organic matter in the soil.

☐ **vein**

n The vascular tissue in plants responsible for transporting water, minerals, and nutrients

- The intricate patterns of <u>veins</u> in a leaf provide support and nutrient transport.

☐ **outline**

v To draw or sketch the outer edges or main features of something

- The artist began to <u>outline</u> the shape of the mountain on the canvas.

☐ **define**

v To establish the precise meaning or boundaries of something

- The dictionary helps to <u>define</u> the meanings of words.

☐ **dissolve**

v To become incorporated into a liquid and form a solution

- The sugar began to <u>dissolve</u> in the warm water.

☐ **replace**

v To put something back in the place of another or substitute for

- They had to <u>replace</u> the old machinery with new, more efficient equipment.

☐ **pigment**   **n** A substance that provides color, especially in biological tissues

- Melanin is a <u>pigment</u> responsible for skin color in humans.

☐ **hide A from view**   To conceal or keep A from being seen

- The curtains were drawn to <u>hide</u> the room <u>from view</u>.

☐ **camouflage**   **n** The use of disguises or colors to conceal and blend with the surroundings

- Animals use <u>camouflage</u> to avoid being seen by predators.

☐ **marvel**   **v** To be filled with wonder or astonishment

- As she gazed at the breathtaking landscape, she couldn't help but <u>marvel</u> at the beauty of nature.

☐ **vivid**   **a** Strikingly bright or intense, especially in color

- The artist used <u>vivid</u> hues to create a vibrant and lively painting.

☐ **glowing**   **a** Emitting a bright, warm light or displaying intense colors

- The sunset cast a <u>glowing</u> light over the horizon, painting the sky in hues of orange and pink.

☐ **odd**   **a** Strange, peculiar, or unconventional; different from what is expected

- He had an <u>odd</u> sense of humor that always made people laugh.

☐ **be predisposed to**   To have a tendency or inclination toward a particular behavior or condition

- Some individuals <u>are predisposed to</u> anxiety due to genetic factors.

UNIT

5

☐ **respond**   **v** To react or reply to something

- The audience clapped and cheered, <u>responding</u> positively to the performer's exceptional talent.

☐ **shimmer**   **v** To shine with a flickering or wavering light; to glisten

- The moonlight caused the water to <u>shimmer</u> like a field of diamonds.

☐ **sunset**   **n** The daily disappearance of the sun below the horizon

- They enjoyed a romantic picnic by the beach, watching the spectacular <u>sunset</u>.

☐ **tawny**   **a** Having a light brown or yellowish-brown color

- The lion's fur was a beautiful shade of <u>tawny</u>, blending perfectly with the savannah grass.

☐ **buff**   **n** A dull yellow-brown color

- The old parchment had turned a soft <u>buff</u> color over the years.

☐ **colt**   **n** A young male horse, especially one less than four years old

- The <u>colt</u> galloped playfully in the meadow.

☐ **rump**   **n** The hindquarters or buttocks of an animal, especially a quadruped

- The kangaroo's powerful legs and muscular <u>rump</u> helped it to hop great distances.

☐ **shuddering**   **a** Experiencing a tremor or involuntary shiver, often due to fear or cold

- The eerie sound in the dark forest left her <u>shuddering</u> with fear.

blush

v To become red in the face, typically due to embarrassment or shyness

- She couldn't help but blush when complimented on her achievements.

color

v To give color to; to tint or dye

- The painter carefully mixed the pigments to color the canvas with precision.

adaptation

n The process of adjusting to new conditions or modifying to fit a different environment

- The film adaptation of the novel stayed true to the original story.

adaptive

a Capable of adjusting or adapting to changing circumstances

- Humans are highly adaptive, capable of thriving in various environments.

not A any more than B

Indicates that A is not more likely or feasible than B

- This book isn't suitable for children any more than a horror movie would be.

haphazard

a Lacking any obvious order or organization; random

- The books on the shelf were arranged in a haphazard manner.

marvel

n A wonderful or astonishing thing

- The technological advancements in the last decade are a marvel of human innovation.

bestow

v To give or confer, especially as a gift or honor

- The king decided to bestow knighthood upon the brave warrior for his valor in battle.

☐ **sizzling**

a Producing a hissing or crackling sound, often due to intense heat

- The steaks were <u>sizzling</u> on the hot grill, filling the air with a mouthwatering aroma.

☐ **thrilling**

a Producing excitement or strong emotion; very exciting

- The <u>thrilling</u> climax of the movie kept the audience on the edge of their seats.

☐ **in a sense**

From a certain point of view or in a particular way

- <u>In a sense</u>, every ending marks the beginning of something new.

☐ **dupe**

v To deceive or trick someone by making them believe something that is not true

- She realized she had been <u>duped</u> into buying a fake painting.

☐ **disintegration**

n The process of breaking down or falling apart into smaller parts

- The old building was in a state of <u>disintegration</u>, with crumbling walls and decaying structure.

☐ **in time**

Eventually, over a period of time

- With patience and effort, the wounds healed <u>in time</u>.

☐ **fragile**

a Easily broken or damaged; delicate

- The ancient artifacts were so <u>fragile</u> that they required careful handling.

☐ **dust**

n Fine, dry particles of earth or other matter that can be easily carried by the wind

- She wiped away the <u>dust</u> that had settled on the old bookshelf.

☐ **vanish**   **v** To disappear suddenly or gradually from sight

- As the magician waved his wand, the rabbit seemed to <u>vanish</u> into thin air.

☐ **sublime**   **a** Elevating to a high degree of moral or spiritual excellence

- The breathtaking view from the mountaintop was a <u>sublime</u> experience.

☐ **state**   **n** The particular condition that someone or something is in at a specific time

- After the storm, the once tranquil beach was in a chaotic and battered <u>state</u>.

☐ **bloom**   **v** To produce flowers; to be in full beauty or health

- In spring, the cherry blossoms <u>bloom</u>, covering the trees with delicate pink flowers.

☐ **urgent colors**   Colors associated with immediacy or intensity, often brighter or more striking

- The <u>urgent colors</u> of the sunset painted the sky in vibrant reds and oranges.

☐ **mummify**   **v** To preserve a body by drying and wrapping it in bandages

- In ancient Egypt, pharaohs were <u>mummified</u> to ensure the preservation of their bodies for the afterlife.

☐ **carnal**   **a** Relating to the physical or sensual aspects of human nature, especially sexual desires

- The novel explored both the spiritual and <u>carnal</u> dimensions of human existence.

☐ **mute**   **a** Silent or refraining from speech; not emitting sound

- He stood <u>mute</u>, unable to express the overwhelming emotions within him.

☐ **radiant**   **a** Emitting a bright, glowing light; full of brightness

- The bride looked <u>radiant</u> in her wedding gown as she walked down the aisle.

☐ **lead**   **v** To guide or direct; to be in charge or command

- He was chosen to <u>lead</u> the expedition into the uncharted territory.

☐ **leafy**   **a** Covered with or having a lot of leaves

- The quaint cottage was surrounded by a <u>leafy</u> garden, providing a serene and peaceful atmosphere.

☐ **abundance**   **n** A very large quantity of something; plentifulness

- The orchard was filled with an <u>abundance</u> of ripe apples, ready for harvest.

☐ **remind A of B**   To evoke memories or bring thoughts of something or someone to mind

- The old photograph <u>reminded</u> her of the carefree days of her youth.

☐ **fig**   **n** A fruit-bearing tree or its pear-shaped edible fruit

- She enjoyed a fresh <u>fig</u> picked from the tree in her backyard.

☐ **wither**   **v** To shrivel, fade, or decay; to lose freshness or vitality

- The flowers began to <u>wither</u> under the scorching sun.

☐ **scale**   **n** A small, thin, flat piece of a protective layer; often referring to the small plates on a fish or reptile

- The fish's <u>scales</u> shimmered in the sunlight as it swam in the clear water.

☐ **spring up**   To emerge or appear suddenly and rapidly

- New buildings began to <u>spring up</u> across the city as it experienced rapid urbanization.

☐ **simmer**

v To cook or be cooked gently at or just below the boiling point

- The soup continued to <u>simmer</u> on the stove, filling the kitchen with a savory aroma.

☐ **whine**

v To make a high-pitched, complaining sound; to express discontent

- The puppy would <u>whine</u> when it wanted attention from its owner.

☐ **pile**

n A heap or mass of things laid or lying one on top of another

- She stacked a <u>pile</u> of books on the table, ready to be sorted.

☐ **hurl**

v To throw with great force; to propel forcefully

- He angrily decided to <u>hurl</u> the pebble into the pond.

☐ **leap**

v To jump or spring a long way, to a great height, or with great force

- The gazelle could <u>leap</u> gracefully across the savannah.

☐ **unruly**

a Disorderly and difficult to control; disobedient

- The <u>unruly</u> crowd disrupted the peaceful demonstration.

☐ **mattress**

n A large pad filled with resilient material, often used as a bed

- She chose a <u>mattress</u> with extra padding for a more comfortable night's sleep.

☐ **odder**

a More strange or unusual

- The abandoned house appeared even <u>odder</u> in the pale moonlight.

UNIT
5

☐ **figment** n Something invented or imaginary; a fabrication of the mind

- The ghostly figure turned out to be a mere <u>figment</u> of his imagination.

☐ **hailstone** n A pellet of hail; a small, hard ball of ice that falls during a hailstorm

- The roof echoed with the sound of <u>hailstones</u> during the storm.

☐ **snowflake** n A single ice crystal that falls as snow

- Each <u>snowflake</u> is unique, with its own intricate pattern.

☐ **overhung** a Suspended or extended downward

- The balcony <u>overhung</u> the garden, providing a shaded retreat.

☐ **never-never** a Unrealistic, fantastical, or beyond reality

- The landscapes in the fantasy novel were described as being in the <u>never-never</u> realm, where magic prevailed.

☐ **sheer** a Complete, pure, entire

- The waterfall was a <u>sheer</u> spectacle of natural beauty.

☐ **delicious** a Highly pleasing to the senses, especially taste and smell; very enjoyable

- The chef prepared a <u>delicious</u> meal that left everyone satisfied.

☐ **spill** n To overturn or allow something to fall out of a container; to leak

- Be careful not to <u>spill</u> the coffee as you carry the tray.

☐ **lost** a Deeply absorbed or engrossed in something; distracted or preoccupied

- She was <u>lost</u> in thought as she contemplated the beautiful sunset.

conceal — **v** To hide or keep something secret; to prevent from being seen or known

- He tried to conceal his surprise when she entered the room unexpectedly.

awkward — **a** Lacking skill or dexterity; causing discomfort or embarrassment

- The dancer felt awkward during the unfamiliar routine.

the colored leaves — Leaves that have changed color, typically in the fall, displaying vibrant hues

- Autumn brings a breathtaking display of the colored leaves on the trees.

age — **v** To grow older; the process of getting older

- With age comes wisdom and a deeper understanding of life.

growth hormone — **n** A hormone responsible for stimulating growth, particularly in humans and animals

- The doctor prescribed growth hormone therapy for the child with a growth deficiency.

fade — **v** To gradually weaken or lose brightness; to diminish over time

- The colors of the painting began to fade after years of exposure to sunlight.

petiole — **n** The stalk that joins a leaf to a stem; leafstalk

- The petiole allowed the leaf to sway gently in the breeze.

rows of — Arranged in lines or linear formations

- The orchard was filled with rows of apple trees.

☐ **angle**

n The space between two intersecting lines or surfaces; a perspective or standpoint

- The photographer captured the scene from a unique <u>angle</u>.

☐ **at right angles**

Perpendicular; forming a 90-degree angle

- The shelf was mounted <u>at right angles</u> to the wall.

☐ **axis**

n An imaginary line about which a body rotates; a central line

- The Earth's <u>axis</u> is tilted, causing seasons to change.

☐ **react with**

To undergo a chemical reaction with a substance

- Certain metals <u>react with</u> acids to produce hydrogen gas.

☐ **come apart**

To break or separate into pieces; to disassemble

- The old book began to <u>come apart</u> at the seams.

☐ **airborne**

a Suspended in the air; carried or transmitted through the air

- <u>Airborne</u> particles can spread infectious diseases.

☐ **glide**

v To move smoothly and effortlessly; to slide or sail

- The skater seemed to <u>glide</u> across the ice with grace.

☐ **swoop**

v To descend rapidly and aggressively; to make a sudden, sweeping movement

- The eagle made a <u>swoop</u> down to catch its prey.

☐ **cradle**

n A small bed for an infant; a place of origin or early life

- The baby slept peacefully in the <u>cradle</u>.

☐ **wing**

v To fly or allow something to fly; a structure that enables flight in birds

- Birds <u>wing</u> their way across the sky during migration.

☐ **flutter**

v To move quickly and lightly; the rapid motion of wings or similar structures

- The butterfly began to <u>flutter</u> from flower to flower.

☐ **whirlwind**

n A column of rapidly rotating air; a swift and turbulent movement

- The leaves were lifted into the air by the <u>whirlwind</u>.

☐ **updraft**

An upward current of air, especially in the atmosphere

- The glider rode the <u>updraft</u> to gain altitude.

☐ **swivel**

v To rotate or pivot, especially around a fixed point; a device allowing rotation

- The chair could <u>swivel</u> to face any direction.

☐ **from yard to yard**

Across different yards or open spaces

- The children played tag <u>from yard to yard</u> in the neighborhood.

☐ **firmly**

ad In a strong, secure, or determined manner

- She held onto the rope <u>firmly</u> as she climbed the mountain.

☐ **tether**

v To tie or limit the movement of something; a rope or chain used for restraint

- The dog was <u>tethered</u> to a post in the yard.

☐ **capricious**

a Subject to sudden and unpredictable changes; whimsical or impulsive

- The weather in spring can be quite <u>capricious</u>, with sunny days followed by sudden rain.

2 Text Reading

: Why Leaves Turn Color in the Fall

Text **1**

The stealth of autumn catches one unaware. Was that a goldfinch perching in the early September woods, or just the first turning leaf? A red-winged blackbird or a sugar maple closing up shop for the winter? Keen-eyed as leopards, we stand still and squint hard, looking for signs of movement. Early-morning frost sits heavily on the grass, and turns barbed wire into a string of stars. On a distant hill, a small square of yellow appears to be a lighted stage. At last the truth dawns on us: Fall is staggering in, right on schedule, with its baggage of chilly nights, macabre holidays, and spectacular, heart-stoppingly beautiful leaves. Soon the leaves will start cringing on the trees, and roll up in clenched fists before they actually fall off. Dry seedpods will rattle like tiny gourds.

But first there will be weeks of gushing color so bright, so pastel, so confetti-like, that people will travel up and down the East Coast just to stare at it— a whole season of leaves. Where do the colors come from? Sunlight rules most living things with its golden edicts. When the days begin to shorten, soon after the summer solstice on June 21, a tree reconsiders its leaves. All summer it feeds them so they can process sunlight, but in the dog days of summer the tree begins pulling nutrients back into its trunk and roots, pares down, and gradually chokes off its leaves. A corky layer of cells forms at the leaves' slender petioles, then scars over.

* Mature cork cells are plant cells that form the protective water-resistant tissue in the outer covering of stems or trunks

 핵심 PLUS!

1 The stealth of autumn **catches** one **unaware**.

- 5형식 동사로 쓰인 catch
- catch someone unaware: ~을/를 놀래키다

2 Was that a goldfinch perching in the early September woods, or just the first turning leaf?

- 2형식 문장의 의문문으로 보어자리에서 병치되는 명사는 goldfinch와 leaf임.

3 (**Keen-eyed** as leopards), we stand still and squint hard, **looking** for signs of movement.

- 양보절이 생략된 분사구문: **Even though we are** keen-eyed as leopards,
- 분사구문: **while we are** looking for ~

4 Early-morning frost sits heavily on the grass, and turns barbed wire into a string of stars. On a distant hill, a small square of yellow appears to be a **lighted** stage.

- 서술부를 이끄는 동사 병치
- 명사 앞에서 수식하는 과거분사: lighted

5 At last the truth dawns on us: Fall is staggering in, right on schedule, with its baggage of chilly nights, macabre holidays, and spectacular, heart-stoppingly beautiful leaves.

- 콜론은 명사절을 이끄는 that의 대용
  → At last the truth dawns on us: Fall is ~ = At last the truth dawns on us **that** fall is ~
- 의미강조 부사 right
  → on schedule 〈 right on schedule

6 But first there will be weeks of gushing color (**so** bright, **so** pastel, **so** confetti-like, **that** people will travel up and down the East Coast just to stare at it — a whole season of leaves).

- weeks of ~: 수 주간의 ~
- so ~ that 구문: so에 이어지는 괄호의 전체 표현이 앞의 명사 color를 수식하는 형용사구임을 파악.

7 (All summer) it feeds them so (that) they can process sunlight, but (in the dog days of summer) the tree begins pulling nutrients back into its trunk and roots, pares down, **and** gradually chokes off its leaves.

- 목적의 부사절 접속사 so that에서 that이 생략된 형태.
- 주어 the tree의 서술부를 이끄는 동사의 병치: S V1, V2, and V3

8 A corky layer of cells forms at the leaves' slender petioles, (and) then scars over.

- 문법적으로 서술부를 연결하는 and를 넣어야 함.

Undernourished, the leaves stop producing the pigment chlorophyll, and photo-synthesis ceases. Animals can migrate, hibernate, or store food to prepare for winter. But where can a tree go? It survives by dropping its leaves, and by the end of autumn only a few fragile threads of fluid-carrying xylem hold leaves to their stems.

A turning leaf stays partly green at first, then reveals splotches of yellow and red as the chlorophyll gradually breaks down. Dark green seems to stay longest in the veins, outlining and defining them. During the summer, chlorophyll dissolves in the heat and light, but it is also being steadily replaced. In the fall, on the other hand, no new pigment is produced, and so we notice the other colors that were always there, right in the leaf, although chlorophyll's shocking green hid them from view. With their camouflage gone, we see these colors for the first time all year, and marvel, but they were always there, hidden like a vivid secret beneath the hot glowing greens of summer.

어구 및 표현 연구

핵심 PLUS!

1 **Undernourished**, the leaves stop producing the pigment chlorophyll, and photo-synthesis ceases.

• 분사구문: **If they are** undernourished,

2 Animals can migrate, hibernate, or store food **to prepare for** winter.

• 조동사 can에 걸리는 동사 병치
• to부정사의 부사적 용법의 목적: ~하기 위해서

3 It survives by dropping its leaves, and (by the end of autumn) S [only **a few** fragile threads of fluid-carrying xylem] hold leaves to their stems.

• a few: (셀 수 있는 명사와 함께) 몇 개의

4 A turning leaf |stays| partly green at first, (and) then |reveals| splotches of yellow and red (as the chlorophyll gradually breaks down).

• 서술부의 동사와 동사 병치
• breaks는 접속사 as에 걸리는 부사절 내 동사임.

5 Dark green seems to stay **longest** in the veins, outlining and defining them.

• 최상급에 정관사가 붙지 않는 경우: 다른 상대와의 비교가 아닌 경우

6 During the summer, chlorophyll dissolves in the heat and light, but it is also **being** steadily **replaced**.

• 수동 진행: being replaced

7 In the fall, on the other hand, no new pigment is produced, and so we notice the other colors (**that** were always there, right in the leaf), (although chlorophyll's shocking green hid them from view).

• 선행사 colors를 수식하는 주격 관계대명사 that
• shocking은 의미강조 부사: 몹시, 지독히 (= shockingly)

8 (**With** their camouflage **gone**), we see these colors for the first time all year, and marvel, but they **were** always there, **hidden** like a vivid secret beneath the hot glowing greens of summer.

• 부대구문: with + N + v-ed
• they **were** always there, hidden ~에 서 were는 완전자동사로 쓰이고 있으며, hidden은 분사구문 또는 유사보어로도 볼 수 있음.

An odd feature of the colors is that they don't seem to have any special purpose. We are predisposed to respond to their beauty, of course. They shimmer with the colors of sunset, spring flowers, the tawny buff of a colt's pretty rump, the shuddering pink of a blush. Animals and flowers color for a reason–adaptation to their environment– but there is no adaptive reason for leaves to color so beautifully in the fall any more than there is for the sky or ocean to be blue. It's just one of the haphazard marvels the planet bestows every year. We find the sizzling colors thrilling, and in a sense they dupe us. Colored like living things, they signal death and disintegration. In time, they will become fragile and, like the body, return to dust. They are as we hope our own fate will be when we die: Not to vanish, just to sublime from one beautiful state into another. Though leaves lose their green life, they bloom with urgent colors, as the woods grow mummified day by day, and Nature becomes more carnal, mute, and radiant.

어구 및 표현 연구

핵심 PLUS!

1 An odd feature of the colors is [**that** they don't seem to have any special purpose].

• 보어자리에 위치한 명사절 that

2 They shimmer with the colors of sunset, spring flowers, the tawny buff of a colt's pretty rump, (and) the shuddering pink of a blush.

• 전치사 with에 걸리는 명사구의 병치에서 and가 생략된 상황: A, B, C, (and) D

3 Animals and flowers **color** for a reason— adaptation to their environment — but there is **no** adaptive reason (**for leaves**) **to color** so beautifully in the fall **any more than** there is for the sky or ocean to be blue.

• color는 "(색으로) 물들다"의 뜻으로 쓰인 자동사임.
• to color의  for leaves
• A is no B any more than C is D: A는 C가 D가 아닌 것만큼 B가 아니다

4 It's just **one of** the haphazard **marvels** (that) the planet **bestows** every year.

- one of Ns: one of 다음에 복수명사
- 타동사 bestow 뒤에 목적어가 생략된 것으로 보아 목적격 관계대명사가 생략됨.

5 We **find** / the sizzling colors / **thrilling**, and in a sense they dupe us.

- find가 5형식 동사이므로 thrilling이 목적보어임.

6 (**Colored** like living things), they signal death and disintegration. In time, they will become fragile and, (like the body), return to dust.

- they를 수식하는 과거분사가 이끄는 분사구문

7 Though leaves lose their green life, they bloom with urgent colors, as the woods **grow** mummified day by day, and Nature becomes more carnal, mute, and radiant.

- become류 동사: grow

We call the season "fall," from the Old English feallan, to fall, which leads back through time to the Indo-European phol, which also means to fall. So the word and the idea are both extremely ancient, and haven't really changed since the first of our kind needed a name for fall's leafy abundance. As we say the word, we're reminded of that other Fall, in the garden of Eden, when fig leaves never withered and scales fell from our eyes. Fall is the time when leaves fall from the trees, just as spring is when flowers spring up, summer is when we simmer, and winter is when we whine from the cold. Children love to play in piles of leaves, hurling them into the air like confetti, leaping into soft unruly mattresses of them. For children, leaf fall is just one of the odder figments of Nature, like hailstones or snowflakes. Walk down a lane overhung with trees in the never-never land of autumn, and you will forget about time and death, lost in the sheer delicious spill of color. Adam and Eve concealed their nakedness with leaves, remember? Leaves have always hidden our awkward secrets.

어구 및 표현 연구

핵심 PLUS!

1 We <u>call</u> / the season / "**fall**," from the Old English feallan, to fall, [<u>which</u> leads back through time to the Indo-European phol, (<u>which</u> also means to fall)].

- 5형식 call: call A B로 call A as B라고 하지 않도록 주의할 것.

- 선행사 fallen를 수식하는 계속적 용법의 주격 관계대명사 which가 이끄는 절 내 phol을 수식하는 주격 관계대명사가 반복되는 점에 유의할 것.

2 So the word and the idea are both extremely ancient, and haven't really changed (since the first of our kind needed a name for fall's leafy abundance).

- 서술부 병치: are ~, and haven't ~

3 As we say the word, we**'re reminded of** that other Fall, in the garden of Eden, when fig leaves never withered and scales fell from our eyes.

- be reminded of: ~가 상기되다

4 Fall is the time (when leaves fall from the trees), just as spring is (**the time**) when flowers spring up, summer is (**the time**) when we simmer, and winter is (**the time**) when we whine from the cold.

- 시간의 선행사 time을 수식하는 관계부사 when의 병치와 등위접속사를 중심으로 대등관계의 생략된 표현을 확인할 것.

5 Children love to play in piles of leaves, **hurling** them into the air like confetti, **leaping** into soft unruly mattresses of them.

- 분사구문: , and they hurl ~, and leap ~

6 Walk down a lane (**overhung** with trees in the never-never land of autumn), **and** you will forget about time and death, (**lost** in the sheer delicious spill of color).

- 명령문 ~ , and S will V: ~해라 그러면 ~할 것이다
- a lane을 수식하는 과거분사 overhung
- 분사구문 lost ~: **as you are** lost ~

But how do the colored leaves fall? As a leaf ages, the growth hormone, auxin, fades, and cells at the base of the petiole divide. Two or three rows of small cells, lying at right angles to the axis of the petiole, react with water, then come apart, leaving the petioles hanging on by only a few threads of xylem. A light breeze, and the leaves are airborne. They glide and swoop, rocking in invisible cradles. They all wing and may flutter from yard to yard on small whirlwinds or updrafts, swiveling as they go. Firmly tethered to earth, we love to see things rise up and fly–soap bubbles, balloons, birds, fall leaves. They remind us that the end of a season is capricious, as is the end of life.

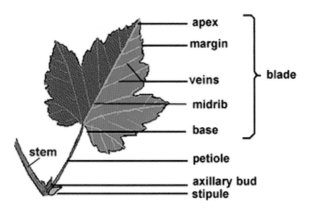

 핵심 PLUS!

1 (As a leaf ages), the growth hormone, auxin, / fades, and cells at the base of the petiole / divide.

- 동격의 코마: the growth hormone = auxin
- 1형식 문장이 등위접속사 and로 연결된 중문

2 S [Two or three rows of small cells, **lying** at right angles to the axis of the petiole,] react with water, (and) (then) come apart, (**leaving** the petioles **hanging** on by only a few threads of xylem).

- cells를 수식하는 현재분사 lying
- 서술부 병치: S react ~ , (and) (then) come ~
- 계속적 용법 관계대명사를 활용한 문장으로 전환:
  Two or three rows of small cells, lying at right angles to the axis of the petiole, react with water, then come apart, **which leaves** the petioles hanging on by only a few threads of xylem.
- 5형식 동사 leave: leave + 목적어 + **v-ing**

3 They glide and swoop, **rocking** in invisible cradles.

- 주어 They를 설명하는 형용사 용법의 분사구문

4 They all wing and may flutter (from yard to yard) **on** small whirlwinds or updrafts, (**swiveling** as they go).

- on: ~을 타고
- swiveling이 이끄는 분사구문

5

5 (Firmly **tethered** to earth), we love to see things rise up and fly—soap bubbles, balloons, birds, fall leaves.

- tethered가 이끄는 분사구문: **As we are** firmly tethered to earth,

6 They **remind** us **that** the end of a season is capricious, (**as** is the end of life).

- remind + 사람 + that S V
- 접속사 as뒤 생략 도치:
  as the end of life is (**capricious**)의 표현에서 capricious를 생략하면서 도치가 발생한 경우임.
  = as is the end of life

PART

3 Voca Check

* 빈칸에 들어갈 적절한 단어를 박스에서 찾아 넣으시오.

1

keen-eyed / lighted / unaware / a string of / close up shop / stealth /
squint / barbed / perch / distant

1　The cat moved with _____ through the dark alley, avoiding any noise.

2　She was _____ of the surprise party planned by her friends.

3　The owl found a comfortable _____ on the branch to observe its surroundings.

4　The small business had to _____ after facing financial difficulties.

5　The detective's _____ observation skills helped him notice even the smallest details.

6　Trying to read the tiny print, he had to _____ to see the words clearly.

7　The conversation took a _____ turn when sensitive topics were brought up.

8　The detective investigated _____ burglaries in the neighborhood.

9　The mountain range seemed _____ as it faded into the horizon.

10　The _____ candles created a warm and inviting atmosphere in the room.

2

dawn on / gushing / spectacular / roll up / confetti / fall off / rattle / in clenched fists / cringe / macabre

1   The realization of her mistake began to _____ her just as the consequences unfolded.

2   The horror movie had a _____ atmosphere, with scenes that were both eerie and disturbing.

3   The fireworks display was truly _____, lighting up the night sky with vibrant colors.

4   Witnessing the embarrassing moment made him _____ in discomfort.

5   To prepare for the performance, the magician started to _____ his sleeves for a trick.

6   The angry protestor approached the podium _____, expressing frustration with the government.

7   As the race progressed, some participants began to _____ from the leading group.

8   The noise from the construction site continued to _____ throughout the day.

9   Water started _____ out of the broken pipe, creating a messy situation.

10 At the end of the celebration, the air was filled with _____, creating a festive atmosphere.

3   choke off / pare / migrate / photosynthesis / solstice / slender / undernourished / edict / cease / petiole

1 The king issued an _____, declaring a new law that all citizens must obey.

2 During the winter _____, the day is shortest, and the night is longest.

3 To improve financial stability, the company decided to _____ costs by reducing unnecessary expenses.

4 The oppressive regime tried to _____ any form of dissent by suppressing free speech.

5 The _____ thread hanging from the delicate fabric seemed fragile and easily breakable.

6 The leaf's _____ connected it to the stem, providing support and nourishment.

7 Children in impoverished regions may suffer from being _____ due to inadequate access to nutritious food.

8 Plants utilize _____, a process that converts sunlight into energy for growth.

9 The ongoing conflict led the two nations to _____ diplomatic relations, leading to a state of war.

10 Birds often _____ to warmer climates during the colder months to find better living conditions.

4

dissolve / fragile / pigments / vein / define / vivid / splotch / replaced / hibernate / camouflage

1 Many animals _____ during the winter to conserve energy and survive harsh conditions.

2 The glass was so _____ that even a slight impact could cause it to break.

3 A random _____ of paint on the canvas created an interesting and unexpected pattern.

4 The surgeon carefully dissected the leaf to examine its _____ and structure.

5 Can you _____ the main characteristics of the new policy for better understanding?

6 Sugar will quickly _____ in water, creating a sweet solution.

7 The old machinery was outdated and needed to be _____ with more advanced equipment.

8 The artist used various _____ to create a vibrant and colorful painting.

9 The chameleon's ability to change color is a form of natural _____.

10 The artist painted a _____ picture of the bustling city with vivid details.

5

adaptive / shimmer / sizzling / tawny / shuddering / odd / glowing / haphazard / thrilling / be predisposed to

1 The night sky was filled with _____ stars, creating a breathtaking view.

2 His behavior was quite _____ and unpredictable, making it challenging

to understand.

3   Some people may _____ certain health conditions due to genetic factors.

4   The lake reflected the moonlight, causing it to _____ on the water's surface.

5   The lion's fur had a _____ hue, blending with the dry grass of the savannah.

6   The unexpected loud noise left everyone _____ with fear.

7   _____ changes in the environment can lead to the evolution of new species.

8   The project was completed in a somewhat _____ manner, lacking proper planning.

9   The sound of the steak _____ on the hot grill added to the excitement of the barbecue.

10 The roller coaster ride was both exhilarating and _____, providing an unforgettable experience.

6

fragile / disintegration / bloom / sublime / mummify / radiate / radiant / vanish / sublime / mute

1   The delicate glass vase was so _____ that it shattered with the slightest touch.

2   The ancient manuscript was on the verge of _____, with its pages crumbling away.

3   The magician performed a trick that made a flower suddenly _____ on the empty table.

4   As the sun set, the colors in the sky created a _____ and awe-inspiring scene.

5   The mummy was carefully wrapped to _____ it for preservation over the centuries.

6   The sweet fragrance of the flowers began to _____, filling the room with a pleasant scent.

7   The artist used a variety of colors to capture the _____ beauty of the landscape.

8   The once lively city seemed to _____, as if swallowed by the encroaching darkness.

9   The forbidden ritual was said to have the power to _____ the soul from the mortal body.

UNIT

5

10 Despite the chaos, the monk remained _____, maintaining a solemn and silent demeanor.

7   never-never / abundance / awkward / simmer / whine / unruly / figment / sheer / conceal / fade / leafy / glide / swoop / wither / airborne

1   The forest was filled with the soothing sound of _____ trees in the gentle breeze.

2   The garden displayed an _____ of colorful flowers, creating a vibrant and lively scene.

3   As the summer heat persisted, the once lush flowers began to _____ and lose their vibrancy.

4   The soup was left to _____ on the stove, allowing its flavors to meld and intensify.

Voca Check | 269

5   The child continued to _____ about wanting a toy, making a constant complaining noise.

6   The students became _____ when the teacher left the classroom, causing chaos.

7   The unicorn in the story was not real but merely a _____ of the protagonist's imagination.

8   The mysterious forest was often referred to as the _____, a place of enchantment.

9   The view from the mountaintop was breathtaking in its _____ beauty, extending as far as the eye could see.

10 The spy attempted to _____ himself in the shadows, avoiding any attention.

11 His _____ dance moves drew laughter from the crowd, making the situation even more embarrassing.

12 As the sun began to set, the colors of the sky started to _____ into a palette of warm hues.

13 The parachute allowed the skydivers to remain _____, gracefully descending to the ground.

14 With wings outstretched, the eagle could _____ effortlessly through the open sky.

15 The owl made a sudden _____, silently diving down to catch its unsuspecting prey.

[1-4] Read the passage and answer each question.

The stealth of autumn catches one unaware. Was that a goldfinch perching in the early September woods, or just the first turning leaf? A red-winged blackbird or a sugar maple closing up shop for the winter? (가)Keen-eyed as leopards, we stand still and squint hard, looking for signs of movement. Early-morning frost sits heavily on the grass, and turns barbed wire into a string of stars. On a distant hill, a small square of yellow appears to be a lighted stage. At last the truth ㉠dawns on us: Fall is staggering in, right on schedule, with its baggage of chilly nights, macabre holidays, and spectacular, ㉡heart-stoppingly beautiful leaves. (나)Soon the leaves will start cringing on the trees, and roll up in clenched fists before they actually fall off. Dry seedpods will rattle like tiny gourds. But first there will be weeks of gushing color so bright, so pastel, so confetti-like, that people will travel up and down the East Coast just to stare at it- a whole season of leaves. Where do the colors come from? Sunlight rules most living things with its golden ㉢edicts. When the days begin to shorten, soon after the summer solstice on June 21, a tree reconsiders its leaves. All summer it feeds them so they can process sunlight, but in the dog days of summer the tree begins pulling nutrients back into its trunk and roots, ㉣pares down, and gradually chokes off its leaves. A corky layer of cells forms at the leaves' slender petioles, then scars over.

Undernourished, the leaves stop producing the pigment chlorophyll, and photo-synthesis ceases. (다)Animals can migrate, hibernate, or store food to prepare for winter. But where can a tree go? It survives by dropping its leaves, and by the end of autumn only a few fragile threads of fluid-carrying xylem hold leaves to their stems.

A turning leaf stays partly green at first, then reveals ㉤splotches of yellow and red as the chlorophyll gradually breaks down. Dark green seems to stay longest in the veins, outlining and defining them. During

UNIT

5

the summer, chlorophyll dissolves in the heat and light, but (라)<u>it is also being steadily replaced</u>. In the fall, on the other hand, no new pigment is produced, and so we notice Ⓐ<u>the other colors</u> that were always there, right in the leaf, although chlorophyll's shocking green hid Ⓑ<u>them</u> from view. With Ⓒ<u>their</u> Ⓓ<u>camouflage</u> gone, we see these colors for the first time all year, and marvel, but Ⓔ<u>they</u> were always there, hidden like a vivid secret beneath the hot glowing greens of summer.

1 What is the purpose of the underlined (가)?
① The realm of nature beyond human perception
② Secret attributes of Autumn
③ The piercing eyes of leopards
④ The nature of Autumn that never ceases to stimulate human curiosity
⑤ Capriciousness of nature

2 밑줄 친 (나) ~ (라)에 대한 설명 중 옳은 것을 <u>모두</u> 고른 것은?

> ㉠ (나): Visual and auditory imagery is maximized through figurative descriptions.
> ㉡ (다): It emphasizes how agilely trees relocate for the winter.
> ㉢ (라): It explains why the leaves keep wearing green clothes during the summer.

① ㉠ only
② ㉠ and ㉡
③ ㉢ only
④ ㉠ and ㉢
⑤ ㉠, ㉡, and ㉢

3 Among Ⓐ ~ Ⓔ, the odd one is

① Ⓐ the other colors

② Ⓑ them

③ Ⓒ their

④ Ⓓ camouflage

⑤ Ⓔ they

4 밑줄 친 ㉠~㉢의 문맥상 영영풀이 또는 동의어로 적절하지 <u>않은</u> 것은?

① ㉠ dawn on: to begin to be understood or realized by someone for the first time

② ㉡ heart-stoppingly: breathtakingly

③ ㉢ edict: order

④ ㉣ pare down: to make smaller or less in amount, degree or intensity

⑤ ㉤ splotch: a mark or spot that has a regular shape

[5-9] Read the passage and answer each question.

[A] ㉠The stealth of autumn catches one unaware. Was that a goldfinch perching in the early September woods, or just the first turning leaf? A red-winged blackbird or a sugar maple closing up shop for the winter? Keen-eyed as leopards, we stand still and squint hard, looking for signs of movement. ㉡Early-morning frost sits heavily on the grass, and turns barbed wire into a string of stars. On a distant hill, a small square of yellow appears to be a lighted stage. At last the truth ㉢dawns on us: **Fall is staggering in, right on schedule, with its baggage of chilly nights, macabre holidays, and spectacular, heart-stoppingly beautiful leaves**. Soon the leaves will start cringing on the trees, and roll up in clenched fists before they actually fall off. ㉣Dry seedpods will rattle like tiny gourds.

[B] (가)But first there will be weeks of gushing color so bright, so pastel, so confetti-like, that people will travel up and down the East Coast just to stare at it—a whole season of leaves. Where do the colors come from? Sunlight rules most living things with its golden edicts. When the days begin to shorten, soon after the summer solstice on June 21, a tree reconsiders its leaves. (A) All summer it feeds them so they can process sunlight, but (나)in the dog days of summer the tree begins pulling nutrients back into its trunk and roots, pares down, and gradually chokes off its leaves. A corky layer of cells forms at the leaves' slender petioles, then scars over.

[C] (다)Undernourished, we see the leaves stop producing the pigment chlorophyll, and photo-synthesis ceases. Animals can migrate, hibernate, or store food to prepare for winter. But where can a tree go? ㉤It survives by dropping its leaves, and by the end of autumn only a few fragile threads of fluid-carrying xylem hold leaves to their stems. (B)

[D] A turning leaf stays partly green at first, then reveals splotches of yellow and red as the chlorophyll gradually breaks down. (라)Dark green seems to stay longest in the veins, outlining and defining them. During the summer, chlorophyll dissolves in the heat and light, but it is also being steadily replaced. In the fall, on the other hand, no new pigment is produced, and so we notice the other colors that were always there, right in the leaf, although chlorophyll's shocking green hid them from view. (마)With their camouflage gone, we see these colors for the first time all year, and marvel, but they were always there, hidden like a vivid secret beneath the hot glowing greens of summer.

ⓗAn odd feature of the colors is that they don't seem to have any special purpose. We are predisposed to respond to their beauty, of course. (C) They shimmer with the colors of sunset, spring flowers, the tawny buff of a colt's pretty rump, the shuddering pink of a blush. Animals and flowers color for a reason—adaptation to their environment—but there is no adaptive reason for leaves to color so beautifully in the fall any more than there is for the sky or ocean to be blue. (D) We find the sizzling colors thrilling, and in a sense they Ⓐ _____ us. Colored like living things, they signal death and disintegration. In time, they will become fragile and, like the body, return to dust. They are as we hope our own fate will be when we die: Not to vanish, just to sublime from one beautiful state into another.

(E) Though leaves lose their green life, they bloom with urgent colors, as the woods grow mummified day by day, and Nature becomes more carnal, mute, and radiant.

5   Which of the literary devices is found in the underlined sentence in [A]?

> Fall is staggering in, right on schedule, with its baggage of chilly nights, macabre holidays, and spectacular, heart-stoppingly beautiful leaves.

① Simile   ② Alliteration
③ Allusion   ④ Personification
⑤ hyperbole

6 (가) ~ (마) 중 어법상 <u>어색한</u> 것을 <u>한 개</u> 고르시오.

① (가)   ② (나)

③ (다)   ④ (라)

⑤ (마)

7 Find the best place that is best suitable for the sentence given below.

> It's just one of the haphazard marvels the planet bestows every year.

① (A)   ② (B)

③ (C)   ④ (D)

⑤ (E)

8 Which of the following is <u>NOT</u> correct?

① In [A], descriptive writing is distinctly used help the reader vividly visualize the situation.

② ㉠ means that when the season changes to autumn it does so, slowly, so that most people don't even realize it is happening.

③ In ㉡, imagery is used to allow the reader to experience the changing of leaves in the fall so vividly through the visual senses.

④ ㉢ means to become known or obvious to someone, often suddenly.

⑤ ㉣ refers to people watching the turning leaves.

9 Which of the following is <u>NOT</u> correct?

① In [B], the author details the scientific process that leaves go through in order to change colors.

② ㉤ shows how trees adapt to the changing environment around them.

③ The underlined sentence in (마), the simile is used.

④ The "odd feature of the colors" in ㉥ is the difference between animals and trees because animals change colors to adapt to their environment, and trees do not.

⑤ ㉦ can be filled in with "enlighten."

[10-11] Read the passage and answer each question.

 NOTE

Animals and flowers color for a reason—adaptation to their environment—but there is no adaptive reason for leaves to color so beautifully in the fall any more than there is for the sky or ocean to be blue.

[A] Though leaves lose their green life, they bloom with urgent colors, as the woods grow mummified day by day, and Nature becomes more carnal, mute, and radiant.

[B] It's just one of the haphazard marvels the planet bestows every year. We find the sizzling colors thrilling, and in a sense they dupe us.

[C] Colored like living things, they signal death and disintegration. In time, they will become fragile and, like the body, return to dust. They are as we hope our own fate will be when we die: Not to vanish, just to sublime from one beautiful state into another.

We call the season "fall," from the Old English feallan, to fall, which leads back through time to the Indo-European phol, which also means to fall. So the word and the idea are both extremely ancient, and haven't really changed since the first of our kind needed a name for fall's leafy abundance. As we say the word, we're reminded of ㉠that other Fall, in the garden of Eden, when fig leaves never withered and scales fell from our eyes. ㉡Fall is the time when leaves fall from the trees, just as spring is when flowers spring up, ㉢summer is when we simmer, and winter is when we whine from the cold. Children love to play in piles of leaves, hurling them into the air like confetti, leaping into soft unruly mattresses of them. For children, leaf fall is just one of the odder figments of Nature, like hailstones or snowflakes. Walk down a lane overhung with trees in the never-never land of autumn, and you will forget about time and death, lost in the sheer delicious spill of color. Adam and Eve concealed their nakedness with leaves, remember? Leaves have always hidden our awkward secrets.

But how do the colored leaves fall? As a leaf ages, the growth hormone, auxin, fades, and cells at the base of the petiole divide. Two or three rows of small cells, lying at right angles to the axis of the petiole, react with water, then come apart, leaving the petioles hanging on by only a few threads of xylem. A light breeze, and the leaves are airborne. They glide and swoop, rocking in invisible cradles. They are all wing and may flutter from yard to yard on small whirlwinds or updrafts, swiveling as they go. Firmly tethered to earth, we love to see things rise up and fly—soap bubbles, balloons, birds, fall leaves. They remind us that the end of a season is capricious, as is the end of life.

10 Which is the best order of [A] - [C]?

① [B] - [A] - [C]
② [B] - [C] - [A]
③ [A] - [B] - [C]
④ [C] - [B] - [A]
⑤ [C] - [A] - [B]

11 Which of the following statements is <u>NOT</u> correct?

① In ㉠, allusion is used.
② In ㉡, simile is used.
③ In ㉢, alliteration is used.
④ The author compares colored leaves to living things in that phenomena in nature occur in a cycle that is characteristic of the life cycle of human beings.
⑤ The author deplores on the moodiness of the changing of seasons and on life and death.

PART

5 Sentence Completion

1 His qualifications for the diplomatic job were _____, and as a result his nomination was confirmed, and he became the ambassador to the United Nations.

① terrible   ② stingy
③ impeccable   ④ simple
⑤ retroactive

어휘
qualification 자격, 기준 diplomatic job 외교관 일 as a result 결과적으로(인과를 이끄는 접속사) nomination 지명 또는 임명권 confirmed 확정된, 일이 성사된 ambassador to ~의 대사관 terrible 끔찍한, 형편없는 stingy 구두쇠의, 인색한 impeccable 결함이 없는, 죄를 범하는 일이 없는, 완벽한 retroactive 퇴행의, 역행의

2 Human activity wipes out more than a thousand plant and animal species every year, and many more species are pushed to the edge of _____.

① habitat   ② extinction
③ survival   ④ erosion

어휘
wipe out 쓸어버리다(= brush up) be pushed to N ~에 몰리다 the edge of extinction 멸종의 벼락 be pushed to the edge of extinction 멸종의 벼락에 몰리다 habitat 서식지 survival 생존 cf. the survival of the fittest 적자생존 (= natural selection) erosion 부식, 침식 (= corrosion, wear out)

3 Criticism that tears down without suggesting areas of improvement is not _____ and should be avoided if possible.

① violent   ② dangerous
③ conventional   ④ constructive

어휘
criticism 비판 tear down 찢어 뭉개다, 부수다 suggest areas of improvement 개선할 부분에 대해 언급하다 avoid 피하다 if possible 가능하면 violent 폭력적인 dangerous 위험한 conventional 전통적인, 재래식의 constructive 생산적인

4 There are many people who hate violence and are convinced that it is one of their foremost and at the same time one of their most hopeful tasks to work for its reduction and, if possible, for its _____ from human life.

① redemption

② retaliation

③ elimination

④ retrogression

5 In the rest of the Western world religious ardor was _____ and church building was consequently declining.

① coalescing

② changing

③ dissipating

④ diminishing

⑤ diversifying

6 The shift from manufacturing to service has resulted in _____ paying jobs and a _____ in the strength of labor unions.

① lower – decline

② scanty – burst

③ meager – representation

④ lugubrious – decrease

7 It is characteristic of many groups to resist change, for, they argue, change is not necessarily for the better but may also be for the worse. Change means disorganization, and many groups tend to view it _____.

① as inevitable   ② as desirable

③ with complacency   ④ with suspicion

8 The scientist vehemently defended her research practices and she claimed that her results were _____.

① mauve

② delusive

③ indubitable

④ acetic

⑤ tutelary

9 The North in May conducted its second nuclear test and consequently _____ the U. N. members including South Korea and the United States.

① approbated with

② endorsed with

③ contended with

④ negotiated with

10 The president's secretary and his chief aide adored him, and both wrote obsessively _____ personal memoirs about him; unfortunately, however, _____ does not make for true intimacy.

① fatuous – frankness

② devoted – idolatry

③ garrulous – confidentiality

④ candid – discretion

⑤ rancorous – criticism

어휘

secretary 장관 chief aide 보좌관 adore 칭송하다 obsessively 비정상적일 정도로 memoir 회고록 make for 조장하다, 형성하다 true intimacy 진실한 친밀감 fatuous 어리석은, 얼빠진 devoted 헌신적인, 충실한, 종교적인 (= dutiful, faithful, loyal, devout) idolatry 우상숭배 garrulous 수다스러운, 말 많은 confidentiality 기밀성 candid 정직한, 노골적인 discretion 신중, 분별 rancorous 원한이 사무친, 악의에 불타는

문학_단편소설

The Tell-Tale Heart

by Edgar Allan Poe

☐ **mediocre**   **a** Neither good nor bad; average; of moderate quality

- The movie received <u>mediocre</u> reviews, neither praised nor criticized.

☐ **talented**   **a** Having natural aptitude or skill in a particular area

- She is a <u>talented</u> musician who can play multiple instruments.

☐ **desert**   **v** To abandon or leave; a dry, barren area with little or no vegetation

- He decided to <u>desert</u> the old car in the junkyard.

☐ **be taken in by**   To be deceived or fooled by someone or something

- She <u>was taken in by</u> the scam and lost a significant amount of money.

☐ **charitable**   **a** Generous in giving to those in need; relating to or involved in charity

- They organized a <u>charitable</u> event to raise funds for the local orphanage.

☐ **self-righteous**   **a** Morally superior and judgmental; convinced of one's own righteousness

- His <u>self-righteous</u> attitude made it difficult for others to work with him.

☐ **guardian**   **n** A person who has the legal responsibility to care for and make decisions for someone unable to do so

- The older sister became the legal <u>guardian</u> of her younger siblings.

☐ **make no secret of** — To be open or public about something; not hide or conceal

- She <u>made no secret of</u> her plans to start a new business.

☐ **idleness** — **n** The state of being inactive or doing nothing; laziness

- He realized that <u>idleness</u> was not conducive to personal growth.

☐ **indifference (to)** — **n** Lack of interest or concern towards something

- His <u>indifference to</u> the environmental issues surprised many.

☐ **moody** — **a** Prone to unpredictable changes in mood; having gloomy or irritable tendencies

- She can be quite <u>moody</u> during rainy days.

☐ **resentful** — **a** Feeling bitterness or anger towards someone or something

- She became <u>resentful</u> when her ideas were consistently ignored.

☐ **meager** — **a** Lacking in quantity or quality; inadequate or insufficient

- The <u>meager</u> salary was not enough to cover basic expenses.

☐ **go deep into** — To become deeply involved or immersed in a particular activity or subject

- He decided to <u>go deep into</u> research to understand the complex issue.

☐ **withdraw** — **v** To remove or take back; to retreat or disengage

- The army decided to <u>withdraw</u> from the battle due to unfavorable conditions.

☐ **bitter** — **a** Harsh or unpleasant in disposition; expressing strong resentment

- Their <u>bitter</u> argument left a lasting impact on their relationship.

☐ **quarrel** **n** A heated argument or disagreement

- They had a <u>quarrel</u> over the division of household chores.

☐ **run off to** To leave or escape to a particular place

- She decided to <u>run off to</u> the countryside for a weekend getaway.

☐ **make one's own way** To achieve success independently; to carve out one's path in life

- Despite facing challenges, she was determined to <u>make her own way</u> in the competitive industry.

☐ **in despair** In a state of hopelessness or extreme sadness

- After numerous failed attempts, he found himself <u>in despair</u>.

☐ **promote** **v** To advance or elevate someone to a higher position or rank

- After years of hard work, she was finally <u>promoted</u> to the position of manager.

☐ **sergeant major** **n** In the U.S. Army and Marine Corps, a senior non-commissioned officer holding the rank of sergeant major

- During the military exercise, the <u>sergeant major</u> commanded the troops with unwavering authority and precision.

☐ **enlisted man** A member of the military who is not a commissioned officer; typically a soldier

- <u>Enlisted men</u> are trained for ground combat and often operate on foot, carrying out missions such as patrolling, securing areas, and engaging enemy forces.

☐ **appeal to A for help** To request assistance from someone

- He decided to <u>appeal to</u> his colleagues <u>for help</u> with the project.

☐ **intercede**　**v** To mediate or intervene in a situation on behalf of others

- The diplomat tried to <u>intercede</u> in the conflict to bring about a peaceful resolution.

☐ **recognition**　**n** Acknowledgment or appreciation of someone's achievements or status

- Her hard work and dedication finally led to the <u>recognition</u> she deserved.

☐ **heir**　**n** A person who inherits or is entitled to inherit the property, title, or privileges of another

- The eldest son was the rightful <u>heir</u> to the family fortune.

☐ **dismiss**　**v** To disperse or send away; to terminate someone's employment or involvement

- The meeting was <u>dismissed</u> after reaching a resolution.

☐ **move in with**　To relocate and live with someone

- After getting married, they decided to <u>move in with</u> his parents temporarily.

☐ **odd**　**a** Not matching or not part of a set; strange or unusual

- She noticed an <u>odd</u> piece of artwork among the regular paintings.

☐ **housemate**　**n** A person with whom one shares a house or living space

- They get along well as <u>housemates</u>, sharing responsibilities and chores.

☐ **editor**　**n** The person responsible for overseeing and editing the content of a newspaper or other publication

- The <u>editor</u> made significant changes to improve the clarity of the article.

☐ **full-length**   **a** Referring to a work of art or literature that is not abridged or shortened; complete and unabridged

- She wrote a <u>full-length</u> novel that became a bestseller.

☐ **intuitive**   **a** Based on intuition or instinct rather than conscious reasoning

- Her <u>intuitive</u> understanding of people's emotions made her an excellent counselor.

☐ **sleuth**   **n** A detective or investigator; also refers to tracking or following clues

- The <u>sleuth</u> solved the mystery by piecing together various clues.

☐ **ghastly**   **a** Extremely unpleasant, horrifying, or causing great fear

- The <u>ghastly</u> scene in the horror movie made the audience scream.

☐ **grotesque**   **a** Comically or repulsively ugly or distorted; bizarre or absurd

- The artist created a <u>grotesque</u> sculpture that challenged traditional notions of beauty.

☐ **be peopled with**   To be inhabited or populated by certain kinds of people

- The novel <u>is peopled with</u> eccentric characters who add depth to the story.

☐ **distraught**   **a** Deeply agitated, anxious, or troubled

- She was <u>distraught</u> when she couldn't find her missing pet.

☐ **deranged**   **a** Mentally disturbed, insane, or irrational

- The criminal's actions were so <u>deranged</u> that they left the community in shock.

☐ **doomed**
a Condemned to an unfortunate or disastrous outcome; marked by a sense of unavoidable failure or destruction

- The ship was <u>doomed</u> from the moment it hit the iceberg.

☐ **convincing**
a Capable of persuading or causing someone to believe in the validity or truth of something

- She presented a <u>convincing</u> argument that swayed the jury in her favor.

☐ **likeness**
n Similarity or resemblance in appearance or characteristics

- The artist captured the <u>likeness</u> of the subject with incredible detail.

☐ **frighten**
v To cause fear or apprehension; to make someone scared or alarmed

- The sudden loud noise <u>frightened</u> the small child.

☐ **unsettling**
a Causing discomfort, disturbance, or a feeling of unease

- The mysterious sounds in the dark forest were quite <u>unsettling</u>.

☐ **considerable**
a Large in size, amount, or degree; noteworthy or substantial

- The project required a <u>considerable</u> amount of time and resources.

☐ **body**
n A group or mass of people or things; an organized whole

- A <u>body</u> of protesters gathered in the square to voice their concerns.

☐ **humiliating**
a Causing a loss of pride or self-respect; embarrassing or degrading

- His public defeat was a <u>humiliating</u> experience that he wanted to forget.

UNIT
6

☐ **senseless**

a Lacking sense, meaning, or purpose; without logical or reasonable basis

- The act of violence was <u>senseless</u> and left everyone in shock.

☐ **agonizing**

a Causing extreme physical or mental pain; distressing or tormenting

- Waiting for the test results was an <u>agonizing</u> experience for the patient.

☐ **elude**

v To cleverly or skillfully avoid or escape from something

- The fugitive managed to <u>elude</u> the police for weeks.

☐ **tuberculosis**

n An infectious bacterial disease affecting the lungs, commonly known as TB

- Many lives were lost to <u>tuberculosis</u> before effective treatments were developed.

☐ **relentless**

a Unyielding, persistent, or harsh; not easing or letting up

- The <u>relentless</u> pursuit of success sometimes takes a toll on one's well-being.

☐ **romance**

n A feeling or atmosphere of love, excitement, and mystery; a love story

- She was swept away by the <u>romance</u> of the novel.

☐ **delirious**

a In a state of mental confusion or excitement; experiencing hallucinations

- The fever left him <u>delirious</u> and unable to distinguish reality from imagination.

☐ **raging**

a Violently moving or behaving; intense, furious, or vehement

- The storm brought <u>raging</u> winds and torrential rain.

delirium

n A state of mental confusion characterized by restlessness, illusions, and incoherent speech

- The patient experienced <u>delirium</u> as a result of the high fever.

pass in and out of

To move back and forth between different states or conditions

- His memories seemed to <u>pass in and out of</u> focus as he reminisced about the past.

dreadfully

ad Extremely or excessively; causing great fear or distress

- She felt <u>dreadfully</u> alone in the empty house.

sharpen

v To make something sharper or more acute; to enhance or intensify

- The knife needed to be <u>sharpened</u> before slicing the vegetables.

dull

v ① To make or become less sharp or clear
② To alleviate or reduce (pain, suffering, etc.)

- Years of use had <u>dulled</u> the blade of the knife.
- The medication helped <u>dull</u> the intensity of the pain.

acute

a Sharp, keen, or perceptive; having a strong effect or impact

- She had an <u>acute</u> sense of hearing and could detect even the faintest sounds.

hearken

v To listen attentively or give heed; to pay close attention

- They <u>hearkened</u> to the distant sounds of music echoing through the forest.

conceive

v To form or develop an idea, opinion, or emotion in the mind

- She couldn't <u>conceive</u> the idea of leaving her hometown.

UNIT

6

☐ **haunt**　**v** ① To persistently follow or trouble
　　　　　　　② To visit or appear frequently in the mind

- The memories of the accident <u>haunted</u> him for years.
- The ghostly figure seemed to <u>haunt</u> her dreams.

☐ **day and night**　Continuously; without interruption, throughout the entire day and night

- They worked <u>day and night</u> to meet the deadline.

☐ **wrong**　**v** ① To harm or cause injury to someone
　　　　　　② To treat someone unfairly or unjustly

- It is not right to <u>wrong</u> others for personal gain.
- She felt <u>wronged</u> by the unjust decision.

☐ **insult**　**n** A disrespectful or offensive remark or action that causes offense

- His remarks were intended as an <u>insult</u>, and they hurt deeply.

☐ **vulture**　**n** A large bird of prey known for scavenging on carrion; metaphorically, a person who preys on others' misfortunes

- In times of crisis, <u>vultures</u> may gather to exploit the situation.

☐ **pale**　**a** Lacking intensity of color; faint or weak

- The moon cast a <u>pale</u> light over the landscape.

☐ **film**　**n** A thin layer or coating; also, a thin layer of a substance on a surface

- A <u>film</u> of dust had settled on the old bookshelf.

☐ **fall upon**　To drop or descend onto something; to attack or assail suddenly

- As night fell, a hush <u>fell upon</u> the city.

☐ **run cold**　　　To become cold or chilly, either in a literal or figurative sense

- The news made her blood <u>run cold</u>.

☐ **by degrees**　　　Gradually or slowly over time; step by step

- <u>By degrees</u>, he began to understand the complexities of the problem.

☐ **take the life of**　　　To cause the death of; to kill

- The predator sought to <u>take the life of</u> its prey.

☐ **rid A of B**　　　To relieve or free A from the presence or burden of B

- She wanted to <u>rid</u> her life <u>of</u> negativity.

☐ **for ever**　　　**ad** Perpetually; without end; eternally

- Their love for each other was meant to last <u>for ever</u>.

☐ **fancy**　　　**v** ① To imagine or visualize
　　　② To have a preference or desire

- Can you <u>fancy</u> what it would be like to live on another planet?
- She didn't <u>fancy</u> going out in the rain.

☐ **proceed**　　　**v** To move forward or continue; to begin or carry on with an action

- They decided to <u>proceed</u> with the construction project.

☐ **caution**　　　**n** Careful and deliberate actions to avoid potential danger or risks; a warning

- She approached the situation with <u>caution</u>, aware of the potential risks.

☐ **foresight**　　　**n** The ability to predict or anticipate future events; prudence or careful consideration for the future

- His <u>foresight</u> in financial matters helped him navigate economic challenges.

UNIT
6

☐ **dissimulation**　**n** The act of concealing true feelings, thoughts, or intentions; hypocrisy

- Her dissimulation made it difficult to discern her true emotions.

☐ **latch**　**n** A fastening or locking device, often used on doors or gates

- She turned the latch and opened the creaky door.

☐ **sufficient**　**a** Adequate or enough to meet a particular need or purpose

- The information provided was sufficient for the task at hand.

☐ **shine out**　To emit or display light brightly; to become prominent or outstanding

- As the clouds cleared, the stars began to shine out in the night sky.

☐ **thrust in**　To forcefully insert or push something inward

- He thrust in the key and turned it, unlocking the door.

☐ **lie**　**v** to be in or move into a horizontal position on a surface (lie - lay - lain)

- She lies on the grass every afternoon; yesterday, she laid the blanket out; she has lain there for hours.

☐ **hinge**　**n** A jointed or flexible device that allows the turning or pivoting of a door or lid

- The door swung open on its creaky hinges.

☐ **creak**　**n** / **v** ① A harsh, grating sound, often produced by something moving slowly or with friction ② To make or cause to make a harsh squeaking sound ③ To make such sounds while moving

- The old floorboards creaked as she walked across the room.

☐ **vex** **v** To annoy, irritate, or cause distress

- His constant complaints began to <u>vex</u> her.

☐ **the day breaks** The moment when daylight begins; sunrise

- They rose early to watch as <u>the day breaks</u> over the horizon.

☐ **boldly** **ad** In a courageous or daring manner; without fear or hesitation

- She <u>boldly</u> confronted the challenges that came her way.

☐ **chamber** **n** A room, especially a bedroom; in some contexts, a private office or meeting room

- The cozy <u>chamber</u> had a beautiful view of the garden.

☐ **hearty** **a** Warm and friendly; enthusiastic or vigorous

- They received a <u>hearty</u> welcome from the locals.

☐ **inquire** **v** To ask about or seek information; to make an inquiry

- He decided to <u>inquire</u> about the availability of tickets for the event.

☐ **profound** **a** Deep or intense in quality; having great depth or seriousness

- The speaker's words had a <u>profound</u> impact on the audience.

☐ **suspect** **v** To believe or have a feeling that someone or something is guilty, unreliable, or dishonest

- The detective began to <u>suspect</u> foul play in the mysterious case.

☐ **minute hand** **n** The hand on a clock or watch that indicates the minutes

- The <u>minute hand</u> moved slowly around the clock face.

UNIT

6

extent

n ① The degree or scope of something
② A large area or range

- We didn't realize the extent of the damage until later.
- The extent of the forest was vast and untouched.

sagacity

n The quality of being wise, discerning, or mentally sharp

- His sagacity in decision-making earned him the respect of his peers.

contain

v To keep something within limits; to control or restrain

- She struggled to contain her excitement as the surprise was revealed.

little by little

Gradually or slowly, in small increments

- With persistence, the project advanced little by little.

deeds

n Actions or accomplishments; something done, especially something notable or significant

- His noble deeds were celebrated throughout the kingdom.

fairly

v To a moderate or reasonable extent; reasonably; justly

- The results were fairly consistent across all experiments.

chuckle

v To laugh quitely, often expressing amusement or satisfaction

- He couldn't help but chuckle at the amusing story.

startle

v To cause someone to suddenly feel shocked, surprised, or alarmed

- The sudden loud noise did startle the sleeping cat.

draw back

To move backward; to retreat or step back

- He had to draw back from the edge of the cliff to ensure safety.

☐ **as black as pitch**	Completely black or dark; pitch-black
	• During the power outage, the room became <u>as black as pitch</u>.
☐ **thick darkness**	A state of complete and dense darkness
	• In the forest at night, there was <u>thick darkness</u> with no visible light.
☐ **shutter**	**n** A hinged cover for a window or camera lens; a device to block or allow light
	• He closed the <u>shutters</u> to keep the room dark during the daytime.
☐ **be close fastened**	To be securely or tightly fixed or closed
	• The door <u>was close fastened</u>, and no light seeped through the cracks.
☐ **have one's head in**	To have one's attention or focus on something
	• I <u>had my head in</u> the book and didn't notice the time passing.
☐ **be about to**	To be on the verge of doing something; to be ready or prepared to do
	• She <u>was about to</u> leave when the phone rang.
☐ **thumb**	**n** The short, thick first digit of the human hand, set lower and apart from the other four and opposable to them
	• He counted the pages by running his <u>thumb</u> along the edge.
☐ **slip**	**v** To slide or move smoothly and quietly
	• She tried not to <u>slip</u> on the icy pavement.
☐ **tin**	**n** A soft, silvery-white metallic element often used in alloys, characterized by its resistance to corrosion
	• The kitchen utensils were made of <u>tin</u>.

fastening

n ① A device used to close or secure something
② The action of securing or attaching something

- The <u>fastening</u> on the gate was a simple latch.
- She inspected the <u>fastening</u> to ensure it was secure.

keep still

To remain in a motionless or quiet state

- The teacher requested the students to <u>keep still</u> during the exam.

sit up in the bed

To assume an upright or sitting position while in bed

- She <u>sat up in the bed</u>, wide awake and alert.

night after night

Every night continuously or repeatedly

- They performed <u>night after night</u> to enthusiastic audiences.

death watch

n ① A vigil kept beside a dying person ② A person or group assigned to watch over a condemned prisoner

- The ticking sound made by the <u>death watch</u> beetle, believed in superstition to be an omen of death.
- The family maintained a <u>death watch</u> at the bedside of their ailing grandfather.

press corps

A group of journalists representing different media outlets covering the same event or topic, especially major announcements

- The president addressed the nation, and the <u>press corps</u> eagerly awaited to report on the latest developments.

presently

ad ① In a short time; soon
② In the current circumstances; at present

- I am busy right now, but I will be with you <u>presently</u>.

slight

a Small in degree; not considerable; minor

- There was only a <u>slight</u> difference between the two options, making it difficult to choose.

☐ **groan** | **n** A low, mournful sound indicative of pain, discomfort, or unhappiness; also used metaphorically for expressions of disapproval or dissatisfaction

- The old floorboards let out a <u>groan</u> as I walked across the room.

☐ **mortal** | **a** Subject to death; having a limited lifespan

- All living beings, including humans, are <u>mortal</u> and will eventually face death.

☐ **terror** | **n** Extreme fear; intense dread

- The sudden loud noise filled them with <u>terror</u>, and they ran for cover.

☐ **grief** | **n** Deep sorrow, especially that caused by someone's death

- The whole community shared in the collective <u>grief</u> after the tragic accident.

☐ **stifle** | **v** To suppress or hold back, often in reference to sounds or emotions

- She <u>stifled</u> her laughter during the serious meeting to avoid attracting attention.

☐ **arise** | **v** To come into existence; to originate or emerge

- Unexpected challenges can <u>arise</u> at any moment, requiring quick problem-solving.

☐ **be overcharged with** | To be filled or loaded excessively with something

- Her heart <u>was overcharged with</u> emotions as she received the unexpected news.

☐ **awe** | **n** A feeling of reverential respect mixed with fear or wonder

- The majestic view of the Grand Canyon filled them with a sense of <u>awe</u>.

UNIT

6

☐ **well up**   To rise to the surface, often used to describe emotions or tears

- Emotions began to <u>well up</u> as they listened to the heartfelt speech.

☐ **bosom**   **n** The chest, especially when considered as the seat of emotions

- She held the letter close to her <u>bosom</u>, treasuring the words within.

☐ **deepening**   **a** Becoming more intense or more profound

- The <u>deepening</u> darkness signaled the approaching storm.

☐ **dreadful**   **ad** Extremely bad, unpleasant, or shocking

- The news of the accident was truly <u>dreadful</u>, leaving everyone in shock.

☐ **distract**   **v** To draw away the attention or focus

- The noisy surroundings began to <u>distract</u> him from his reading.

☐ **pity**   **n** A feeling of sorrow and compassion for the suffering or misfortunes of others

- It's impossible not to feel <u>pity</u> for the stray animals roaming the streets.

☐ **chuckle**   **n** A quiet or suppressed laugh

- He couldn't help but <u>chuckle</u> at the amusing story his friend shared.

☐ **lie awake**   To remain in bed without sleeping

- She had to <u>lie awake</u> for hours, unable to find peace in her thoughts.

fancy | **v** To imagine or visualize; to have a whimsical or unrealistic idea

- He would often <u>fancy</u> himself as a famous explorer, embarking on thrilling adventures.

causeless | **a** Without a specific cause or reason; happening without explanation

- The sudden and <u>causeless</u> disappearance of the old building puzzled the historians.

nothing but | **ad** Only; just; emphasizing the exclusivity of a particular thing

- The landscape was covered in <u>nothing but</u> snow, creating a serene and white environment.

cricket | **n** An insect known for its distinctive chirping sound

- The rhythmic sound of <u>crickets</u> filled the night air, creating a peaceful atmosphere.

chirp | **n** The sound made by birds or insects, such as crickets

- The birds began to <u>chirp</u> as the sun rose, signaling the start of a new day.

comfort | **v** ① To soothe or console someone in distress ② A state of physical ease and freedom from pain or constraint

- She tried to <u>comfort</u> her friend who was going through a difficult time.

supposition | **n** An assumption or belief based on inconclusive evidence; a conjecture

- The theory was built on the <u>supposition</u> that ancient civilizations had advanced knowledge.

in vain | Without success or a desired outcome; futilely

- He tried to fix the broken device, but his efforts were <u>in vain</u> as it remained non-functional.

☐ **stalk** | **v** ① To walk with a stiff or proud gait ② To pursue stealthily or in a threatening manner

- The predator began to <u>stalk</u> its prey, moving silently through the tall grass.

☐ **envelop** | **v** To wrap or cover completely; to surround

- The dense fog began to <u>envelop</u> the entire town, reducing visibility.

☐ **mournful** | Expressing or inducing sadness; filled with sorrow

- The <u>mournful</u> melody of the song brought tears to the eyes of the listeners.

☐ **unperceived** | **a** Not noticed or detected; not observed by others

- The cat moved <u>unperceived</u> through the shadows, hunting its prey.

☐ **patiently** | **ad** With forbearance and calmness; without getting frustrated

- She waited <u>patiently</u> for the train, knowing that delays were common during rush hours.

☐ **resolve to V** | To make a firm decision or commitment to do something

- After much contemplation, he <u>resolved to</u> pursue his passion for art.

☐ **crevice** | **n** A narrow opening or crack, especially in a rock or wall

- Light streamed through the <u>crevice</u> in the door, revealing a dimly lit room.

☐ **lantern** | **n** A portable light source with a protective enclosure, often used outdoors

- They carried a <u>lantern</u> to guide them through the dark forest at night.

☐ **stealthily**

ad In a cautious and secretive manner; avoiding detection

- The cat moved stealthily through the house, trying not to wake anyone.

☐ **at length**

After a long period of time; finally or eventually

- The negotiations continued at length before a consensus was reached.

☐ **dim**

a ① Lacking in brightness; not well-lit
② Lacking clarity or distinctness

- As the sun set, the room grew dim, and shadows filled the space.

☐ **furious**

a Extremely angry or intense in its activity or force

- The storm grew furious, with strong winds and heavy rain causing chaos.

☐ **mid**

ad ① In the middle of; surrounded by or mixed with
② During the middle of a particular period

- The house is located mid the beautiful mountains.

☐ **dreadful**

a Extremely bad, unpleasant, or shocking

- The storm caused dreadful damage to the coastal area.

☐ **burst**

v Break open or apart suddenly and violently

- The balloon burst with a loud noise during the celebration.

☐ **anxiety**

n A feeling of worry, nervousness, or unease, typically about an imminent event or something with an uncertain outcome

- His anxiety about the upcoming exam kept him awake all night.

☐ **seize**

v To take hold of suddenly and forcibly

- The police officer tried to <u>seize</u> the suspect as he attempted to flee.

☐ **throw open**

To open something, such as a door or window, wide and quickly

- The bride <u>threw open</u> the doors to welcome the guests into the wedding hall.

☐ **shriek**

n A loud, sharp, shrill cry or sound

- The sudden <u>shriek</u> of the alarm frightened everyone in the building.

☐ **gaily**

ad In a cheerful and lively way

- The children danced <u>gaily</u> around the maypole during the festival.

☐ **deed**

n An action that is performed intentionally or consciously

- His heroic <u>deed</u> saved a life during the accident.

☐ **muffled**

a (of a sound) not loud because it is hindered in its passage

- The voices from the other room were <u>muffled</u>, making it difficult to understand.

☐ **cease**

v To bring or come to an end

- The rain will <u>cease</u> by evening, according to the weather forecast.

☐ **remove**

v To take away from a place

- Please <u>remove</u> your shoes before entering the house.

☐ **corpse**

n A dead body, especially of a human being

- The detective examined the <u>corpse</u> to determine the cause of death.

stone dead　　Completely lifeless or without any sign of life

- The plant, once vibrant, is now <u>stone dead</u> due to neglect.

pulsation　　**n** A rhythmic beating or throbbing, especially of the heart

- The doctor measured the <u>pulsation</u> to check the patient's heart rate.

trouble　　**v** To cause distress or worry to; upset

- Don't <u>trouble</u> yourself; everything will be fine.

precaution　　**n** A measure taken in advance to prevent something dangerous, unpleasant, or inconvenient from happening

- Wearing a helmet is a necessary <u>precaution</u> when riding a bike.

conceal　　**v** to hid something or preventing it from being known

- The detective discovered the <u>concealed</u> weapon during the search.

wane　　**v** To decrease in vigor, power, or extent; become weaker

- As the days <u>wane</u>, the temperature gradually drops in autumn.

hastily　　**ad** In a hurried or rash manner; quickly and without much thought

- She packed her bags <u>hastily</u>, afraid that she might miss her flight.

dismember　　**v** To cut off or remove the limbs of a person or an animal

- The gruesome crime scene suggested that someone had tried to <u>dismember</u> the victim.

☐ cut off

To sever or detach from something; to interrupt or terminate

- Due to the storm, the town was <u>cut off</u> from the rest of the region for several days.

☐ plank

n A thick, flat piece of timber, wider than a board

- The old house had creaky wooden <u>planks</u> that added to its rustic charm.

☐ scantling

v A small piece of lumber used in construction, typically with a square or rectangular cross-section

- The carpenter measured the <u>scantling</u> before cutting it to the required length.

☐ replace

v To put something back in its original position; to provide a substitute for something

- They had to <u>replace</u> the broken window with a new one.

☐ cunningly

ad In a clever, sly, or deceitful manner

- The fox <u>cunningly</u> outsmarted the other animals to get its meal.

☐ wash out

To remove or clean something with water; to cancel or nullify plans

- Heavy rain threatened to <u>wash out</u> the outdoor event.

☐ stain

n A discoloration or mark caused by a foreign substance; to color with a stain

- The red wine left a stubborn <u>stain</u> on the white tablecloth.

☐ wary

a Cautious, watchful, and alert, especially in the face of possible danger

- The hiker remained <u>wary</u> of the wild animals in the dense forest.

tub

n A large, open container for holding liquids; a bathtub

- She filled the <u>tub</u> with warm water for a relaxing bath.

make an end of

To bring something to a conclusion; to finish or put an end to

- The detective vowed to <u>make an end of</u> the criminal's activities.

a light heart

Cheerful and carefree; having a happy disposition

- Despite the challenges, she faced each day with <u>a light heart</u>.

street door

n The main door that opens directly onto the street from a building

- The delivery person left the package outside the <u>street door</u>.

suavity

n Graceful politeness and sophistication

- The diplomat addressed the sensitive issue with remarkable <u>suavity</u>.

with perfect suavity

Acting or speaking with impeccable politeness and charm

- He handled the difficult situation <u>with perfect suavity</u>, calming everyone present.

suspicion

n A feeling or belief that something is possible or likely; a slight trace

- There was a <u>suspicion</u> of foul play in the mysterious disappearance.

foul play

Unfair or dishonest conduct; illegal or dishonest behavior

- The investigators suspected <u>foul play</u> in the financial scandal.

□ arouse

v ① To awaken someone from sleep ② To stimulate or provoke someone or something; to bring about interest, debate, etc.

- The loud noise outside the window did not <u>arouse</u> the sleeping cat.

□ lodge

v ① To submit information, objections, or complaints to a person or authority ② To provide accommodation or shelter; to stay or reside temporarily

- She decided to <u>lodge</u> a formal complaint with the management about the noisy neighbors.

□ depute

v To appoint or instruct someone as a representative; to delegate someone for a specific task

- The manager <u>deputed</u> the experienced employee to handle the client's concerns.

□ premises

n The land and buildings on it

- The company decided to expand its <u>premises</u> to accommodate the growing workforce.

□ bid

v To utter a greeting or farewell; to command or direct someone to do something

- He <u>bid</u> farewell to his colleagues as he left the office for the last time.

□ at length

After a long period of time; finally

- The negotiations continued, and <u>at length</u>, an agreement was reached.

□ chamber

n A room, especially a bedroom; in British English, it can also refer to a set of rooms or an apartment

- The hotel room had a spacious <u>chamber</u> with a beautiful view.

□ undisturbed　　**a** ① Not interrupted or bothered; quiet and peaceful
② Calm and composed, without losing one's tranquility

- The undisturbed atmosphere of the library was perfect for studying.

□ treasure　　**n** ① Valuables, precious items, wealth, or belongings, either as a collection or individually
② Something highly valued or cherished

- The old chest was filled with family treasures passed down through generations.

□ desire　　**v** To wish for or want something; a strong feeling of longing or craving

- She expressed her desire to travel to exotic destinations.

□ fatigue　　**n** ① Extreme tiredness or exhaustion
② The result of labor, toil, or hard work

- After a day of hiking, the fatigue set in, and they welcomed the rest.

□ wild　　**ad** To an extreme or unrestrained degree; excessively

- They partied wild into the early hours of the morning.

□ audacity　　**n** Boldness or daring, often with a disregard for normal constraints or rules

- The young entrepreneur had the audacity to challenge established industry practices.

□ beneath　　**prep** Under or below; in a lower place

- The treasure was buried beneath the old oak tree.

□ repose　　**v** To rest or be at peace, especially in death

- The ancient king's remains were laid to repose in a grand mausoleum.

☐ **be(feel) at ease** To feel comfortable, relaxed, and free from worry or tension

- After the successful presentation, she finally <u>felt at ease</u>.

☐ **singularly** `ad` In a remarkable or exceptional manner; exceptionally

- The singer was <u>singularly</u> talented, captivating the audience with each note.

☐ **cheerily** `ad` In a cheerful and upbeat manner; happily

- The children played <u>cheerily</u> in the sunlit garden.

☐ **chat** `v` To engage in informal conversation; to talk or discuss casually

- Friends often gather to <u>chat</u> about their day over a cup of coffee.

☐ **ere** `prep` Before; earlier than

- They arrived <u>ere</u> the sun began to set.

☐ **pale** `a` / `ad` ① Having a light complexion; lacking color; feeble or weak ② To become pale in color

- Her face turned <u>pale</u> when she heard the shocking news.

☐ **ringing** `n` The sound of something resonating or echoing loudly

- The <u>ringing</u> of the church bells filled the air.

☐ **fancy** `v` / `a` ① To imagine or envision; to have a preference for ② Elaborate or decorative

- She <u>fancied</u> a world where anything was possible.

☐ **distinct** `a` ① Separate or different from something else; unique ② Clearly perceived or easily distinguished

- Each fingerprint is <u>distinct</u> and unique to an individual.
- Mules are <u>distinct</u> from donkeys in various ways.

get rid of   To eliminate or dispose of; to remove or free oneself from something unwanted

- They decided to <u>get rid of</u> old furniture to make room for new ones.

gain   **v** To obtain or acquire through effort; to achieve or win

- He worked hard to <u>gain</u> the trust of his colleagues.

definitiveness   **n** The quality of being conclusive or having a clear and definite nature

- The <u>definitiveness</u> of the decision left no room for doubt.

grow pale   The phrase "grow pale" typically refers to a person's complexion becoming lighter or losing color, often due to fear, shock, illness, or other strong emotions

- As the news unfolded, her face began to <u>grow pale</u> with shock.

heightened   **a** Intensified or increased in degree or intensity

- The <u>heightened</u> tension in the room was palpable.

gasp for breath   To struggle or breathe heavily, often due to exhaustion or distress

- After running the marathon, he <u>gasped for breath</u> at the finish line.

vehemently   **ad** In a forceful, passionate, or intense manner

- The speaker <u>vehemently</u> defended his point of view.

trifle   **n** Something of little value or importance; to treat something as unimportant

- She dismissed the issue as a mere <u>trifle</u>.

☐ **in a high key**	With great intensity or loudness

- The singer performed the song <u>in a high key</u> to showcase her vocal range.

☐ **gesticulation**	**n** The act of making gestures or movements, especially while speaking

- His <u>gesticulation</u> emphasized the passion in his speech.

☐ **pace the floor to and fro**	To walk nervously or anxiously back and forth in a confined space

- Unable to sleep, she <u>paced the floor to and fro</u>.

☐ **with heavy strides**	Walking with long and forceful steps, often indicating determination or anger

- He approached <u>with heavy strides</u>, clearly upset.

☐ **fury**	**n** Intense anger or violent rage

- His face turned red with <u>fury</u> as he realized the extent of the betrayal.

☐ **observation**	**n** The action or process of closely watching or monitoring something or someone

- The scientist conducted careful <u>observations</u> to gather data for the experiment.

☐ **foam**	**v** ① To produce foam, especially as a liquid boils or agitates ② (of a horse or a person) To excrete foam, typically due to exertion or anger

- The waves <u>foamed</u> as they crashed against the shore.

☐ **rave**	**v** ① To speak or write in an extravagant or enthusiastic manner ② To speak or shout wildly, especially in anger or excitement

- She <u>raved</u> about the incredible performance she witnessed.

☐ **swing** **v** To move back and forth or from side to side in a regular arc or rhythm

- The pendulum swung gently, marking the passage of time.

☐ **grate** **v** ① To rub or wear something away by friction
② To make an unpleasant rasping sound

- The sound of the rusty gate grated on his nerves.

☐ **over all** ① Everywhere; in any place ② Including everything; overall

- He searched over all the rooms but couldn't find his keys.

☐ **pleasantly** **ad** In a pleasing or agreeable manner

- The garden was pleasantly fragrant with blooming flowers.

☐ **mockery** **n** Ridicule or contempt expressed through derisive imitation or scornful language

- The sarcastic applause was a mockery of their failed attempt.

☐ **make a mockery of** To treat something with disrespect or scorn; to ridicule or undermine the seriousness of

- His careless actions made a mockery of their hard work.

☐ **agony** **n** Intense physical or mental suffering; extreme pain or anguish

- The patient endured hours of agony before the pain subsided.

☐ **tolerable** **a** Capable of being endured or tolerated; moderately good or acceptable

- The heat was barely tolerable without air conditioning.

☐ **derision** **n** Contemptuous ridicule or mockery; the act of expressing scorn or contempt

- Her suggestion was met with derision from the group.

☐ **bear**

v To endure or tolerate; to carry the weight or burden of something

- She had to <u>bear</u> the weight of responsibility as the team leader.

☐ **hypocritical**

a Behaving in a way that contradicts one's stated beliefs or feelings; characterized by hypocrisy

- It's <u>hypocritical</u> to preach honesty while practicing deception.

☐ **hark**

v To listen carefully or pay attention

- <u>Hark</u>! Do you hear the distant sound of music?

☐ **dissemble**

v To conceal one's true motives, feelings, or beliefs; to disguise or pretend

- She tried to <u>dissemble</u> her disappointment with a forced smile.

☐ **tear up**

To rip or destroy something, typically a piece of paper, by tearing it into pieces

- Frustrated with the rejection, he decided to <u>tear up</u> the rejection letter.

☐ **plank**

n A thick, flat piece of timber, typically intended for use in construction or flooring

- The carpenter measured and cut the <u>plank</u> to fit the floor.

☐ **hideous**

a Extremely ugly or repulsive; shocking in appearance

- The creature in the horror movie was truly <u>hideous</u> and terrifying.

2 Text Reading

: The Tell-Tale Heart

1 About the author

> **About Childhood**
>
> "The want of parental affection," wrote Poe, "has been the heaviest of my trials."
> Edgar Allan Poe was, indeed, most unfortunate in his parents. His father, David Poe,
> was a mediocre travelling actor who drank heavily. His mother, Elizabeth Arnold,
> was a talented actress who was deserted by her husband when Edgar was still a baby.
> She died on tour in Richmond, Virginia, leaving Edgar virtually an orphan before his
> third birthday.
>
> The boy was taken in by John and Frances Allan, a charitable and childless couple in
> Richmond. John Allan, an ambitious and self-righteous merchant, became Edgar's
> guardian (and the source of the writer's middle name). He provided generously for
> Edgar's early education, but he never formally adopted the boy.
>
> Although Frances Allan was kind to Edgar, the boy grew up feeling both the lack of
> a natural father and the disapproval of his foster father. John Allan made no secret of
> his disappointment in Edgar—in his idleness, in his indifference to business life, and
> in his literary ambitions. Surely Allan's criticism added to Edgar's growing moodiness.

Quick Quiz

1 본문과 일치하는 진술일 경우 True, 틀린 진술일 경우 False를 고르시오.

① Edgar Allan Poe considered the absence of parental affection as his
most significant trial.(True/False)

② Edgar Allan Poe's mother, Elizabeth Arnold, was a mediocre actress
who deserted him when he was a baby.(True/False)

③ Edgar Allan Poe's father, David Poe, was a traveling actor with a
penchant for heavy drinking.(True/False)

④ Edgar Allan Poe was taken in by John and Frances Allan, a childless
couple in Richmond.(True/False)

⑤ John Allan formally adopted Edgar Allan Poe as his son.(True/False)

⑥ Frances Allan, Edgar's foster mother, disapproved of his literary ambitions.
(True/False)

핵심 PLUS!

1 "The want of parental affection," wrote Poe, "has been the heaviest of my trials."

- 간접화법으로 바꾸면 다음과 같다.
  → Poe wrote **that** the want of parental affection **had** been the heaviest of **his** trials.

2 His father, David Poe, was a mediocre travelling actor (**who** drank heavily). His mother, Elizabeth Arnold, was a talented actress [**who** was deserted by her husband (when Edgar was still a baby)].

- 동격의 코마: His father = David Poe
  His mother = Elizabeth Arnold
- 주격 관계대명사 who

3 She died on tour in Richmond, Virginia, **leaving** Edgar virtually an orphan before his third birthday.

- 계속적 용법의 관계대명사로 전환하면 아래와 같다.
  = She died on tour in Richmond, Virginia, **which left** Edgar virtually an orphan before his third birthday.

4 The boy **was taken in by** John and Frances Allan, a charitable and childless couple in Richmond.

- 수동태: be taken in by
- 동격의 코마: John and Frances Allan = a charitable and childless couple

5 S[John Allan, an ambitious and self-righteous merchant], became Edgar's guardian (and the source of the writer's middle name).

- 동격의 코마: John Allan = an ambitious and self-righteous merchant

6 (Although Frances Allan was kind to Edgar), the boy grew up feeling both the lack of a natural father and the disapproval of his foster father.

- 유사보어 feeling에 걸리는 목적어 병치: grow up feeling (N구) and (N구)

Breaking Away

At seventeen, Edgar entered the University of Virginia. He did well in his studies but was resentful of the meager allowance Allan gave him. When he tried to earn extra money by gambling, he went deep into debt. On discovering this, Allan refused to help his foster son and instead withdrew him from college.

After an especially bitter quarrel with Allan, Poe ran off to Boston to make his own way in the world. There, in 1827, he published a small volume of poems, Tamerlane. The book did not attract much attention, and Poe could find no other work. In despair he joined the army. He was promoted to the rank of sergeant major, but he disliked the enlisted man's life and appealed to Allan for help. At the request of his wife, who was dying, Allan interceded for Poe (for the last time) and agreed to help him enter the U.S. Military Academy at West Point. Poe's motive in going to the academy was probably to please his foster father.

While waiting to get into the academy, Poe published a second book of poems, Al Aaraaf, in 1829 and received his first real recognition as a writer. The next year, while at West Point, Poe learned that Allan (now a widower) had remarried and that the woman was young enough to have children. Since this appeared to end all hope of becoming Allan's heir, Poe had himself dismissed from West Point.

UNIT

6

어구 및 표현 연구

핵심 PLUS!

1 He did well in his studies but <u>was resentful</u> <u>of</u> the meager allowance (<u>that</u>) Allan <u>gave</u> him.

- be resentful of: ~ 분개하다
- 4형식 동사로 쓰인 give 다음의 직접목적어가 없는 목적격 관계대명사 생략 파악.

2 <u>On discovering</u> this, Allan refused to help his foster son and (instead) withdrew him from college.

- on v-ing: ~하자마자
- 서술부 동사 병치

3 (After an especially bitter quarrel with Allan), Poe ran off (<u>to</u> Boston) (**to make** his own way in the world).

- 장소/방향의 전치사 to와 부사적 용법의 목적에 해당하는 to부정사

4 He **was promoted** to the rank of sergeant major, but he disliked the enlisted man's life and <u>appealed to</u> Allan <u>for help</u>.

- 수동태 be promoted
- appeal to + 사람 + for help: ~에게 도움을 호소하다

5 [At the request of his wife, (<u>who</u> was dying)], Allan <u>interceded</u> for Poe (for the last time) and <u>agreed</u> to help him enter the U.S. Military Academy at West Point.

- 부사구 내 his wife를 수식하는 주격 관계대명사 who
- 서술부 동사 병치: S **v-ed** ~ and **v-ed**

6 Poe's motive in going to the academy **was** probably **to** please his foster father.

- to부정사의 형용사 용법의 be to: ~할 의도이다

7 (While **waiting** to get into the academy), Poe <u>published</u> a second book of poems, Al Aaraaf, in 1829 and <u>received</u> his first real recognition as a writer.

- 분사구문: While he was waiting ~,
- 서술부 동사 병치: S **v-ed** ~ and **v-ed**

8 (The next year), [while (<u>he was</u>) at West Point], Poe <u>learned</u> that Allan (now a widower) <u>had remarried</u> and that the woman was **young enough to** have children.

- 부사절 while 내 he was가 생략된 분사구문
- 서술부 내 동사의 시제차 확인: had p.p
- [형용사 + enough + to부정사]의 구조

9 Since this appeared to end all hope of becoming Allan's heir, Poe <u>had</u> himself <u>dismissed</u> from West Point.

- 5형식 사역동사 have의 목적보어 자리에 과거분사형 동사: have + 목적어 + p.p

Exploring the Darkness and the Depths

Poe moved in with an aunt, Maria Poe Clemm, in Baltimore, Maryland. In 1835, he married her thirteen-year-old daughter, Virginia. The difference in their ages and Virginia's poor health resulted in a very odd marriage, but need and a strong sense of family drew the three housemates together.

Poe supported his family by working as an editor at various magazines. He wrote when he could find the time, completing his only full-length novel, *The Narrative of Arthur Gordon Pym*, several years after his marriage. It was his short stories, however, that had the greatest effect on other writers.

In "The Gold Bug" and in the tales built around the intuitive sleuth C. Auguste Dupin, "The Purloined Letter" and "The Murders in the Rue Morgue," Poe laid the foundations for the modern detective story. In fact, he inspired Sir Arthur Conan Doyle to create Sherlock Holmes. In tales such as "The Tell-Tale Heart" and "The Cask of Amontillado," Poe inspired the Russian novelist Fyodor Dostoyevsky(1821~1881) to explore the criminal mind.

Poe was a master of the psychological thriller. His tale of the ghastly and the grotesque are peopled with distraught narrators, deranged heroes, and doomed heroines, yet his purpose in creating such characters was not to present readers with convincing likenesses of human beings—nor merely to shock and frighten. Instead, Poe wanted to take us behind the curtain that separates the everyday from the incredible. He wanted to leave behind the sunlit, tangible, rational world and discover the unsettling truth that lies in the dark, irrational depths of the human mind.

어구 및 표현 연구

 핵심 PLUS!

1 S [The difference in their ages and Virginia's poor health] resulted in a very odd marriage, but S [need and a strong sense of family] drew the three housemates together.

- (원인) result in (결과)
- draw ~ together: 한데 모으다[모이다], ~을 단결[협력]시키다

2 He wrote when he could find the time, **completing** his only full-length novel, *The Narrative of Arthur Gordon Pym*, (several years after his marriage).

- 분사구문: , **and (as a result) he completed** ~
- 동격의 코마: his only full-length novel = *The Narrative of Arthur Gordon Pym*

3 **It** was his short stories, however, **that** had the greatest effect on other writers.

- 주어를 강조하는 it ~ that 강조용법

  his short stories had the greatest effect on other writers.

  → **It** was his short stories **that** had the greatest effect on other writers.

4 [In "The Gold Bug" and in the tales (built around the intuitive sleuth C. Auguste Dupin), "The Purloined Letter" and "The Murders in the Rue Morgue,"] Poe laid the foundations for the modern detective story.

- tales를 수식하는 과거분사 built
- 동격의 코마: the tales = "The Purloined Letter" and "The Murders in the Rue Morgue"
- lay the foundations for: ~의 기반을 닦다

5 In fact, he **inspired** Sir Arthur Conan Doyle **to create** Sherlock Holmes. In tales such as "The Tell-Tale Heart" and "The Cask of Amontillado," Poe **inspired** the Russian novelist Fyodor Dostoyevsky(1821~1881) **to explore** the criminal mind.

- 5형식 동사 inspire의 목적보어 자리에 to 부정사

6 His tale of the ghastly and the grotesque are peopled with distraught narrators, deranged heroes, and doomed heroines, yet S [his purpose in creating such characters] **was not to** present readers with convincing likenesses of human beings—**nor** merely **to** shock and frighten.

- be people with의 people이 타동사로 쓰여 "많이 살게 하다《보통 수동형으로》"의 뜻으로 쓰이고 있음.
- 전치사 with에 걸리는 명사구 병치: N구, N구, and N구
- to부정사의 "의도"에 해당하는 be to용법
- not to ~ , nor to ~의 병렬구조

7   Instead, Poe wanted to take us behind the curtain (**that** separates the everyday from the incredible). He wanted to leave behind the sunlit, tangible, rational world and discover the unsettling truth (**that** lies in the dark, irrational depths of the human mind).

• 주격 관계대명사 that

Small Triumphs and Great Tragedy

Poe produced a considerable body of work in spite of humiliating poverty and a serious drinking problem. The slightest amount of alcohol made him senseless, yet he drank to escape a reality he found agonizing. Publication of his poem "The Raven" in 1845 brought Poe some fame at last, but financial security still eluded him.

When Virginia died of tuberculosis in 1847, Poe and "Muddy" (Virginia's mother) were left alone. Poe grew more unstable. He pursued romance relentlessly, always looking for someone to "adopt" him. In 1849, on his way home after a visit to Virginia to see a woman he hoped to marry, Poe disappeared. A week later, he was found in a Baltimore tavern—delirious and in cheap clothing that was not his, wet through from a raging storm. Four days later, having passed in and out of delirium, Poe died, leaving critics to argue endlessly about this final mystery. What happened during those last days in Baltimore?

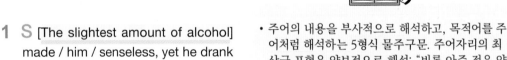

어구 및 표현 연구

 핵심 PLUS!

1 S [The slightest amount of alcohol] made / him / senseless, yet he drank to escape a reality [(that) he found agonizing)].

- 주어의 내용을 부사적으로 해석하고, 목적어를 주어처럼 해석하는 5형식 물주구문. 주어자리의 최상급 표현은 양보적으로 해석: "비록 아주 적은 양의 술을 마시더라도 (그것이)"
- 5형식 동사 find 뒤 목적어가 탈락된 목적격 관계대명사의 생략: a reality **that** he found (목적어) agonizing

2 S [Publication of his poem "The Raven" in 1845] brought / Poe / some fame at last, but financial security still eluded him.

- 4형식 수여동사로 쓰인 bring: 가져오다 + 주다 = 가져다 주다

3 When Virginia died of tuberculosis in 1847, Poe and "Muddy" (Virginia's mother) were left alone.

- die of의 경우 "내부"에 의한 사망을 표현할 때 씀. 참고로 "외부"에 의한 사망은 die from을 주로 씀.

4 Poe **grew** more unstable. He pursued romance relentlessly, always **looking** for someone to "adopt" him.

- become류 동사 grow와 분사구문

5 (In 1849), [on his way home after a visit to Virginia **to see** a woman (that) he hoped to marry], Poe disappeared.

- 문장 앞쪽에 부사구가 길게 이어지는 구조 파악: to부정사의 부사적 용법 내 see에 걸리는 목적어 woman이 생략된 목적격 관계대명사의 수식을 받고 있음.

6 A week later, he was found in a Baltimore tavern—**delirious and in cheap clothing** (**that** was not his), (**wet** through from a raging storm).

- 유사보어 격으로 he를 수식하는 형용사(구): **delirious and in cheap clothing**
- 주격 관계대명사 that이 이끄는 절과 wet이 이끄는 형용사구 모두 clothing을 수식하는 형용사적 용법임.

7 (Four days later), **having passed** in and out of delirium, Poe died, **leaving** critics to argue endlessly about this final mystery.

- 분사구문: **after he had passed** in and out of delirium
- 분사구문의 계속적 용법의 주격 관계대명사로 전환: Four days later, having passed in and out of delirium, Poe died, **which left** critics to argue endlessly about this final mystery.

2 The Tell-Tale Heart

TRUE! nervous, very, very dreadfully nervous I had been and am; but why WILL you say that I am mad? The disease had sharpened my senses, not destroyed, not dulled them. Above all was the sense of hearing acute. I heard all things in the heaven and in the earth. I heard many things in hell. How then am I mad? Hearken! and observe how healthily, how calmly, I can tell you the whole story.

It is impossible to say how first the idea entered my brain, but, once conceived, it haunted me day and night. Object there was none. Passion there was none. I loved the old man. He had never wronged me. He had never given me insult. For his gold I had no desire. I think it was his eye! Yes, it was this! One of his eyes resembled that of a vulture—a pale blue eye with a film over it. Whenever it fell upon me my blood ran cold, and so by degrees, very gradually, I made up my mind to take the life of the old man, and thus rid myself of the eye for ever.

Quick Quiz

2 본문의 주인공에 대한 설명으로 <u>부적절한</u> 것은?

① The protagonist was extremely nervous and fearful.

② The protagonist's senses became more acute without being dulled.

③ The protagonist expressed aversion to the old man's eye using a metaphor like a vulture's eye.

④ The protagonist has never been wronged or insulted by the old man.

⑤ The protagonist harbors a desire for the old man's wealth.

핵심 PLUS!

1 TRUE! <u>nervous, very, very dreadfully nervous</u> I had been and am; but why WILL you say that I am mad? The disease had sharpened my senses, not destroyed, not dulled them.

- TRUE 앞에 It is가 생략된 형태
- I had been and am (nervous, very, very dreadfully nervous)에서 괄호의 형용사구가 문두로 이동한 경우

2 (Above all) <u>was</u> S[the sense of hearing acute].

- 부사구 above all이 문장의 맨 앞으로 이동하면 서 도치된 문장

3 How then am I mad? Hearken! and observe [<u>how</u> healthily, <u>how</u> calmly, I can tell you the whole story].

- Hearken은 고어로 "귀를 기울이다, 경청하다"의 뜻으로 목적어를 필요로 할 때 전치사 to를 가짐.
- 타동사 observe의 목적어 자리에 의문사가 이끄 는 명사절 및 어순 확인: (의문부사 + 부사/형용 사) + 주어 + 동사

4 **It** is impossible **to say** (<u>how</u> first the idea entered my brain), but, [once (it was) conceived], it haunted me (day and night).

- 가주어(it)/진주어(to say ~) 파악. 진주어의 타 동사 say에 걸리는 목적어 자리에 의문사가 이끄 는 명사절: 의문부사 + 주어 + 동사
- 분사구문: once it(the idea) was conceived

5 He had never <u>wronged</u> me. He had never <u>given</u> me <u>insult</u>.

- wrong "…에게 해를 끼치다; 모욕을 주다"의 타 동사로 활용된 경우로 결국 두 문장이 같은 의미 로 반복에 의한 의미 강조

6 For his gold I had no desire. I think **it** was his eye! Yes, it was this! One of his eyes resembled **that** of a vulture— a pale blue eye <u>with a film over it</u>.

- it = the reason I wanted to kill
- that = **one** of his eyes
- with a film over it(= a pale blue eye)

7 [(Whenever <u>it</u> fell upon me my blood ran cold), and so (<u>by degrees</u>), (<u>very gradually</u>)], I made up my mind **to take** the life of the old man, and thus <u>rid</u> myself <u>of</u> the eye for ever.

- it = the old man's eye
- 동의 표현을 반복해서 사용함으로써 의미 강조: by degrees = (very) gradually
- to부정사의 부사적 용법: ~하기 위해서
- rid A of B: A에게서 B를 제거하다

Now this is the point. You fancy me mad. Mad men know nothing. But you should have seen me. You should have seen how wisely I proceeded—with what caution— with what foresight—with what dissimulation I went to work! I was never kinder to the old man than during the whole week before I killed him. And every night, about midnight, I turned the latch of his door and opened it—oh, so gently! And then, when I had made an opening sufficient for my head, I put in a dark lantern, all closed, closed, so that no light shone out, and then I thrust in my head. Oh, you would have laughed to see how cunningly I thrust it in! I moved it slowly—very, very slowly, so that I might not disturb the old man's sleep.

It took me an hour to place my whole head within the opening so far that I could see him as he lay upon his bed. Ha!—would a madman have been so wise as this? And then, when my head was well in the room, I undid the lantern cautiously—oh, so cautiously—cautiously (for the hinges creaked)—I undid it just so much that a single thin ray fell upon the vulture eye. And this I did for seven long nights—every night just at midnight—but I found the eye always closed; and so it was impossible to do the work; for it was not the old man who vexed me, but his Evil Eye. And every morning, when the day broke, I went boldly into the chamber, and spoke courageously to him, calling him by name in a hearty tone, and inquiring how he had passed the night. So you see he would have been a very profound old man, indeed, to suspect that every night, just at twelve, I looked in upon him while he slept.

1 You <u>fancy</u> / me / mad. Mad men know nothing.

- 5형식 동사로 쓰인 fancy는 "…라고 생각하다, …같은 생각이 들다, …이라고 믿다"는 뜻으로 쓰이고 있음.

2 You <u>should have seen</u> (<u>how</u> wisely I proceeded)—[(**with what** caution)—(**with what** foresight)—(**with what** dissimulation)] I went to work!

- 조동사 과거표현 중 아쉬움을 드러내는 should have p.p "~했어야 했다"
- 의문부사가 이끄는 명사절: 의문(부)사 + 부사 + 주어 + 동사
- 의문형용사가 이끄는 명사절: 전치사 + 의문형용사 + 명사 + 주어 + 동사

3 I was **never** kind**er** to the old man **than** (during the whole week before I killed him).

- 부정어 + 비교급 = 최상급 표현

4 And then, when I had made an opening (<u>sufficient</u> for my head), I put in a dark lantern, <u>all</u> closed, closed, so that no light shone out, and then I thrust in my head.

- sufficient가 이끄는 형용사구가 앞의 명사 opening을 수식
- all은 강조 부사로 "완전히" 정도의 의미

5 Oh, you <u>would have laughed</u> <u>to see</u> (<u>how</u> cunningly I thrust it in)!

- 과거 추측의 조동사 would have p.p: "~했을 거다"
- if 대용의 to부정사: ~한다면
- 의문부사가 이끄는 명사절: 의문(부)사 + 부사 + 주어 + 동사

6 <u>It took me an hour to</u> place my whole head within the opening <u>so</u> far <u>that</u> I could see him (as he lay upon his bed).

- it takes + 사람 + 시간 + to V: ~가 ~하는데 ~가 걸리다
- so ~ that S V: ~할 수 있도록 (아주) ~하게

7 Ha!—<u>would</u> a madman <u>have been</u> so wise as this? And then, (when my head was <u>well</u> in the room), I <u>undid</u> the lantern cautiously—oh, so cautiously—cautiously (for the hinges creaked)—I undid it **just so much that** a single thin ray fell upon the vulture eye.

- would have p.p를 활용한 의문문으로 "~이었 겠는가" 정도로 해석
- well은 부사로 "잘, 충분히, 완전히 (thoroughly)"라는 강조의 기능
- 여기서 undo는 랜턴을 노인의 눈에만 딱 비치도록 "덮개를 벗기다"의 의미로 쓰이고 있음.
- ~ so much that S V: 딱 S V 할 정도만

8 And **this** I did for seven long nights— every night just at midnight—but I <u>found</u> the eye (always) <u>closed</u>; and so <u>it</u> was impossible **to do** the work; for <u>it</u> was not the old man <u>who</u> vexed me, but his Evil Eye.

- I did this for ~에서 목적어 this가 문두로 나간 형태
- find + 목적어 + 목적보어(p.p)
- 가주어 it/진주어 to V와 it ~ that 강조구문 구별할 것.

Upon the eighth night I was more than usually cautious in opening the door. A watch's minute hand moves more quickly than did mine. Never before that night had I felt the extent of my own powers—of my sagacity. I could scarcely contain my feelings of triumph. To think that there I was, opening the door, little by little, and he not even to dream of my secret deeds or thoughts. I fairly chuckled at the idea; and perhaps he heard me; for he moved on the bed suddenly, as if startled. Now you may think that I drew back—but no. His room was as black as pitch with the thick darkness (for the shutters were close fastened, through fear of robbers), and so I knew that he could not see the opening of the door, and I kept pushing it on steadily, steadily.

I had my head in, and was about to open the lantern, when my thumb slipped upon the tin fastening, and the old man sprang up in the bed, crying out—"Who's there?"

I kept quite still and said nothing. For a whole hour I did not move a muscle, and in the meantime I did not hear him lie down. He was still sitting up in the bed listening;—just as I have done, night after night, hearkening to the death watches in the wall.

UNIT

6

Quick Quiz

3 다음은 본문의 밑줄 친 두 문장에서 공통으로 활용된 문학 장치에 대한 설명이다. 빈칸에 공통으로 들어갈 단어를 쓰시오. (단, 문맥에 따른 품사의 형태에 유의하여 넣을 것)

The common literary device used in the extracted sentences from the passage is _____. In both sentences, exaggeration is employed to emphasize the slow passage of time or the stillness of the protagonist. The minute hand of a watch moving more quickly than the protagonist's indicates an exaggerated perception of time, and the claim of not moving a muscle for a whole hour is a _____ expression of absolute stillness.

1 Upon the eighth night I was more than usually cautious **in opening** the door.

- in V-ing: ~할 때

---

2 A watch's minute hand moves more quickly **than did mine**.

- 접속사 than 뒤 대동사 도치로 my hand 는 소유대명사와 moved의 대동사 did의 자리가 바뀐 형태
  A watch's minute hand moves more quickly **than my hand moved**.
  = A watch's minute hand moves more quickly **than did mine**.

---

3 **(Never before that night)** <u>had I felt</u> the extent (of my own powers)—(of my sagacity). I could scarcely <u>contain</u> my feelings of triumph.

- 부정어와 부사구가 함께 문두로 이동하면서 도치가 발생: I had **never** felt ~ **before that night**
- extent를 수식하는 of가 이끄는 전치사구 병치
- 타동사 contain은 "억누르다"라는 의미로 사용되고 있다.

---

4 <u>To think</u> that there I was, opening the door, little by little, <u>and</u> he (<u>was</u>) not even to dream of my secret deeds or thoughts.

- to think: ~을 생각하자면
- 등위접속사를 중심으로 be동사 생략

---

5 I fairly chuckled at the idea; and perhaps he heard me; **for** he moved on the bed suddenly, as if (<u>he were</u>) startled.

- 등위접속사 for와 가정법 as if 내 주어 동사의 생략

---

6 His room was <u>as black as pitch</u> (<u>with</u> the thick darkness) (for the shutters were close fastened, <u>through</u> fear of robbers), and so I knew that he could not see the opening of the door, and I kept pushing it on steadily, steadily.

- as black as pitch는 "칠흑처럼 검은"이란 관용표현이고 이어지는 전치사 with는 "~로 인해서"의 의미
- through 뒤에 이유/원인의 명사(보통 추상명사)가 오면 "…으로 인하여, … 때문에"의 의미로 해석

7 I <u>had</u> my head <u>in</u>.

- have는 여기서 5형식 사역동사로 쓰이고 있고, 목적보어에 in이 위치

8 For a whole hour I did not move a muscle, and in the meantime I did not <u>hear</u> him <u>lie down</u>.

- 5형식 지각동사 hear와 목적보어 자리에 동사원형

9 He was still sitting up in the bed <u>listening</u>;—just as I have done, night after night, **hearkening** to the death watches in the wall.

- 자동사 sit up 뒤 현재분사가 이끄는 분사 구문으로 해석도 가능하지만, 유사보어로 파악 가능

Presently I heard a slight groan, and I knew it was the groan of mortal terror. It was not a groan of pain or of grief—oh, no!—it was the low stifled sound that arises from the bottom of the soul when overcharged with awe. I knew the sound very well. Many a night, just a midnight, when all the world slept, it has welled up from my own bosom, deepening, with its dreadful echo, the terrors that distracted me. I say I knew it well. I knew what the old man felt, and pitied him, although I chuckled at heart. I knew that he had been lying awake ever since the first slight noise, when he had turned in the bed. His fears had been ever since growing upon him. He had been trying to fancy them causeless, but could not. He had been saying to himself—"It is nothing but the wind in the chimney—it is only a mouse crossing the floor," or "it is merely a cricket which has made a single chirp." Yes, he had been trying to comfort himself with these suppositions; but he had found all in vain. All in vain; because Death, in approaching him, had stalked with his black shadow before him, and enveloped the victim. And it was the mournful influence of the unperceived shadow that caused him to feel—although he neither saw nor heard—to feel the presence of my head within the room.

어구 및 표현 연구

핵심 PLUS!

1 It was not a groan of pain or of grief—oh, no!—it was the low stifled sound [that arises from the bottom of the soul ((when (it was) overcharged with awe))].

- 선행사 sound를 수식하는 주격 관계대명사 that과 when절 내 it was가 생략된 분사구문

2 Many a night, just a midnight, (when all the world slept), it has welled up from my own bosom, deepening, (with its dreadful echo), the terrors (that distracted me). I say I knew it well.

- many a N(단수): 많은 ~들
- 분사구문의 deepening의 목적어는 관계대명사의 수식을 받는 the terrors (that distracted me)임.

3 I knew (**what** the old man felt), and pitied him, although I chuckled at heart.

- 관계대명사 what이 이끄는 명사절

4 I knew that he had been lying awake ever since the first slight noise**, when** he had turned in the bed.

- 관계부사의 계속적 용법의 코마 다음에 when은 "바로 그때"로 해석

5 His fears / had been (ever since) growing / upon him. He had been trying to <u>fancy</u> / them / causeless, but could not.

- 5형식 동사 fancy

6 He had been saying to himself—"It is <u>nothing but</u> the wind in the chimney—it is only a mouse (**crossing** the floor)," or "it is merely a cricket (**which** has made a single chirp)."

- nothing but = only(merely)
- a mouse를 수식하는 현재분사 crossing
- 주격 관계대명사 which

7 All in vain; because Death, <u>in approaching</u> him, <u>had stalked</u> with his black shadow before him, and enveloped the victim.

- had p.p로 보아 in V-ing는 "~했을 때"로 해석

8 And <u>it</u> was the mournful influence of the unperceived shadow **that** caused him **to feel**—although he neither saw nor heard—**to feel** the presence of my head within the room.

- it ~ that 강조구문
- to feel은 cause의 목적보어임.

When I had waited a long time, very patiently, without hearing him lie down, I resolved to open a little—a very, very little crevice in the lantern. So I opened it—you cannot imagine how stealthily, stealthily—until, at length, a single dim ray, like the thread of the spider, shot from out for crevice and full upon the vulture eye.

It was open—wide, wide open—and I grew furious as I gazed upon it. I saw it with perfect distinctness—all a dull blue, with a hideous veil over it that chilled the very marrow in my bones; but I could see nothing else of the old man's face or person: for I had directed the ray as if by instinct, precisely upon the damned spot.

And now have I not told you that what you mistake for madness is but over-acuteness of the sense?—now, I say, there came to my ears a low, dull, quick sound, such as a watch makes when enveloped in cotton. I knew that sound well too. It was the beating of the old man's heart. It increased my fury, as the beating of a drum stimulates the soldier into courage.

어구 및 표현 연구

 핵심 PLUS!

1 When I <u>had waited</u> (a long time), (very patiently), (<u>without</u> hearing him lie down), I <u>resolved</u> to open a little—a very, very little crevice in the lantern.

- 주절의 과거동사 resolved 보다 앞선 시제 표현 had waited: had p.p
- without: ~않은 채

2 So I opened it—you cannot imagine [<u>how</u> stealthily, stealthily (<u>I opened a little crevice</u>)—until, at length, <u>a single dim ray</u>, (like the thread of the spider), <u>shot</u> from out for crevice and full upon the vulture eye.

- how + 부사 + (주어 + 동사)에서 생략된 형태: I opened a little crevice
- until에 걸리는 주어와 동사 파악: a single dim ray shot ~

3 It was open—wide, wide open—and I <u>grew</u> furious (as I gazed upon it).

- become류 동사: grew

4 I saw it **with** perfect **distinctness**—all a dull blue, [with a hideous veil over it (**that** chilled the very marrow in my bones)];

- with + 추사명사 = 부사
- 선행사 veil을 수식하는 주격 관계대명사

5 but I could see nothing else of the old man's face or person: **for** I had **directed** the ray (as if by instinct), precisely **upon** the damned spot.

- 등위접속사 for: 왜냐하면
- as if by instinct는 direct A upon B의 숙어 표현 사이에 들어간 삽입구

6 And now have I not told you that S [**what** you mistake for madness] is **but** over-acuteness of the sense?—now, I say, there came (to my ears) a low, dull, quick **sound**, [**such as** a watch makes (when it is enveloped in cotton)].

- that절의 주어 자리에 관계대명사 what이 이끄는 명사절
- but = only와 there come S(sound) 구문
- such as S V의 구문에서 such는 코마(,)로 이어지는 동격의 대명사이고, as는 유사관계대명사

7 It increased my fury, **as** the beating of a drum stimulates the soldier into courage.

- 비유적 표현에 해당하는 접속사 as가 이끄는 부사절
- stimulate A into B: A를 자극해 B하도록 하다

But even yet I refrained and kept still. I scarcely breathed. I held the lantern motionless. I tried how steadily I could maintain the ray upon the eye. Meantime the hellish tattoo of the heart increased. It grew quicker and quicker, and louder and louder, I say, louder every moment!—do you mark me well? Mark my words. I have told you that I am nervous: so I am. And now at the dead hour of the night, amid the dreadful silence of that old house, so strange a noise as this excited me to uncontrollable terror. Yet, for some minutes longer I refrained and stood still. But the beating grew louder, louder! I thought the heart must burst. And now a new anxiety seized me—the sound would be heard by a neighbor! The old man's hour had come! With a loud yell, I threw open the lantern and leaped into the room. He come! He shrieked once—once only. In an instant I dragged him to the floor, and pulled the heavy bed over him. I then smiled gaily, to find the deed so far done. But, for many minutes, the heart beat on with a muffled sound. This, however, did not vex me; it would not be heard through the wall. At length it ceased. The old man was dead. I removed the bed and examined the corpse. Yes, he was stone, stone dead. I placed my hand upon the heart and held it there many minutes. There was no pulsation. He was stone dead. His eye would trouble me no more.

 어구 및 표현 연구

 핵심 PLUS!

1 But even yet I refrained and kept <u>still</u>. I <u>held</u> / the lantern / <u>motionless</u>.

- still은 형용사로 "움직이지 않는, 정지한"의 의미다.
- <u>hold</u>는 5형식 동사로 쓰이고 있음.

2 I tried (<u>how</u> steadily I could maintain the ray upon the eye).

- 의문사가 이끄는 명사절과 어순: 의문부사 + 부사 + S V

3 Meantime the hellish <u>tattoo</u> of the heart increased.

- tattoo는 "똑똑[둥둥] 두드리는 소리"의 의미로 사용되고 있음.

4 It grew quicker and quicker , and louder and louder , I say, louder every moment!—do you mark me well?

- 2형식 become류 동사와 [비교급 and 비교급] 표현 병치

5 I have told you that I am nervous: **so I am**.

- So S V는 앞의 내용에 동조하여 "정말 그러하다"의 의미

6 And now (at the dead hour of the night), (amid the dreadful silence of that old house), S[so strange a noise as this] excited me to uncontrollable terror.

- 주어 자리에 [so + 형용사 + a(an) + 명사]의 어순
- 결과의 전치사 to는 "~하게 되기까지"의 의미
- excite A **to** B: A를 자극해서 B하게까지 만들다

7 (In an instant) I dragged him to the floor, and pulled the heavy bed over him.

- S **v-ed** ~ and **v-ed**의 서술부 동사 병치

8 I then smiled gaily, **to find** the deed so far done. But, for many minutes, the heart beat on (with a muffled sound).

- to부정사의 부사적 용법 to find는 "~을 발견하고선, 알아채고는" 정도의 의미로 해석하고, beat on에서 on은 부사로 "계속해서"의 의미임.

9 Yes, he was stone, stone dead.

- stone dead는 "완전히 죽은"이란 의미로 쓰이는 관용표현임. (**stone**은 "완전한, 철저한; 훌륭한, 매력적인"의 뜻으로 쓰임.)

10 I placed my hand upon the heart and held **it there** many minutes.

- it = **my hand**, there = **upon the heart**

If still you think me mad, you will think so no longer when I describe the wise precautions I took for the concealment of the body. The night waned, and I worked hastily, but in silence. First of all I dismembered the corpse. I cut off the head and the arms and the legs.

I then took up three planks from the flooring of the chamber, and deposited all between the scantlings. I then replaced the boards so cleverly, so cunningly, that no human eye—not even his—could have detected anything wrong. There was nothing to wash out—no stain of any kind—no bloodspot whatever. I had been too wary for that. A tub(= basin) had caught all—ha! ha!

When I had made an end of these labors, it was four o'clock—still dark as midnight. As the bell sounded the hour, there came a knocking at the street door. I went down to open it with a light heart,—for what had I now to fear? There entered three men, who introduced themselves, with perfect suavity as officers of the police. A shriek had been heard by a neighbor during the night; suspicion of foul play had been aroused; information had been lodged at the police office, and they (the officers) had been deputed to search the premises.

어구 및 표현 연구

핵심 PLUS!

1 If still you think me mad, you will think so no longer when I describe [the wise precautions (that) I took for the concealment of the body].

- 타동사 take 다음에 생략된 목적어로 보아 목적격 관계대명사 that 파악.

2 The night <u>waned</u>, and I worked hastily, but in silence.

- wane: 끝이 가까워지다

3 I then <u>took up</u> three planks <u>from</u> the flooring of the chamber, and deposited all between the scantlings.

- take up A from B: B에서 A를 뜯어 올리다

4 I then replaced the boards **so** cleverly, **so** cunningly, **that** no human eye—not even his— could have detected anything wrong.

- so ~ that 구문: 너무 ~해서 ~한

5 When I had <u>made an end of</u> these labors, it was four o'clock—still dark as midnight. As the bell sounded <u>the hour</u>, there came a knocking at the street door.

- make an end of: ~을 끝내다
- the hour는 여기서 "정각"의 의미

6 I went down to open it with a light heart,—**for what** had I now to fear?

- "~ 때문에 두려워 하다"의 fear for에서 for가 의문사 앞으로 이동하여 for what이라고 표현된 것. (→ I now had nothing to fear for와 같은 의미)

7 There entered three men, **who introduced** themselves, (with perfect suavity) **as** officers of the police.

- 계속적 용법의 주격 관계대명사 who
- introduce A as B의 숙어 표현 중간에 부사적 해석인 [전치사 + 추상명사]가 삽입된 형태

UNIT

6

8 A shriek |had been heard| by a neighbor during the night; suspicion of foul play |had been aroused|; information |had been| |lodged| at the police office, and they (the officers) |had been deputed| to search the premises.

- 경찰이 한 시제 앞서 있었던 일을 설명하는 부분에 수동의 의미가 추가되어 had been p.p로 쓰였음.
- lodge는 "신고하다"의 의미로 쓰이고 있음.

I smiled,—for what had I to fear? I bade the gentlemen welcome. The shriek, I said, was my own in a dream. The old man, I mentioned, was absent in the country. I took my visitors all over the house. I bade them search—search well. I led them, at length, to his chamber. I showed them his treasures, secure, undisturbed. In the enthusiasm of my confidence, I brought chairs into the room, and desired them here to rest from their fatigues, while I myself, in the wild audacity of my perfect triumph, placed my own seat upon the very spot beneath which reposed the corpse of the victim.

The officers were satisfied. My manner had convinced them. I was singularly at ease. They say, and while I answered cheerily, they chatted familiar things. But, ere long, I felt myself getting pale and wished them gone. My head ached, and I fancied a ringing in my years: but still they sat and still chatted. The ringing became more distinct:—it continued and became more distinct: I talked more freely to get rid of the feeling: but it continued and gained definitiveness—until, at length, I found that the noise was not within my ears.

어구 및 표현 연구

핵심 PLUS!

1 I smiled,—for what had I to fear? I <u>bade</u> the gentlemen welcome.

- bid: (인사 따위를) 말하다《to》

  참고. give a person farewell(welcome) = give farewell(welcome) to a person: 아무에게 작별 [환영] 인사를 하다.

2 I <u>bade</u> / them / search—search well. I led them, (at length), to his chamber.

- 앞 문장의 bid와 같이 4형식 구조를 가진 문장이지만, 해당 문장에서 "~에게 명하다"의 뜻으로 쓰이고 있음.

3 I showed them his treasures, <u>secure</u>, <u>undisturbed</u>.

- 전체적으로 4형식 문장으로 직접목적어 자리에 있는 treasures가 형용사의 후치 수식을 받는 형태로 관계대명사를 활용하여 I showed them his treasures, **which were** secure and undisturbed. 와 같이 표현 가능

4 In the enthusiasm of my confidence, I brought chairs into the room, and <u>desired</u> them here <u>to rest</u> from their fatigues, [while I (myself), (in the wild audacity of my perfect triumph), placed my own seat upon the very spot (**beneath which** reposed the corpse of the victim).

- desire가 5형식 동사로 활용됨: desire + 목적어 + to V
- [전치사 + 관계대명사] 내 주어와 동사가 도치된 형태로 아래 문장에서 앞 문장과 관계대명사로 연결되면서 "장소/방향의 부사"가 앞으로 이동하면서 도치 발생
  the corpse of the victim reposed <u>beneath the very spot</u>.
  → beneath **which** reposed the corpse of the victim

5 But, ere long, I <u>felt</u> / myself / getting pale and <u>wished</u> / them / <u>gone</u>.

- feel과 wish 모두 5형식 동사로 사용되고 있음.
- them(= police officers)이 "갔으면"하는 표현인 gone이 사용됨에 주의.

6 The ringing became more distinct:— it continued and became more distinct: I talked more freely to get rid of the feeling: but it continued and gained definitiveness—<u>until</u>, (at length), I found that the noise was not within my ears.

- until이 코마(,) 또는 대쉬(-) 뒤거나 직후에 at last와 같은 부사구가 올 경우 내리 번역하여 "…하여 결국, …하고 그리고"로 해석함.

Three Types of Irony

1. **<u>Verbal Irony</u>**: This occurs when a character says something but means the opposite. It's often used for humor or to emphasize a point. For example, saying "What a beautiful day" during a thunderstorm.

2. **<u>Situation Irony</u>** (or situational irony): This occurs when there is a contrast between what is expected to happen and what actually happens. It can involve a reversal of expectations or a discrepancy between intention and result. For example, a fire station burning down.

3. **<u>Dramatic Irony</u>**: This occurs when the audience or reader knows something that the characters do not. It creates tension and suspense in storytelling. For example, in a horror movie, when the audience sees the killer hiding in a room while the unsuspecting character enters.

UNIT**6**

Text Reading | 341

No doubt I now grew very pale:—but I talked more fluently, and with a heightened voice. Yet the sound increased—and what could I do? It was a low, dull, quick sound—much such a sound as a watch makes when enveloped in cotton. I gasped for breath—and yet the officers heard it not. I talked more quickly—more vehemently; but the noise steadily increased. I arose and argued about trifles, in a high key and with violent gesticulations, but the noise steadily increased. Why would they not be gone? I paced the floor to and fro with heavy strides, as if excited to fury by the observation of the men—but the noise steadily increased. Oh God! what could I do? I foamed—I raved —I swore! I swung the chair upon which I had been sitting, and grated it upon the boards, but the noise arose over all and continually increased. It grew louder—louder—louder! And still the men chatted pleasantly, and smiled. Was it possible they heard not? Almighty God!—no, no! They heard!—they suspected!—they knew!—they were making a mockery of my horror!—this I thought, and this I think. But anything was better than this agony! Any thing was more tolerable than this derision! I could bear those hypocritical smiles no longer! I felt that I must scream or die!—and now—again!—hark! louder! louder! louder! louder!—

"Villains!" I shrieked, "dissemble no more! I admit the deed!—tear up the planks!—here, here!—it is the beating of his hideous heart!"

어구 및 표현 연구

 핵심 PLUS!

1 **No doubt** I now grew very pale:—but I talked more fluently , and with a heightened voice .

- 생략된 표현 (It was) no doubt (that) ~
- 부사(구) 병치

2 Yet the sound increased—and what could I do? It was a low, dull, quick sound—much such a sound [as a watch makes when (it is) enveloped in cotton].

- 선행사를 sound로 하는 유사관계대명사 as (타동사 make 뒤에 목적어가 없는 것으로 보아 목적격 관계대명사와 유사한 성격을 볼 수 있음)
- 시간의 접속사를 여전히 가지는 분사구문: When (it is) enveloped in cotton

3 I arose and argued about trifles, in a high key and with violent gesticulations , but the noise steadily increased. Why would they not be gone?

- 부사구 병치
- they = the officers

4 I paced the floor to and fro with heavy strides, [as if (I were) excited to fury / by the observation of the men]—but the noise steadily increased.

- to and fro: 이리저리, 앞 뒤로
- 가정법 as if 내 I were 생략
- excited to fury: 분노할 만큼 흥분해서

5 Oh God! what could I do? I foamed—I raved —I swore! I swung the chair (upon which I had been sitting), and grated it upon the boards, but the noise arose over all and continually increased.

- [전치사 + 관계대명사 + 완전절]
- 서술부 동사의 병치: I swung ~ and grated ~

6 It grew louder—louder—louder! And still the men chatted pleasantly, and smiled.

- 2형식 become류 동사: grew

7 Was it possible (that) they heard not? Almighty God!—no, no! They heard!—they suspected!—they knew!—they were making a mockery of my horror!—this I thought, and this I think. But anything was better than this agony! Any thing was more tolerable than this derision!

- 가주어 it/진주어 that에서 that 생략된 형태
- make a mockery of: ~을 조롱하다
- 비교급을 활용한 최상급 표현: anything ~ better than ~

Voca Check

* 빈칸에 들어갈 적절한 단어를 박스에서 찾아 넣으시오.

1

desert / indifference / intercede / self-righteous / meager / idleness / mediocre / moody / resentful / charitable / talented / quarrel / in despair / recognition / bitter

1 The restaurant received _____ reviews, neither excellent nor terrible.

2 Mozart was an incredibly _____ composer, creating masterpieces at a young age.

3 After being mistreated for years, the loyal dog decided to _____ its unkind owner.

4 The millionaire's _____ acts, including regular donations to charities, were widely appreciated.

5 The politician's _____ attitude alienated many voters who disagreed with his views.

6 Long hours of _____ led to a lack of productivity in the workplace.

7 Her _____ to environmental issues made her indifferent to the concerns of others.

8 His _____ temperament made it challenging to predict his mood swings.

9 The employee remained _____ after being passed over for a promotion.

10 The refugees received only a _____ amount of food and shelter in the overcrowded camp.

11 The _____ criticism from the opposing party created tension in the political debate.

12 A minor _____ escalated into a heated argument between the neighbors.

13 Overwhelmed by financial troubles, she found herself _____ and without hope.

14 The mediator tried to _____ between the conflicting parties to find a resolution.

15 The actor's outstanding performance earned him widespread _____ for his talent.

2

distraught / dismiss / peopled / body / ghastly / frighten / grotesque / considerable / doomed / heir / convincing / likeness / deranged / unsettling / intuitive

1 The wealthy businessman passed away, leaving his only son as the sole _____ to the family fortune.

2 After a series of conflicts, the company decided to _____ several employees to cut costs.

3 Maria had an _____ sense of when her friends needed support, even without them saying a word.

4 The horror movie had a _____ scene that left the audience horrified and unable to look away.

5 The haunted house seemed to be _____ with ghostly apparitions and mysterious shadows.

6 Losing her job left Emma feeling _____ and uncertain about her future.

7 The novel depicted a _____ creature that defied the laws of nature and terrified the characters.

8 The protagonist in the psychological thriller appeared _____, haunted by traumatic memories.

9　The expedition was _____ from the start due to a lack of essential supplies and poor planning.

10　The lawyer presented a _____ argument that persuaded the jury to rule in favor of his client.

11　The portrait captured a remarkable _____ to the late king, showcasing the artist's skill.

12　The unexpected loud noise in the dark alley was enough to _____ anyone passing by.

13　The mysterious events in the town were _____, causing fear and confusion among the residents.

14　Despite facing a _____ challenge, the team managed to overcome the obstacles and succeed.

15　The forest was home to a diverse _____ of wildlife, each species playing a unique role in the ecosystem.

3

senseless / haunt / dreadfully / raging / pursue / delirious / acute / relentless / delirium / sharpen / agonizing / dull / humiliating / wrong / elude

1　The _____ experience of being publicly criticized left him feeling deeply ashamed.

2　The accident left him in a _____ state, unable to feel pain or respond to stimuli.

3　The _____ wait for news about her missing child was incredibly distressing.

4　The elusive criminal managed to _____ capture by slipping away unnoticed.

5 Despite facing numerous setbacks, she continued to _____ her dream of becoming a successful entrepreneur.

6 The _____ patient spoke incoherently, lost in a state of mental confusion.

7 The _____ storm caused havoc, with strong winds and heavy rainfall.

8 The crowd erupted into _____ cheers as the underdog team secured an unexpected victory.

9 The movie depicted a _____ state where characters experienced wild and unrealistic joy.

10 She had a _____ fear of spiders, to the point of being terrified at the sight of them.

11 The constant pressure and demands of the job were _____, leading to high stress levels.

12 The _____ pain in his leg made it difficult for him to walk.

13 The _____ blade of the knife easily sliced through the tough meat.

14 The monotonous routine of daily life became increasingly _____, lacking excitement or challenge.

15 The patient's _____ condition required immediate medical attention.

UNIT

6

4

hearty / deeds / contain / foresight / sagacity / vex / boldly / proceed / caution / inquire / profound / pale / creak / insult / fairly

1 Despite the _____ remarks from his colleague, John remained composed and focused on his work.

2 The room was filled with a _____ light as the sun began to set, casting long shadows across the floor.

3   Before we _____ with the project, let's take a moment to discuss the potential challenges and risks involved.

4   The teacher advised her students to approach the experiment with great _____ to ensure everyone's safety.

5   The old door would _____ loudly every time it was opened, creating an eerie atmosphere in the abandoned house.

6   Trying to _____ the teacher with irrelevant questions, the student hoped to distract the class from the upcoming test.

7   She _____ entered the meeting room, ready to present her proposal with confidence and conviction.

8   The mountaineer's _____ appetite for adventure led him to explore the most challenging and remote peaks.

9   If you have any questions or concerns, feel free to _____, and I'll do my best to provide the information you need.

10 The philosopher's _____ of human nature allowed him to anticipate the consequences of various actions.

11 The rusty gate continued to _____ as it swung back and forth in the gentle breeze.

12 The wise elder was known for his _____, offering valuable advice to those seeking guidance.

13 It's essential to _____ our emotions and approach the situation with a calm and rational mindset.

14 The detective carefully examined the suspect's past _____ to understand their motives and behavior.

15 The distant mountains were visible, but their features were _____ in the fading light of the evening.

5 causeless / deepening / distract / terror / mortal / stifled / arise / overcharged / groan / dreadful / awe / supposition / grief / stalk / startle

1 The sudden loud noise was enough to _____ everyone in the quiet room.

2 A _____ escaped his lips as he lifted the heavy box, feeling the strain on his back.

3 _____ beings are destined to face the inevitable reality of death.

4 The horror movie filled the audience with _____ as unexpected events unfolded on the screen.

5 _____ overwhelmed her as she mourned the loss of her beloved pet.

6 He _____ a yawn during the boring lecture to avoid drawing attention to his fatigue.

7 Unforeseen challenges can _____ at any moment, requiring us to adapt and overcome.

8 The room seemed to be _____ with tension, making the air thick with discomfort.

9 _____-stricken, they gazed at the majestic waterfall, captivated by its sheer beauty.

10 The _____ darkness signaled the approach of night, casting shadows across the landscape.

11 The _____ sight of the abandoned house sent shivers down their spines.

12 Trying to _____ himself from the pain, he immersed himself in a book.

13 The _____ fear lingered, leaving an unsettling feeling in the pit of her stomach.

14 The _____ that aliens exist is based more on imagination than concrete evidence.

15 The predator began to _____ its prey, moving silently through the dense underbrush.

6

dim / hideous / gaze upon / unperceived / patiently / resolve / crevice / stealthily / mournful / acuteness / distinctness / dull / chill / veil / furious

1 The _____ melody echoed through the empty halls, filling the space with a sense of sadness.

2 His presence was so quiet and _____ that he could move through the crowded room unnoticed.

3 She waited _____ for hours, hoping that the train would finally arrive.

4 With determination, she made a strong _____ to overcome the challenges that lay ahead.

5 A small beam of light seeped through the _____ in the ancient wall, revealing a hidden passage.

6 The thief moved _____ through the darkness, avoiding any detection.

7 As the sun set, the room grew _____, and the shadows danced on the walls.

8 The crowd grew _____ as they demanded answers from the unresponsive official.

9 He couldn't help but _____ the breathtaking beauty of the sunset over the horizon.

10 The _____ of her voice made her stand out in the choir, captivating everyone's attention.

11 The city's nightlife seemed strangely _____ that evening, lacking its usual vibrancy.

12 The old mansion looked even more _____ in the moonlight, casting eerie shadows.

13 She wore a delicate _____ that added an air of mystery to her appearance.

14 The sudden gust of wind sent a _____ through the air, causing everyone to shiver.

15 The _____ of his observations made him an excellent detective, noticing details others overlooked.

7

refrain / motionless / envelop / fury / muffled / remove / tattoo / seize / cease / gaily / deed / corpse / vex / dull / shriek

1 The _____ atmosphere in the room made it difficult to focus on the lecture.

2 The fog began to _____ the city, creating an eerie and mysterious ambiance.

3 Her eyes blazed with _____ as she confronted the person who betrayed her.

4 It's essential to _____ from making hasty decisions in moments of anger.

5 The soldiers remained _____, awaiting the command to initiate the next phase of the mission.

6 The rhythmic _____ echoed through the night, signaling the start of the ceremonial procession.

7 He tried to _____ the opportunity and take advantage of the situation.

8 A sudden _____ pierced the air as the haunted house sent shivers down our spines.

9   The children played _____ in the park, laughing and enjoying the sunny day.

10 The heroic _____ of the firefighter saved lives during the blazing inferno.

11 The sound of footsteps was _____, making it challenging to identify the approaching figure.

12 Don't let trivial matters _____ your peace of mind; focus on what truly matters.

13 The city _____ its vibrant colors as the sun set behind the skyline.

14 The mysterious figure seemed to _____ into the shadows, disappearing from sight.

15 The detective carefully examined the _____ to gather clues about the crime scene.

8

wane / foul play / suavity / concealment / precaution / deposit / hastily / suspicion / cunningly / stain / with perfect suavity / wary / trouble / lodge / stone dead

1   The once lively garden now appeared _____, with no sign of movement or growth.

2   His continuous attempts to _____ his colleagues led to a strained work environment.

3   Taking _____, she locked all the doors and windows before leaving for the weekend.

4   The _____ of the treasure was carefully executed, leaving no trace for prying eyes.

5   As the night progressed, the excitement of the party began to _____, and guests started leaving.

6 Realizing the urgency of the situation, they acted _____ to address the unforeseen crisis.

7 The archaeologist carefully uncovered the ancient artifacts, revealing the _____ of a forgotten civilization.

8 The thief _____ maneuvered through the crowded market, evading capture with ease.

9 The spilled coffee left an unsightly _____ on the white tablecloth.

10 The detective remained _____ as he observed the suspicious activities in the dark alley.

11 His _____ and friendly demeanor made him well-liked among his peers.

12 The diplomat handled the delicate negotiations _____, ensuring a smooth and positive outcome.

13 The sudden disappearance of funds raised _____ among the investors.

14 The sports match was marred by allegations of _____, tarnishing the spirit of fair competition.

15 Visitors were required to _____ their belongings before entering the secure area.

9

depute / repose / corpse / vehemently / gesticulation / audacity / beneath / wild / premises / agony / definitiveness / fatigue / trifle / fury / undisturbed

1 The manager decided to _____ the task of coordinating the event to his assistant.

2 The company's _____ included the office building, parking lot, and surrounding land.

3   The ancient ruins remained _____ by modern development.

4   After a long day of physical _____, she felt completely drained and
    exhausted.

5   His decision to invest in the risky venture was _____ and ultimately led to
    financial loss.

6   With surprising _____, he challenged the authority figures, voicing his
    strong opinions.

7   The hidden treasure was buried _____ the old oak tree, waiting to be
    discovered.

8   After a lifetime of hard work, the old man found eternal _____ in his final
    resting place.

9   The detective carefully examined the _____, looking for clues to solve the
    mysterious case.

10 The speaker delivered the message with _____, leaving no room for
    interpretation.

11 The protesters _____ expressed their dissatisfaction with the government's
    policies.

12 She didn't want to waste time on a mere _____, preferring to focus on
    significant matters.

13 The actor's passionate _____ added intensity to his portrayal of the
    character.

14 The storm approached with great _____, unleashing its destructive force
    upon the landscape.

15 She was in _____, unable to decide whether to accept the job offer or
    pursue further studies.

[1-2] Read the passage and answer each question.

NOTE

[A] True!—nervous—very, very dreadfully nervous I had been and am; but why will you say that I am mad? The disease had sharpened my senses—not destroyed—not dulled them. Above all was the sense of hearing acute. (a)I heard all things in the heaven and in the earth. I heard many things in hell. How, then, am I mad? Hearken! and observe how healthily—how calmly I can tell you the whole story.

[B] It is impossible to say how first the idea entered my brain; but conceived, (b)it haunted me day and night. Object there was none. Passion there was none. (c)I loved the old man. He had never wronged me. He had never given me insult. For his gold I had no desire. I think it was his eye! yes, it was this! One of his eyes resembled that of a vulture—a pale blue eye, with a film over it. Whenever it fell upon me, my blood ran cold; and so by degrees—very gradually—I made up my mind to take the life of the old man, and thus rid myself of the eye for ever.

[C] (d)Now this is the point. You fancy me mad. Madmen know nothing. But you should have seen me. You should have seen how wisely I proceeded—with what caution—with what foresight—with what dissimulation I went to work! I was never kinder to the old man than during the whole week before I killed him. And every night, about midnight, I turned the latch of his door and opened it—oh, so gently! And then, when I had made an opening sufficient for my head, I put in a dark lantern, all closed, closed, so that no light shone out, and then I thrust in my head. Oh, you would have laughed to see how cunningly I thrust it in! I moved it slowly—very, very slowly, so that I might not disturb the old man's sleep. (e)It took me an hour to place my whole head within the opening so far that I could see him as he lay upon his bed. Ha!—would a madman have been so wise as this? And then, when my head was well in the room, I undid the lantern

UNIT

6

cautiously—oh, so cautiously—cautiously (for the hinges creaked)—
I undid it just so much that a single thin ray fell upon the vulture eye.
And this I did for seven long nights—every night just at midnight—
but I found the eye always closed; and so it was impossible to do the
work; for it was not the old man who vexed me, but his Evil Eye. And
every morning, when the day broke, I went boldly into the chamber,
and spoke courageously to him, calling him by name in a hearty tone,
and inquiring how he had passed the night. So you see he would have
been a very profound old man, indeed, to suspect that every night, just
at twelve, I looked in upon him while he slept.

1 Choose the number of all the options that are correct about paragraph [A]?

> I.   The unnamed narrator is called crazy by someone.
> II. The person calling the narrator crazy is also unknown just like the narrator himself.
> III. The narrator clearly distinguishes between "being nervous" and being crazy.
> IV. The narrator thinks he knows better than "you."
> V.   The words such as "dreadfully nervous" and "how healthily or how calmly" are contradictory, which reveals the narrator's mental status.

① 1개   ② 2개   ③ 3개   ④ 4개   ⑤ All of the above

2 Which of the following is correct about each underlined sentence? (multiple correct answers)

① (a) shows the character of the narrator whose words cannot be trusted because he acts irrational.

② (b) means that the idea of killing the old man to put an end to the evil eye keeps returning.

③ (c) shows the unreliable character of the narrator considering that he actually made up his mind to take the life of the old man.

④ In (d), the highly dubious nature of the narrator's sanity can be detected from the fact that he makes a virtue out of his ability to deceive, and specifically to fool the old man.

⑤ (e) may not only show an exaggeration, but also portray how the narrator is so devoted to accomplishing his goal of killing the old man.

[3-4] Read the passage and answer each question.

NOTE

[A] True!—nervous—very, very dreadfully nervous I had been and am; but why will you say that I am mad? The disease had sharpened my senses—not destroyed—not dulled them. Above all was the sense of hearing acute. I heard all things in the heaven and in the earth. I heard many things in hell. How, then, am I mad? Hearken! and observe how healthily—how calmly I can tell you the whole story.

[B] (가)If still you think me mad, you will think so no longer when I describe the wise precautions I took for the concealment of the body. The night waned, and I worked hastily, but in silence. First of all I dismembered the corpse. I cut off the head and the arms and the legs.

I then took up three planks from the flooring of the chamber, and deposited all between the scantlings. I then replaced the boards so cleverly, so cunningly, that no human eye—not even his—could have detected anything wrong. There was nothing to wash out—no stain of any kind—no bloodspot whatever. I had been too wary for that. A tub had caught all—ha! ha!

When I had made an end of these labors, it was four o'clock—still dark as midnight. As the bell sounded the hour, there came a knocking at the street door. I went down to open it with a light heart,—for what had I now to fear? There entered three men, who introduced themselves, with perfect suavity, as officers of the police. A shriek had been heard by a neighbor during the night; suspicion of foul play had been aroused; information had been lodged at the police office, and they (the officers) had been deputed to search the premises.

I smiled,—for what had I to fear? I bade the gentlemen welcome. The shriek, I said, was my own in a dream. The old man, I mentioned, was absent in the country. I took my visitors all over the house. I bade them search—search well. I led them, at length, to his chamber. I showed them his treasures, secure, undisturbed. In the enthusiasm of my confidence, I brought chairs into the room, and desired them here to rest from their fatigues, while I myself, in the wild audacity of my perfect triumph, placed my own seat upon the very spot beneath which reposed the corpse of the victim.

(나)The officers were satisfied. My manner had convinced them. I was singularly at ease. They say, and while I answered cheerily, they chatted familiar things. But, ere long, I felt myself getting pale and wished them gone. My head ached, and I fancied a ringing in my years: but still they sat and still chatted. The ringing became more distinct:—it continued and became more distinct: I talked more freely to get rid of the feeling: but it continued and gained definitiveness—until, at length, I found that the noise was not within my ears. No doubt I now grew very pale:—but I talked more fluently, and with a heightened voice. (다)Yet the sound increase—and what could I do? It was a low, dull, quick sound—much such a sound as a watch makes when enveloped in cotton. I gasped for breath—and yet the officers heard it not. I talked more quickly—more vehemently; but the noise steadily increased. I arose and argued about trifles, in a high key and with violent gesticulations, but the noise steadily increased. Why would they not be gone? I paced the floor to and fro with heavy strides, as if excited to fury but the observation of the men—but the noise steadily increased. Oh God! what could I do? I foamed—I raved—I swore! I swung the chair upon which I had been sitting, and grated it upon the boards, but the noise arose over all and continually increased. It grew louder—louder—louder! And still the men chatted pleasantly, and smiled. Was it possible they heard not? Almighty God!—no, no! (라)They heard!—they suspected!—they knew!—they were making a mockery of my horror!—this I thought, and this I think. But anything was better than this agony! Any thing was more tolerable than this derision! I could bear those hypocritical smiles no longer! I felt that I must scream or die!—and now—again!—hark! louder! louder! louder! louder!—"Villains!" I shrieked, "dissemble no more! I admit the deed!—tear up the planks!—

here, here!—it is the beating of his hideous heart!"

3 Which of the following statements can <u>NOT</u> be inferred from the passage?

① The narrator's newly heightened sensitivity overcomes him, as he shows an inability to distinguish between real and imagined sounds.

② The fact that the narrator thinks that he hears the beating of the dead man shows the deranged state of his mind.

③ The narrator's obsession with the low beat of the man's heart contradicts his little concern about the man's shriek, which is loud enough to attract a neighbor's attention.

④ The beating of the man's heart leads the narrator to confess his crime.

⑤ Since the old man is now dead, the narrator is convinced that the beating of the man's heart must be coming from his own heart.

4 Which of the following can be the <u>LEAST</u> appropriate explanation from each underlined sentence?

① (가): The narrator believes he is not insane because he is very careful and precise when plotting to murder the old man.

② (나): It is odd that the police officers do not show any indication of suspecting that the narrator is guilty, but only a full satisfaction over the situation.

③ (다): Edgar Allan Poe here compares the sound of the heart to the sound of a watch wrapped in cotton to show that the source of the beating sound is only from the actual clock on the wall, not from the dead man's heart.

④ (라): The police would not have suspected the narrator of murder if he had not confessed.

⑤ (라): Though the narrator himself killed and dismembered an old man due to his eye, it is the policemen who are called the villains. This demonstrates the extent of the narrator's madness.

[5-6] Read the passage and answer each question.

True!—nervous—very, very dreadfully nervous I had been and am; but why will you say that I am mad? The disease had sharpened my senses—not destroyed—not dulled them. Above all was the sense of hearing acute. I heard all things in the heaven and in the earth. I heard many things in hell. How, then, am I mad? Hearken! and observe how healthily—how calmly I can tell you the whole story.

(A)It is impossible to say how first the idea entered my brain; but conceived, it haunted me day and night. Object there was none. Passion there was none. I loved the old man. He had never wronged me. He had never given me insult. For his gold I had no desire. I think it was his eye! yes, it was this! One of his eyes resembled that of a vulture—a pale blue eye, with a film over it. Whenever it fell upon me, my blood ran cold; and so by degrees—very gradually—I made up my mind to take the life of the old man, and thus rid myself of the eye for ever.

(B)Now this is the point. You fancy me mad. Madmen know nothing. But you should have seen me. You should have seen how wisely I proceeded—with what caution—with what foresight—with what dissimulation I went to work! I was never kinder to the old man than during the whole week before I killed him. And every night, about midnight, I turned the latch of his door and opened it—oh, so gently! And then, when I had made an opening sufficient for my head, I put in a dark lantern, all closed, closed, so that no light shone out, and then I thrust in my head. Oh, you would have laughed to see how cunningly I thrust it in! I moved it slowly—very, very slowly, so that I might not disturb the old man's sleep. It took me an hour to place my whole head within the opening so far that I could see him as he lay upon his bed. Ha!—would a madman have been so wise as this? And then, when my head was well in the room, I undid the lantern cautiously—oh, so cautiously—cautiously (for the hinges creaked)—I undid it just so much that a single thin ray fell upon the vulture eye. (C)And this I did for seven long nights—every night just at midnight—but I found the eye always closed; and so it was impossible to do the work; for it was not the old man who vexed me, but his Evil Eye. And every morning, when the day broke, I went boldly into the chamber, and spoke courageously to him, calling him by name in a hearty tone, and inquiring how he had passed the night. So you see he would have been a very profound old man, indeed, to suspect that every night, just at twelve, I looked in upon him while he slept. ㉮

Upon the eighth night I was more than usually cautious in opening the door. A watch's minute hand moves more quickly than did mine. Never before that night had I felt the extent of my own powers—of my sagacity. I could scarcely contain my feelings of triumph. To think that there I was, opening the door, little by little, and he not even to dream of my secret deeds or thoughts. I fairly chuckled at the idea; and perhaps he heard me; for he moved on the bed suddenly, as if startled. ㉯

I had my head in, and was about to open the lantern, when my thumb slipped upon the tin fastening, and the old man sprang up in the bed, crying out—"Who's there?"

I kept quite still and said nothing. For a whole hour I did not move a muscle, and in the meantime I did not hear him lie down. He was still sitting up in the bed listening;—just as I have done, night after night, hearkening to the death watches) in the wall. ㉰

Presently I heard a slight groan, and I knew it was the groan of mortal terror. It was not a groan of pain or of grief—oh, no!—it was the low stifled sound that arises from the bottom of the soul when overcharged with awe. I knew the sound very well. Many a night, just a midnight, when all the world slept, it has welled up from my own bosom, deepening, with its dreadful echo, the terrors that distracted me. I say I knew it well. (D)I knew what the old man felt, and pitied him, although I chuckled at heart. I knew that he had been lying awake ever since the first slight noise, when he had turned in the bed. His fears had been ever since growing upon him. He had been trying to fancy them causeless, but could not. He had been saying to himself—"It is nothing but the wind in the chimney—it is only a mouse crossing the floor," or "it is merely a cricket which has made a single chirp." Yes, he had been trying to comfort himself with these suppositions; but he had found all in vain. All in vain; because Death, in approaching him, had stalked with his black shadow before him, and enveloped the victim. And it was the mournful influence of the unperceived shadow that caused him to feel—although he neither saw nor heard—to feel the presence of my head within the room. 가

When I had waited a long time, very patiently, without hearing him lie down, I resolved to open a little—a very, very little crevice in the lantern. So I opened it—you cannot imagine how stealthily, stealthily—until, at length, a single dim ray, like the thread of the spider, shot from out for crevice and full upon the vulture eye.

(E)It was open—wide, wide open—and I grew furious as I gazed upon it. I saw it with perfect distinctness—all a dull blue, with a hideous veil over it that chilled the very marrow in my bones; but I could see nothing else of the old man's face or person: for I had directed the ray as if by instinct, precisely upon the damned spot. 아

And now have I not told you that what you mistake for madness is but over-acuteness of the sense?—now, I say, there came to my ears a low, dull, quick sound, such as a watch makes when enveloped in cotton. I knew that sound well too. It was the beating of the old man's heart. It increased my fury, as the beating of a drum stimulates the soldier into courage.

5 Which of the following statements about the underlined parts (A) ~ (E) is INCORRECT?

① (A) : It reveals the narrator's fixation on killing the old man.

② (B) : The narrator congratulates himself on his wisdom, claiming to have a better grasp on reality than his listener, whoever that person is.

③ (C) : The narrator said that he couldn't kill the old man because the room was too dark to locate him.

④ (D) : The narrator's emotions are in conflict here, as they are in opposite places, with pity and amusement at war.

⑤ (E) : "It" in the sentence means the eye of the old man and the reason why it is dull is that it has a film over it, and the fact that he only sees the old man's eye shows his obsession with it.

6 Among ㉮~㉲, choose the best place to insert the sentence given below.

> Now you may think that I drew back—but no. His room was as black as pitch with the thick darkness (for the shutters were close fastened, through fear of robbers), and so I knew that he could not see the opening of the door, and I kept pushing it on steadily, steadily.

① ㉮

② ㉯

③ ㉰

④ ㉱

⑤ ㉲

[7-8] Read the passage and answer each question.

 NOTE

Upon the eighth night I was more than usually cautious in opening the door. (A)<u>A watch's minute hand moves more quickly than did mine.</u> Never before that night had I felt the extent of my own powers—of my sagacity. I could scarcely contain my feelings of triumph. To think that there I was, opening the door, little by little, and he not even to dream of my secret deeds or thoughts. I fairly chuckled at the idea; and perhaps he heard me; for he moved on the bed suddenly, as if startled. Now you may think that I drew back—but no. (B)<u>His room was as black as pitch with the thick darkness</u> (for the shutters were close fastened, through fear of robbers), and so I knew that he could not see the opening of the door, and I kept pushing it on steadily, steadily.

I had my head in, and was about to open the lantern, when my thumb slipped upon the tin fastening, and the old man sprang up in the bed, crying out—"Who's there?"

I kept quite still and said nothing. (C)<u>For a whole hour I did not move a muscle</u>, and in the meantime I did not hear him lie down. He was still sitting up in the bed listening;—just as I have done, night after night, hearkening to the death watches in the wall.

Presently I heard a slight groan, and I knew it was the groan of mortal terror. It was not a groan of pain or of grief—oh, no!—it was the low stifled sound that arises from the bottom of the soul when overcharged with awe. I knew the sound very well. Ⓐ Many a night, just a midnight, when all the world slept, it has welled up from my own bosom, deepening, with its dreadful echo, the terrors that distracted me. I say I knew it well. (D)<u>I knew what the old man felt, and pitied him, although I chuckled at heart.</u> Ⓑ I knew that he had been lying awake ever since the first slight noise, when he had turned in the bed. His fears had been ever since growing upon him. He had been trying to fancy them causeless, but could not. Ⓒ He had been saying to himself—"It is nothing but the wind in the chimney—it is only a mouse crossing the floor," or "it is merely a cricket which has made a single chirp." Ⓓ Because Death, in approaching him, had stalked with his black shadow before him, and enveloped the victim. Ⓔ And it was

NOTE

the mournful influence of the unperceived shadow that caused him to feel—although he neither saw nor heard—to feel the presence of my head within the room.

When I had waited a long time, very patiently, without hearing him lie down, I resolved to open a little—a very, very little crevice in the lantern. So I opened it—you cannot imagine how stealthily, stealthily—until, at length, a single dim ray, like the thread of the spider, shot from out for crevice and full upon the vulture eye.

7 Which of the following is <u>NOT</u> a proper explanation for each underlined sentence?

① (A) refers to the narrator's comparable observation of the watch to brag about his being "more than usually cautious".

② (B) is an expression of metaphor, which means the room was "extremely dark".

③ (C) shows the narrator's hyperbolic explanation.

④ (D) implies the narrator's claiming that he knows what others are thinking or feeling.

⑤ (D) shows that his emotions are in conflict here toward the old man.

8 Among Ⓐ ~ Ⓔ, which is the best place to insert the following sentence?

Yes, he had been trying to comfort himself with these suppositions; but he had found all in vain. All in vain;

① Ⓐ
② Ⓑ
③ Ⓒ
④ Ⓓ
⑤ Ⓔ

[9-11] Read the passage and answer each question.

 NOTE

[A] True!—nervous—very, very dreadfully nervous I had been and am; but why will you say that I am mad? The disease had sharpened my senses—not destroyed—not dulled them. Above all was the sense of hearing acute. I heard all things in the heaven and in the earth. I heard many things in hell. How, then, am I mad? Hearken! and observe how healthily—how calmly I can tell you the whole story.

[B] It is impossible to say how first the idea entered my brain; but conceived, it haunted me day and night. Object there was none. Passion there was none. I loved the old man. He had never wronged me. He had never given me insult. For his gold I had no desire. I think it was his eye! yes, it was this! One of his eyes resembled that of a vulture—a pale blue eye, with a film over it. Whenever it fell upon me, my blood ran cold; and so by degrees—very gradually—I made up my mind to take the life of the old man, and thus rid myself of the eye for ever.

[C] Now this is the point. You fancy me mad. Madmen know nothing. But you should have seen me. You should have seen how wisely I proceeded—with what caution—with what foresight—with what dissimulation I went to work! I was never kinder to the old man than during the whole week before I killed him. And every night, about midnight, I turned the latch of his door and opened it—oh, so gently! And then, when I had made an opening sufficient for my head, I put in a dark lantern, all closed, closed, so that no light shone out, and then I thrust in my head. Oh, you would have laughed to see how cunningly I thrust it in! I moved it slowly—very, very slowly, so that I might not disturb the old man's sleep. It took me an hour to place my whole head within the opening so far that I could see him as he lay upon his bed. Ha!—would a madman have been so wise as this? And then, when my head was well in the room, I undid the lantern cautiously—oh, so cautiously—cautiously (for the hinges creaked)— I undid it just so much that a single thin ray fell upon the vulture eye. And this I did for seven long nights—every night just at midnight— but I found the eye always closed; and so it was impossible to do the work; for it was not the old man who vexed me, but his Evil Eye. And every morning, when the day broke, I went boldly into the chamber, and spoke courageously to him, calling him by name in a hearty tone, and inquiring how he had passed the night. So you see he would have been a very profound old man, indeed, to suspect that every night, just at twelve, I looked in upon him while he slept.

[D] Upon the eighth night I was more than usually cautious in opening the door. A watch's minute hand moves more quickly than did mine. Never before that night had I felt the extent of my own powers—of my sagacity. I could scarcely contain my feelings of triumph. To think that there I was, opening the door, little by little, and he not even to dream of my secret deeds or thoughts. I fairly chuckled at the idea; and perhaps he heard me; for he moved on the bed suddenly, as if startled. Now you may think that I drew back—but no. His room was as black as pitch with the thick darkness (for the shutters were close fastened, through fear of robbers), and so I knew that he could not see the opening of the door, and I kept pushing it on steadily, steadily. I had my head in, and was about to open the lantern, when my thumb slipped upon the tin fastening, and the old man sprang up in the bed, crying out—"Who's there?" I kept quite still and said nothing. For a whole hour I did not move a muscle, and in the meantime I did not hear him lie down. He was still sitting up in the bed listening;—just as I have done, night after night, hearkening to the death watches) in the wall.

[E] Presently I heard a slight groan, and I knew it was the groan of mortal terror. It was not a groan of pain or of grief—oh, no!—it was the low stifled sound that arises from the bottom of the soul when overcharged with awe. I knew the sound very well. Many a night, just a midnight, when all the world slept, it has welled up from my own bosom, deepening, with its dreadful echo, the terrors that distracted me. I say I knew it well. I knew what the old man felt, and pitied him, although I chuckled at heart. I knew that he had been lying awake ever since the first slight noise, when he had turned in the bed. His fears had been ever since growing upon him. He had been trying to fancy

UNIT
6

them causeless, but could not. He had been saying to himself—"It is nothing but the wind in the chimney—it is only a mouse crossing the floor," or "it is merely a cricket which has made a single chirp." Yes, he had been trying to comfort himself with these suppositions; but he had found all in vain. All in vain; because Death, in approaching him, had stalked with his black shadow before him, and enveloped the victim. And it was the mournful influence of the unperceived shadow that caused him to feel—although he neither saw nor heard—to feel the presence of my head within the room.

[F] When I had waited a long time, very patiently, without hearing him lie down, I resolved to open a little—a very, very little crevice in the lantern. So I opened it—you cannot imagine how stealthily, stealthily—until, at length, a single dim ray, like the thread of the spider, shot from out for crevice and full upon the vulture eye.

It was open—wide, wide open—and I grew furious as I gazed upon it. I saw it with perfect distinctness—all a dull blue, with a hideous veil over it that chilled the very marrow in my bones; but I could see nothing else of the old man's face or person: for I had directed the ray as if by instinct, precisely upon the damned spot. And now have I not told you that what you mistake for madness is but over-acuteness of the sense?—now, I say, there came to my ears a low, dull, quick sound, such as a watch makes when enveloped in cotton. I knew that sound well too. It was the beating of the old man's heart. It increased my fury, as the beating of a drum stimulates the soldier into courage.

9 Which of the following statements are <u>NOT</u> correct about each paragraph?

① [A] : The narrator tries to convince "you" that he isn't out of mind with his ability to deliver the whole story.

② [B] : It was the old man's eye that made him make up his mind to get rid of him.

③ [C] : The lantern was so tightly covered that it might not leak any light upon the old man.

④ [D] : The underlined sentence is designed to show one of the examples of hyperbole show in the novel.

⑤ [E] : Considering the fact that he "knew the sound well" and the possibility that he is mad, the underlined sentence implies that the slight groan that he thinks comes from the old man can possibly all imaginary coming from his inner body.

⑥ [F] : The underlined phrase "the damned spot" indicates the soft spot that he has for the old man.

10 According to Paragraph [F], what finally caused him to jump on the act of murder?

① The old man's eye

② The beating of the old man's heart

③ The sound of the watch hung on the wall

④ The beating of a drum

⑤ The heart beat of the soldier

11 What character traits do the murderer pride himself on?

① His abilities to lie and steal

② His intelligence and his patience

③ His wit and his confidence

④ His sneakiness and his fear

⑤ His contradictory moods

[12-15] Read the passage and answer each question.

 NOTE

TRUE! nervous, very, very dreadfully nervous I had been and am; but why WILL you say that I am mad? The disease had sharpened my senses, not destroyed, not dulled them. Above all ⓐwere the sense of hearing acute. I heard all things in the heaven and in the earth. I heard many things in hell. How then am I mad? Hearken! and observe how healthily, how calmly, I can tell you the whole story.

It is impossible to say how first the idea entered my brain, but, once ⓑconceived, it haunted me day and night. Object there was none. Passion there was none. I loved the old man. He had never wronged me. He had never given me insult. For his gold I had no desire. I think it was his eye! Yes, it was this! One of his eyes resembled that of a vulture — a pale blue eye with a film over it. Whenever it fell upon me my blood ran cold, and so by degrees, very gradually, I made up my mind to take the life of the old man, and thus rid ©myself of the eye for ever.

Now this is the point. You fancy me mad. Mad men know nothing. But you should have seen me. You should have seen how wisely I proceeded—with what caution—with what foresight—with what ㉠ dissimulation I went to work! I was never kinder to the old man than during the whole week before I killed him. And every night, about midnight, I turned the latch of his door and opened it—oh, so gently! And then, when I had made an opening sufficient for my head, I put in a dark lantern, all closed, closed, so that no light shone out, and then I thrust in my head. Oh, you would have laughed to see how cunningly I thrust it in! I moved it slowly—very, very slowly, so that I might not disturb the old man's sleep.

It took me an hour to place my whole head within the opening so far that I could see him as he ⓓlaid upon his bed. Ha!—would a madman have been so wise as this? And then, when my head was well in the room, I undid the lantern cautiously—oh, so cautiously—cautiously (for the hinges creaked)—I undid it just so much that a single thin ray fell upon the vulture eye. And this I did for seven long nights—every

NOTE

night just at midnight—but I found the eye always closed; and so it was impossible to do the work; for it was not the old man who vexed me, but his Evil Eye. And every morning, when the day broke, I went boldly into the chamber, and spoke courageously to him, calling him by name in a hearty tone, and inquiring how he had passed the night. So you see he would have been a very profound old man, indeed, to suspect that every night, just at twelve, I looked in upon him while he slept.

Upon the eighth night I was more than usually cautious in opening the door. A watch's minute hand moves more quickly than did mine. Never before that night had I felt the extent of my own powers—of my ⓛsagacity. I could scarcely ⓒcontain my feelings of triumph. To think that there I was, opening the door, little by little, and he not even to dream of my secret deeds or thoughts. I fairly chuckled at the idea; and perhaps he heard me; for he moved on the bed suddenly, as if startled. Now you may think that I drew back—but no. His room was as black as pitch with the thick darkness (for the shutters were close fastened, through fear of robbers), and so I knew that he could not see the opening of the door, and I kept pushing it on steadily, steadily.

I had my head in, and was about to open the lantern, when my thumb slipped upon the tin fastening, and the old man sprang up in the bed, crying out—"Who's there?"

I kept quite still and said nothing. For a whole hour I did not move a muscle, and in the meantime I did not hear him lie down. He was still sitting up in the bed listening;—just as I have done, night after night, hearkening to the death watches in the wall.

Presently I heard a slight groan, and I knew it was the groan of mortal terror. It was not a groan of pain or of grief—oh, no!—it was the low ⓔ stifled sound that arises from the bottom of the soul when overcharged with awe. I knew the sound very well. Many a night, just a midnight, when all the world slept, it has welled up from my own bosom, deepening, with its dreadful echo, the terrors that distracted me. I say I knew it well. I knew what the old man felt, and pitied him, although I chuckled at heart. I knew that he had been lying awake ever since the first slight noise, when he had turned in the bed. His fears had been ever since growing upon him. He had been trying to fancy them causeless, but could not. He had been saying to himself—"It is nothing but the wind in the chimney—it is only a mouse crossing the floor," or "it is merely a cricket which has made a single chirp." Yes, he had been trying to comfort himself with these ⓓsuppositions; but he had found all in vain. All in vain; because Death, in approaching him, had stalked with his black shadow before him, and enveloped the victim. And it was the mournful influence of ⓔthe unperceived shadow that caused him to feel—although he neither saw nor heard—to feel the presence of my head within the room.

12 Among the underlined parts ⓐ~ⓓ, how many are grammatically <u>INCORRECT</u>?

① None   ② One

③ Two   ④ Three

⑤ Four

13 According to the passage, which of the following statements is <u>TRUE</u>?

> I. The story starts with a conversation already in progress between the narrator and another person who is identified as an old man.
>
> II. The narrator denies having any feeling of hatred or resentment for the old man.
>
> III. The narrator confesses that he has never been kind to the old man since he made up his mind to kill the old man.
>
> IV. Watching the old man terrified in the dark room, the narrator had sympathy for the old man as well as felt pleasure.

① I and II

② I and III

③ II, III, and IV

④ II and IV

⑤ III and IV

14 Choose one among ㉠~㉢ that describes its meaning in context <u>INCORRECTLY</u>.

① ㉠ dissimulation: disagreement, dissent

② ㉡ sagacity: wisdom, discernment

③ ㉢ contain: restrain, control

④ ㉣ stifled: suppressed, smothered

⑤ ㉤ suppositions: assumptions, speculations

15 Which of the following examples does <u>NOT</u> have the same figure of speech used in ㉣<u>the unperceived shadow</u>?

① "Is she at home?" Jack asked with careful carelessness.

② All your perfect imperfections give yours all to me.

③ The silence was deafening.

④ Parting is such sweet sorrow.

⑤ That piece of chocolate cake is calling my name.

[16-18] Read the passage and answer each question.

 NOTE

When I had waited a long time, very patiently, without hearing him lie down, I resolved to open a little—a very, very little crevice in the lantern. So I opened it—you cannot imagine how stealthily, stealthily—until, at length, a single dim ray, like the thread of the spider, shot from out for crevice and full upon the vulture eye.

It was open—wide, wide open—and I grew furious as I gazed upon it. I saw it with perfect distinctness—all a dull blue, with a hideous veil over it that chilled the very marrow in my bones; but I could see nothing else of the old man's face or person: for I had directed the ray as if by instinct, precisely upon the damned spot.

And now have I not told you that what you mistake for madness is but over-acuteness of the sense?—now, I say, there came to my ears a low, dull, quick sound, such as a watch makes when enveloped in cotton. I knew that sound well too. It was the beating of the old man's heart. It increased my fury, as the beating of a drum stimulates the soldier into courage.

But even yet I refrained and kept still. I scarcely breathed. I held the lantern motionless. I tried how steadily I could maintain the ray upon the eye. Meantime the hellish tattoo of the heart increased. It grew quicker and quicker, and louder and louder, I say, louder every moment!—do you mark me well? I have told you that I am nervous: so I am. And now at the dead hour of the night, amid the dreadful silence of that old house, so strange a noise as this excited me to uncontrollable terror. Yet, for some minutes longer I refrained and stood still. But the beating grew louder, louder! I thought the heart must burst.

[A] With a loud yell, I threw open the lantern and leaped into the room. He come! He shrieked once—once only.

[B] This, however, did not vex me; it would not be heard through the wall. At length it ceased. The old man was dead. I removed the bed and examined the corpse.

[C] In an instant I dragged him to the floor, and pulled the heavy bed over him. I then smiled gaily, to find the deed so far done. But, for many minutes, the heart beat on with a muffled sound.

[D] And now a new anxiety seized me—the sound would be heard by a neighbor! The old man's hour had come!

Yes, he was stone, stone dead. I placed my hand upon the heart and held it there many minutes. There was no pulsation. He was stone dead. His eye would trouble me no more.

If still you think me mad, you will think so no longer when I describe the wise precautions I took for the concealment of the body. The night waned, and I worked hastily, but in silence. First of all I dismembered the corpse. I cut off the head and the arms and the legs.

I then took up three planks from the flooring of the chamber, and deposited all between the scantlings. I then replaced the boards so cleverly, so cunningly, that no human eye—not even his—could have detected anything wrong. There was nothing to wash out—no stain of any kind—no bloodspot whatever. I had been too wary for that. A tub(= basin) had caught all—ha! ha!

When I had made an end of these labors, it was four o'clock—still dark as midnight. As the bell sounded the hour, there came a knocking at the street door. I went down to open it with a light heart,—for what had I now to fear? There entered three men, who introduced themselves, with perfect suavity, as officers of the police. A shriek had been heard by a neighbor during the night; suspicion of foul play had been aroused; information had been lodged at the police office, and they (the officers) had been deputed to search the premises.

I smiled,—for what had I to fear? I bade the gentlemen welcome. The shriek, I said, was my own in a dream. The old man, I mentioned, was absent in the country. I took my visitors all over the house. I bade them search—search well. I led them, at length, to his chamber. I showed them his treasures, secure, undisturbed. In the enthusiasm of my confidence, I brought chairs into the room, and desired them here to rest from their fatigues, while I myself, in the wild audacity of my perfect triumph, placed my own seat upon the very spot beneath which reposed the corpse of the victim.

The officers were satisfied. My manner had convinced them. I was singularly at ease. They say, and while I answered cheerily, they chatted familiar things. But, ere long, I felt myself getting pale and wished them gone. My head ached, and I fancied a ringing in my years: but still they sat and still chatted. The ringing became more distinct:—it continued and became more distinct: I talked more freely to get rid of the feeling: but it continued and gained definitiveness—until, at length, I found that the noise was not within my ears.

No doubt I now grew very pale:—but I talked more fluently, and with a heightened voice. Yet the sound increase—and what could I do? [_____(a)_____] It was a low, dull, quick sound—much such a sound as a watch makes when enveloped in cotton. I gasped for breath—and yet the officers heard it not. [_____(b)_____] I talked more quickly—more vehemently; but the noise steadily increased. I arose and argued about trifles, in a high key and with violent gesticulations, but the noise steadily increased. Why would they not be gone? [_____(c)_____] I paced the floor to and fro with heavy strides, as if excited to fury by the observation of the men—but the noise steadily increased. Oh God! what could I do? I foamed—I raved—I swore! [_____(d)_____] I swung the chair upon which I had been sitting, and grated it upon the boards, but the noise arose over all and continually increased. It grew louder—louder—louder! And still the men chatted pleasantly, and smiled. Was it possible they heard not? Almighty God!—no, no! [_____(e)_____] But anything was better than this agony! Any thing was more tolerable than this derision! I could bear those hypocritical smiles no longer! I felt that I must scream or die!—and now—again!—hark! louder! louder! louder! louder!—

"Villains!" I shrieked, "dissemble no more! I admit the deed!—tear up the planks!—here, here!—it is the beating of his hideous heart!"

16 According to the passage above, which of the following statements is <u>INCORRECT</u>?

① The fact that the old man's eye is open stands for the awareness or detection of the narrator's hideous, disturbing and dark nature.

② The heartbeat symbolizes not only the sound of telling the tale of the narrator's murderous deed, but also the sound of his guilty conscience.

③ The use of dash, exclamation marks and word repetition creates the mood such as an anxiety, fear and agitation.

④ Although the old man was dead, his heart-beating sound haunted the narrator and made him confess his crime.

⑤ Readers know the old man is buried under the floorboards while the police search the house without knowing anything. It is called situational irony.

17 According to the context, which of the following is the best order of [A] ~ [D]?

① [A] - [C] - [D] - [B]
② [A] - [D] - [B] - [C]
③ [B] - [D] - [C] - [A]
④ [D] - [A] - [C] - [B]
⑤ [D] - [C] - [B] - [A]

18 According to the context, choose the best place among (a) ~ (e) to insert the sentence in the box below.

> They heard!—they suspected!—they knew!—they were making a mockery of my horror!—this I thought, and this I think.

① (a)
② (b)
③ (c)
④ (d)
⑤ (e)

1 Proposals for appellations have often seemed _____, with delineations that can appear arbitrary. The presence of government-approved marketing labels sometimes seems like a minimal consideration.

① capricious   ② tedious

③ compelling   ④ cautious

어휘 proposal 제안 appellation 명칭, 호칭 delineation 묘사 appear 보이다 arbitrary 임의로, 멋대로, 독재적인 government-approved 정부가 인정한 minimal 아주 적은 consideration 고려 capricious 변덕스러운 tedious 지루한, 짜증나는, 장황한 compelling 강제적인, 강력한, 강한 흥미를 돋우는, 감탄하지 않을 수 없는 cautious 주의 깊은, 신중한, 조심하는

2 Aspirin was originally a brand name used by the Bayer Company, but as use of the product spread rapidly, the name became so common that it was accepted as a _____ term.

① tedious   ② generic

③ specific   ④ selective

어휘 originally 원래 spread rapidly 재빠르게 번지다, 확산되다 be accepted as ~로 받아들여지다 generic 총체적인, 일반적인 tedious 지루한, 짜증나는, 장황한 selective 선택적인, 까다로운 specific 특정한

3 Because his time was limited, Weng decided to read the _____ novel War and Peace in _____ edition.

① wordy – an unedited
② lengthy – an abridged
③ famous – a modern
④ romantic – an autographed
⑤ popular – a complete

어휘 limited 제한된 wordy 말이 많은 lengthy 긴 abridged 축약된 famous 유명한 modern 현대의 romantic 로맨틱한 autographed 서명된 complete 완벽한, 온전한

4 The little boy was so _____ that he couldn't stay awake.

① drowsy   ② dreary

③ hump-backed   ④ versatile

어휘   stay awake 계속 깨어있다 drowsy 졸린 dreary 적적한, 따분한 hump-backed 등이 구부러진 versatile 다재다능한

5 Since no cure for AIDS has yet been discovered, treatment is _____ at best.

① palliative   ② inert

③ abrasive   ④ plausible

어휘   cure 치료(제) has yet been discovered 아직 발견이 되지 않았다 treatment 치료 at best 기껏해야 palliative 완화하는, 경감하는 inert 활발하지 못한 abrasive 닳게 하는 plausible 그럴듯한, 믿을 만한

6 His _____ remarks are often embarrassing because of their frankness.

① sarcastic

② sadistic

③ frank

④ ingenuous

⑤ urbane

어휘   remark 말 embarrassing 당황케 하는 sarcastic 비꼬는 풍자의, 신랄한 sadistic 가학적인 ingenuous 솔직한 urbane 도회풍의, 세련된

7 Now that I realize his brother's _____, I feel that it will be impossible for me to trust his brother sincerely in the future.

① inclemency

② flamboyance

③ ingenuousness

④ chicanery

어휘   sincerely 진지하게 in the future 미래에, 앞으로 inclemency 험악, 무자비 flamboyance 현란함, 화려함 ingenuousness 솔직함, 진지함 chicanery 꾸며댐, 발뺌, 속임수, 궤변

8 The neighbors told me that the flames and extreme heat prevented him from
_____ the apartment.

① seizing

② re-entering

③ constructing

④ renting

9 She was criticized by her fellow lawyers not because she was not _____, but because she so _____ prepared her cases that she failed to bring the expected number to trial.

① well versed – knowledgeably

② well trained – enthusiastically

③ congenial – rapidly

④ hardworking – minutely

⑤ astute – efficiently

10 She was _____ because her plans had gone _____.

① pleased – awry

② imminent – efficiently

③ foiled – well

④ importunate – splendidly

⑤ distraught – awry

Reading A one

2

박지성 저

Step-up

정답/해설

중학 고급 영문 독해

특목고(외고/국제고), 자사고 대비
문학·비문학 고급 영문 독해 수험서

- PART 1 | Voca Master
- PART 2 | Text Reading
- PART 3 | Voca Check
- PART 4 | Reading Comprehension
- PART 5 | Sentence Completion

반석출판사

정답/해설

Part 2 Text Reading

Quick Quiz

1 abab

해설 Tell me not, in mournful numb**ers**,

Life is but an empty dr**eam**!

For the soul is dead that slumb**ers**,

And things are not what they **seem**.

2 ⑤

해설 compare A to B ↔ contrast A with B

The expression "contrasts" in option ⑤ doesn't fit well in the context because the sentence is not about comparing the young man's beauty to something else in a contrasting manner. Instead, it discusses how the poem tries various metaphors and similes but ultimately finds them inadequate, and then introduces a unique simile comparing the young man's beauty to the poem itself. So, a more appropriate word would be <u>one that indicates the development or introduction of this unique simile</u>, rather than a contrasting relationship. The word "contrasts" doesn't accurately reflect the content of the sentence, making it contextually awkward.

3 ① Metaphor ② Simile ③ Simile ④ Metaphor ⑤ Metaphor ⑥ Simile ⑦ Metaphor ⑧ Simile ⑨ Simile ⑩ Simile

참고 **Metaphor vs Simile**

Metaphors and similes are both <u>figures of speech</u> used to make comparisons between <u>two things that are not usually considered to be similar</u>. However, they differ in how the comparison is made.

4 ⑤

해설 This sentence is an example of a metaphor, not a simile. A simile explicitly uses "like" or "as" to compare two unlike things, while a metaphor directly states that one thing is another. In this case, "Love is a battlefield" is a metaphor, as it directly compares love to a battlefield without using "like" or "as."

5 ⓔ

해설 permanently → temporarily

The word "permanently" suggests a sense of enduring or lasting indefinitely, which contradicts the idea of a finite duration conveyed by the word "lease" in this context.

6 ④

> (해설) In the context provided, the speaker describes their beloved as "temperate," which can refer to moderation and self-control in moral behavior, as well as pleasant weather that is neither too hot nor too cold. Therefore, "extremes" in this context likely refers to both moral extremes (such as excessive behavior) and weather extremes (such as extreme heat or cold), suggesting that the beloved avoids both types of extremes.

7 ②

> (해설) Paired with "ow'st," the implication is that summer does not inherently possess its beauty; it merely leases it for a brief period.

8 ①

> (해설) The passage explains that during the Renaissance, calling someone "fair" suggested exceptional beauty, which differs from its modern usage. By mentioning "fair-haired" as an example, the passage emphasizes how the term "fair" was used to denote physical beauty during that time period, particularly in the context of describing someone with blond hair. Therefore, option ① best captures the purpose of mentioning "fair-haired" in the passage.

9 ① False ② False ③ False ④ True ⑤ False

> (해설) ① False: The speaker fails to find a metaphor that adequately reflects his beloved's beauty.
>
> ② False: The first eight lines of the poem document the failure of traditional resources in capturing the young man's beauty.
>
> ③ False: The final six lines argue that the young man's eternal beauty is best compared to the poem itself.
>
> ④ True: The speaker suggests that poetry has the power to reflect and preserve the beloved's beauty.
>
> ⑤ False: Sonnet 18 can be read as honoring both the speaker's beloved and the power of poetry itself in preserving eternal life.

10 ③

> (해설) The engagement with the tradition of using seasons as metaphors. In paragraph [B], "this convention" refers to the tradition of using seasons as symbols in poetry, which the speaker engages with and discusses in "Sonnet 18." The passage mentions the speaker's questioning and rejection of certain aspects of this convention.

11 ④

> (해설) suitable → unsuitable
> The speaker is questioning or challenging the suitability of the conventional symbol (seasons) for his purposes, rather than affirming its suitability. Therefore, "suitable" appears somewhat contradictory in this context.

12 ②

해설 Sonnet 18's Rejection of Traditional Seasonal Metaphors. The passage primarily discusses how "Sonnet 18" engages with and rejects the convention of using seasons as metaphors in poetry. It explores the tension between the speaker and the traditional symbolism of seasons, making option ② the most fitting title.

13 ③

해설 The word "dimmed" in this context implies a reduction in brightness or brilliance, suggesting that the sun's beauty is somewhat obscured or lessened by clouds. The other options—veiled, eclipsed, faded, and obscured—all convey the idea of something being partially or completely hidden or diminished in some way. However, "illuminated" means to be lit up or brightened, which is the opposite of what is being conveyed in the passage. Therefore, "illuminated" does not fit the context.

14 ⑤

해설 The speaker contemplates that the young man's beauty, being more eternal than the sun's, might suggest a rivalry with the divinity, indicating a connection between the sun and divine beauty and importance in Christianity.

15 ①

해설 The passage describes how the speaker occasionally personifies the natural world in the poem, exemplified by the comparison of the sun to the "eye of heaven." However, the heart of the poem lies in the speaker's rejection of personification, particularly in refusing to accept a meaningful resemblance between the summer's day and the young man.

Part 3 Voca Check

1 1 derive from   2 fascinate   3 cover   4 iambic   5 passage of time
6 deliberate   7 line   8 identify   9 take   10 iambic pentameter   11 syllables
12 alternate   13 stressed   14 be made up of   15 iamb   16 metrical
17 foot   18 contain   19 wrestle with   20 capacity

2 1 represent   2 anonymous   3 try out   4 clichéd   5 metaphor   6 simile
7 figure of speech   8 make comparisons   9 differ   10 velvet   11 beloved
12 susceptible to   13 undertone   14 temperance   15 moderation
16 refer to   17 seize upon   18 underscore   19 pleasing   20 nature

3 1 allotted   2 legal contract   3 span   4 implication   5 possess   6 rent
7 complexion   8 personify   9 sense   10 the Renaissance   11 fair
12 exceptionally   13 remnant   14 usage   15 blond-haired   16 stripped of
17 ornament   18 plain   19 contraction   20 address

4 1 assert   2 moderate   3 damage   4 delicate   5 short-lived   6 fade
7 golden   8 dim   9 acknowledge   10 decline   11 chance   12 contrast
13 claim   14 preserve   15 through time   16 admiration   17 immortalize
18 object   19 affection   20 straightforward

5 1 appropriate　2 beloved　3 darling　4 reflect　5 work　6 inevitable
7 decline and death　8 document　9 capture　10 preserve　11 means
12 unfold　13 maturity　14 grounds　15 decay　16 as such　17 represent
18 resurrection　19 reference　20 implicitly

Part 4 Reading Comprehension

1 ①

(해설) 전반적으로 시는 "주장 – 뒷받침 근거"의 패턴을 따르고 있다.

→ The poem presents a clear argument about the superiority of the speaker's friend to a summer's day, and uses a variety of examples and rhetorical strategies to support that argument.

2 ①

(해설) **The natural world is used primarily as a comparison point for the speaker's friend,** and is not given independent value or meaning in the poem.

3 ②

(해설) II. Poet's young beloved friend is addressed to in the poem 'Shall I compare thee to a summer's day', which is an ~~indirect~~ comparison between the friend and a summer's day

(어휘) address …에게 이야기를[말을] 걸다　transcend 초월하다

4 ⑤

5 ⑤

(해설) II. When his beloved friend is compared to 'a summer's day,' he is deemed ~~less beautiful but more enduring~~.

　→ The beloved friend is actually deemed **more beautiful and more temperate** (moderate, pleasant) than a summer's day, not less beautiful. The friend is not only more lovely but also more enduring, as the poem argues that the friend's beauty will be immortalized through poetry.

V. The literary device prominently used in the final two lines is ~~allusion~~.

　→ The literary device prominently used in the final two lines is not allusion, but **rather a combination of metaphor and hyperbole.** The speaker claims that as long as people live and can read the poem, the poem will give life to the friend's beauty, which is an exaggeration to emphasize the power of poetry.

★ allusion 인유
인물이나 사건 혹은 문학 작품, 글의 특정 구절을 직간접적으로 가리키는 것.

(어휘) immortalize 불멸[불후]하게 하다; …에게 영원성[불후의 명성]을 주다
deem A B A를 B로 간주하다 (= A is deemed B A가 B로 간주되다)

6 ③

(해설) ③ ⓗ는 태양이 아니라 시에서 언급하고 있는 그가 흠모하는 사람이다.

⑤ 'death' is being personified as a person who brags or boasts, which gives it human qualities and makes it more tangible and relatable.

7 ③

(해설) ③ The phrase "darling buds" may be interpreted as a term of endearment for the flowers, emphasizing their ~~strength and durability~~.(→ beauty and vulnerability)

(어휘) endearment 친애(의 표시); 총애, 애무; 사랑스러움, 매력 archaic 고풍의, 고체의, 낡은

8 ④

(해설) The poem has **a romantic tone**, with the speaker expressing deep love and admiration for his friend and using the natural world as a metaphor to describe his beauty and worth.

9 ③

(해설) 시인은 자신의 친구를 여름날에 비교하는 것이 적절하고 정확한지 의문을 제기하고 있다. 이어지는 내용에서 자신의 친구가 실제로 자연 세계보다 더 아름답고 오래 가는 이유를 설명하고 있다(뒷받침 근거).

Part 5 Sentence Completion

1 ①

(해설) 인과의 등위접속사 for와 be동사(A = B)를 활용한다.

1) 'S V(결과)... , for S' V'(원인)'

'they must find something to do for either pleasure or profit'에서 알 수 있듯이 미국인들은 언제나 어디서건 무엇인가를 하고 있다. 이는 미국인들이 'inactivity is __부정적__'으로 이해하고 있기 때문이다. 그러므로 빈칸에 들어갈 선택지가 부정적이기 때문에 선택지 ①을 제외하곤 들어갈 수 없다. 나머지 모두 긍정적인 의미를 전달하고 있다.

2) 'A is B(A=B)' 활용

> inactivity is ____A____.
>
> 부정 = 부정

본문에서 'inactivity'는 부정적인 뜻으로 해석되고 있으므로 A에 들어갈 단어도 부정적 의미를 전달하는 단어가 되어야 한다. 고로 선택지 ①이 가장 적절하다.

(해석) 미국인들은 여가 시간의 현명한 활용에 대해 언제나 이야기한다. 이들에게 있어서 활동하지 않는 것은 용서할 수 없는 죄악이기에 즐거움을 위해서건 이익을 얻기 위해서 그들은 무엇인가 할 일을 찾아야만 한다고 생각한다.

2 ④

(해설) 동격의 be동사를 활용한 'A = B'에 따라 동의어 관계를 형성해야 하므로 선택지 ④가 가장 유력하다는 것을 알 수 있다. 다음 두 단계를 거쳐 정확한 답을 제시한다.

> A _____ statement = an _____ comparison.

1) 'comparison'에서 알 수 있듯이, 주어의 빈칸에 들어갈 단어는 두 대상을 전제한다. 고로 선택지에서 두 대상을 비교할 때 활용되는 단어는 선택지 ④의 'metaphorical'을 고를 수 있다.

> A _____ statement = an <u>metaphorical</u> comparison.

2) 'A = B'를 활용하면 'metaphorical = implied'가 된다.

해석 은유적 진술은 두 대상의 내포적 비유이다.

3 ①

해설 다음 두 가지 공식을 활용하자.

1) 관계대명사로 수식을 받는 선행사를 간단히 표현하면 다음과 같다.

'An individual who is _____ = a(an) _____ individual'이므로 다음과 같이 볼 수 있다.

> A(An) _____ individual is incapable of _____.

2) 'be incapable of'는 'can not' 또는 be not'으로 간단히 고칠 수 있으므로, 결국 다음과 같이 반의어를 고르라는 문제가 된다. 선택지에서 반의어로 구성된 것은 ①이다.

> 'A(An) _____ individual is not _____.'
> A ↔ B

해석 구속된 사람은 도망갈 수 없다.

참고

대조를 이루는 전치사구도 함께 외워두자. 아래의 표현은 모두 'A ↔ B'가 된다.

A is at odds with B / A is in line with B / A is in defiance of B / A is in accord with B / A is in contrast to B

4 ⑤

해설 'A is NOT B = A ↔ B'이다.

> _____ something is not _____.
> A ←——————→ B

결국, 'A ≠ B'이므로 'A와 B는 역접/대조의 관계'이다. 선택지 ⑤만이 대조의 관계를 가진다.

해석 진부한 것은 창조성이 결여된 것이다.

5 ④

해설 주부와 술부는 be동사로 연결되어 있다.

$$\text{To } \underline{\hspace{2cm}} = \text{to try to } \underline{\hspace{2cm}} \text{ an individual.}$$
$$A \quad = \quad\quad\quad B$$

결국 'A = B'의 동의어 관계를 고르란 소리다. 문맥에 가장 적절한 짝은 선택지 ④이다.

해석 개종한다는 것은 자신의 종교를 바꾸는 것이다.

6 ④

해설 본문은 'S is to V'구문으로 나가는 문장으로 간략히 'A is B'로 보았을 때, 다음과 같이 볼 수 있다.

S is (=) to V

주어가 부정이면 'to V'의 내용도 부정이 되어야 한다.

---

1) 제시된 본문의 주어가 부정이다.

An example of an illegitimate method of argument

2) 'be'동사 이후의 내용도 부정이 되므로 본문에서 부정적 의미를 전달하는 단어는 'deliberately'이다.

---

to lump dissimilar cases together deliberately under the pretense that the same principles apply to each

---

해석 그릇된 방법의 주장의 예 중 하나는 동일한 법칙을 다른 각자에 적용한다는 구실 아래 의도적으로 서로 다른 사례(경우)를 함께 묶는 것이다.

7 ④

해설 빈칸의 위치는 주어 자리이다. 빈칸에 들어가는 명사의 성격을 'be'동사를 통해 알아내고, 이후 'since(~이기 때문에)'를 활용해 문맥상 가장 적절한 단어를 넣도록 한다.

1) 'A is B(A = B)'의 'be'동사 활용

---

the brain's $\underline{\quad N \quad}$ is all the more remarkable.

→ 밑줄 친 표현은 '훨씬 더 놀라운'이란 의미로 반어법이 아닌 이상 긍정적인 의미를 전달한다.

빈칸의 명사는 긍정적인 단어가 들어갈 것을 예측할 수 있다. 선택지 ③과 ④가 긍정적인 단어에 해당한다.

2) 'since'에 걸리는 내용은 '뇌는 실질적으로 사람이 태어난 후 즉시 퇴화되기 때문에'라고 했다. 고로 1)과 2)를 종합하면, '뇌는 태생 후 바로 노화하기 때문에, 뇌의 장수의 측면은 아주 놀라운 일이다.'라는 문맥이 된다.

해석 뇌는 태생 후 바로 노화하기 때문에, 뇌의 장수의 측면은 아주 놀라운 일이다.

8 ③

해설 'A = B' 및 형용사 후치수식

_____A_____	atmosphere, full of	_____B_____ . 는 다음과 같이 볼 수 있다.
= _____A_____	atmosphere is full of	_____B_____ . (A is full of B 공식 사용)
= _____A_____	atmosphere is	_____B_____ .

고로, 동질의 뉘앙스를 가진 짝을 문맥에 맞게 고르는 문제이다.

선택지 ①의 경우 반대의 의미를 전달하는 단어로 구성되어 있다. 선택지 ③이 답이다. 참고로, 'charged'는 '격앙된, 긴장된, 공격을 당하는'의 의미이다.

해석 이 법은 비난이 가득한 긴장된 분위기에서 제정되었다.

9 ③

해설 A=B와 부연진술의 세미콜론을 활용한다.

1) A includes B에서 B는 A의 속성과 같은 의미를 지녀야 한다.

> A includes B → A = B이므로,
>
> A does not include B → A ↔ B이다.

> The <u>many faults</u> of 대통령 정책 do not include _____B_____ .
>
> A가 부정   ↔   B에 긍정

A와 B는 서로 대조적 관계이므로 B의 내용은 긍정적 내용이 와야 한다. 선택지 ③과 ⑤가 긍정적 답안으로 우선 골라낼 수 있다.

2) 세미콜론 이후의 부연진술은 앞의 내용과 같은 맥락을 전개하고 있으므로, 대통령의 "많은 실수가 포함된" 정책의 결과는 부정적인 표현이어야 한다.

> the <u>bankruptcy</u> of dozens of firms daily

대통령이 실시하려는 정책이 '경제 정책'임을 감안하면 선택지 ③이 답임을 알 수 있다.

해석 대통령의 경제정책의 많은 실수들은 일관성을 포함하지 않는 것이다. 기업환경을 개선할 필요가 있다는 발언 뒤에 수 십 개의 회사들이 도산하는 원인이 되는 제안이 나왔다.

10 ④

해설 A is indicative of B에서 B는 A와 같은 속성을 드러낸다.

> _____ and _____ is indicative of his <u>keen</u> and <u>incisive</u>
>
> A   B   =   C   D

고로, 'A = C', 'B = D'이므로,

> trenchant = keen
>
> penetrating = incisive

해석 신랄하고, 예리한 마음을 나타내는 그의 발언은 정통을 찔렀고, 날카로웠다.

Part 2 Text Reading

Quick Quiz

1 handicapped

2 social equality

3 above average

4 ①

해설 The passage suggests that the world presented by Vonnegut, despite its initial appearance of equality, hints at something sinister, possibly an <u>authoritarian</u> nature, given the mention of handicapping, vigilance, and government interference.

5 ③

해설 ⓒ compromised (손상된, 위태롭게 된): jeopardized

intact 본래대로의, 손대지 않은(untouched), 완전한

The word "compromised" implies that something has been weakened or damaged, which fits well with the idea of George's strength and cognition being affected by the handicaps imposed by the government. Therefore, replacing "compromised" with "intact" contradicts the intended meaning of the sentence.

6 intelligence / equal

7 intelligent

8 ④

해설 Based on George's reaction, which contrasts with Hazel's description of being "little envious," the most appropriate word for the blank is "sadistic." This implies a tendency to derive pleasure from the suffering or unhappiness of others, aligning with Hazel's expression of envy towards George's painful situation. Therefore, the answer is ④ sadistic.

9 equality / handicaps / ordinary / equal / exceptional / exceptional(= extraordinary)

10 ②

해설 The excerpt suggests that Hazel shares similarities with Diana Moon Glampers, implying that the country is being run by people just as clueless as Hazel. Therefore, the most appropriate words for the blanks are "disturbing" and "clueless." This indicates that such similarity is unsettling and that they are ignorant. Hence, the answer is ② disturbing – clueless.

① unsettling 마음을 산란하게 하는, 동요시키는, 소란하게 만드는 – conscious 의식의
② disturbing 교란시키는, 불온한 – clueless 아주 멍청한
③ comforting 격려가 되는, 기운을 돋우는, 위안이 되는 - ignorant 무지한, 무학의, 무식한

④ reassuring 안심시키는, 기운을 돋우는, 마음 든든한, 위안을 주는 – naive 순진한, 미경험의
⑤ pleasing 유쾌한, 호감이 가는, 붙임성 있는 – brainless 머리가 나쁜, 우둔한

11 ③

(해설) inferior → superior

'average' 지능을 가진 Hazel이 오히려 우월한 George을 안타깝게 여기면서 "she does not mind George not being equal to her"라고 말하고 있으므로 안타까움의 대상인 George는 inferior가 아니라 superior로 표현해야 한다.

12 ④

(해설) 산탄총용 탄약이 상징하는 의미를 묻는 내용이다. "While he is not being literally shot for his strength"에서 알 수 있듯이 문자 그대로 "총을 맞은 것은 아니지만" George의 목에 탄약은 "폭력"을 상기한다는 것을 파악할 수 있다.

13 ②

(해설) ② George, despite his superior intelligence, ironically supports a society with limitations rather than one that allows for individual competition, highlighting the paradoxical nature of his preference for equality through enforced handicaps.

14 ⑤

(해설) comply with → protest against

지능이 뛰어난 George가 만약 정부가 생각을 통제하는 라디오를 귀에 틀지 않았고, 곰곰이 생각할 수 있다면(If George were able to think in peace for a few hours) 그가 옹호하는 법이 얼마나 말도 되지 않는지를 알 것이라고 했으므로 이어지는 내용의 그가 "순응하는"에 해당하는 comply with는 문맥에 적절하지 않다. if he could와 같이 가정의 상황이므로 protest against와 같은 표현이 더 적절하다.

15 ⑤

(해설) 본문에서 George는 시민으로서 자신이 해야 할 의무를 잘 수행하는 "바른" 시민으로 묘사되고 있다. 하지만, 그가 자신을 짓누르는 handicaps의 무게, 부담을 느끼지 못하는 멍청한 사람으로 묘사되고 있지는 않다.

16 comfort / removes

(해설) comfort 대신 두 단어로 구성된 표현을 쓰자면 care for도 가능하다.

17 ③

(해설) The announcer is not performing his role properly. But, in Hazel's words, who argue that they should rather get a raise for "not standing out", the government tries every possible way to suppress whatever it is about them that makes them exceptional.

So the correct answer is ③ suppress – exceptional.

① quell (억)누르다, 가라앉히다, 진압[진정]하다, 끝나게 하다, 소멸시키다 - inferior 열등한
② crush 눌러서 뭉개다, 짓밟다, 으깨다 - ordinary 일반적인
③ suppress 억압하다, (반란 등을) 가라앉히다, 진압하다 – exceptional 예외적인, 범상한
④ support – special
⑤ encourage – remarkable

18 ③

🔲해설 The ballerina's apology for her natural beauty and graceful voice, which are considered unfair advantages in the society depicted in the passage, reflects the pressure for compliance with the government-mandated handicap system. By apologizing and making her voice "absolutely uncompetitive," she conforms to the societal norms of equality, where any form of superiority, whether physical or vocal, is suppressed.

① zeal 열중, 열의, 열심; 열성; 열 – ill-mannered 버릇없는
② compliance 승낙, 순종 – uncivil 버릇없는, 무례한, 난폭한《말씨 등》; 야만적인, 미개한
③ negativities 부정성 - equal 평등한
④ antagonism 적대감 - polite 공손한
⑤ suspicion 의심 – impolite 무례함

19 dangerous (또는 동의어 표현이면 정답)

🔲해설 In the given passage, the announcer describes Harrison Bergeron as a genius and an athlete who is under handicapped, meaning that he has not been subjected to the same handicaps as others in society. The announcer then suggests that Harrison should be regarded as extremely dangerous.

20 ②

🔲해설 This metaphor shows that no matter how many handicaps you put on people, some of their talents can still outshine those of others.

🔲어휘 outshine …보다 강하게 빛나다; …보다 우수하다(surpass); …을 무색케 하다

21 이 은유는 사람들에게 아무리 많은 핸디캡을 부여하더라도 그들의 재능 중 일부는 여전히 다른 사람들의 재능을 능가하고, 각 개인의 개별성과 능력을 100% 통제할 수 없다는 의미.

22 ①

🔲해설 "Harrison Bergeron" by Kurt Vonnegut Jr. is a satire that depicts a dystopian society in the future depicted according to science fictions. The narrator tells about the main protagonist Harrison Bergeron who is physically and mentally superior to others. **In order for the people to be all equal, the government made him wear disguises. Concealing his real being is their way of enforcing equality and its policies among all people. Written from an unseen narrator, the story is a satirizing of the ways people would go to extreme lengths just to be deemed equal.**

23 ②

🔲해설 The correct pairing for the blanks in the given context would be:
· reflecting his **extraordinary attributes**
· to mask his **extraordinary looks**
· and so many weights to **calibrate** his prodigious strength
Therefore, the correct choice is ② extraordinary attributes – extraordinary looks – calibrate.

🔲어휘 calibrate (…용으로) 조정하다, 대상을 (…에) 맞추고 궁리하다.
run-of-the-mill: ordinary and not special or exciting in any way

24 ⑤

해설 The sentence uses alliteration, a literary device where there is a repetition of consonant sounds, in this case, the "s" sound in "Scrap metal was hung." The alliteration adds a rhythmic quality to the sentence and emphasizes the visual and auditory impact of the scrap metal on the character's appearance.

25 ⑤

해설 Option ⑤ is not appropriate as it misrepresents the comparison; the passage actually describes Harrison tearing the straps "like wet tissue paper," emphasizing the ease with which he overcomes the supposedly strong and restrictive elements.

26 ②

해설 Personification attributes human-like qualities or actions to non-human entities. In this case, the phrase "his own home had danced to the same crashing tune" personifies the home by suggesting that it "danced" to a "crashing tune," giving it human-like characteristics.

27 ① False ② True ③ True

해설 ① False: The passage describes Harrison and the girl defying not only the laws of the land but also the laws of gravity and motion. Their movements are described as joyful and graceful, and they are not depicted as attempting to impose boundaries or control over their actions. Instead, they embrace the freedom and liberation from constraints.

② True: The simile "They leaped like deer on the moon" emphasizes the weightlessness and otherworldly quality of their movements. Deer on the moon would experience a lack of gravity similar to what Harrison and the girl are experiencing, enhancing the sense of freedom and exuberance in their leaps.

③ True: The culmination of their leaps is described as their intention to "kiss the ceiling," which symbolizes their rebellion against constraints and their reaching towards the seemingly impossible. This action represents their defiance of limitations and their desire to transcend boundaries.

28 ③

해설 George의 의도: "당신 말에 전적으로 동의해."

Hazel의 이해: "또 말해 줄래요?"

Part 3 Voca Check

1
1 unceasing / bursts / vigilance / toy with / elusive
2 breakthroughs / relentless / winced / established / transmit
3 momentum / afoot / over

2 1 attest to 2 compromise 3 placate 4 bear a resemblance to 5 chime

6 glimmeringly   7 salute   8 white   9 rim   10 weigh   11 get away with
12 cheat on   13 blankly   14 unsettling   15 disturbing   16 quell
17 syndicate   18 potent   19 unsettling   20 reflect

3 1 clueless   2 comforting   3 ignorant   4 reassuring   5 naive   6 pleasing
7 brainless   8 interrupt   9 impediment   10 quell   11 crush   12 hideous
13 apologize   14 luminous   15 timeless   16 suspicion   17 plot   18 flash
19 whang   20 hang

4 1 harness   2 symmetry   3 neatness   4 consternation   5 shave off
6 crashing   7 clanking   8 brainless   9 crash   10 clownish   11 delicacy
12 bellow   13 hobble   14 snap   15 willow   16 cower   17 snap
18 delicate   19 reason with   20 crashing

5 1 blinding   2 scramble   3 strip   4 barons and dukes and earls   5 snatch
6 slam   7 gravely   8 synchronize   9 explosion   10 wince   11 shift
12 burn out   13 reel   14 swivel   15 flounce   16 gambol   17 spin
18 neutralize

Part 4 Reading Comprehension

Reading Comprehension 1

1 ③

해설 This statement contradicts the information provided in the passage. The passage clearly states that Hazel has a "perfectly average intelligence," which means her intelligence is average, not overly intelligent.

2 ① - ② ② - ⓒ ③ - ⑦ ④ - ⓒ

3 ③

해설 ㉣ unfairly → perfectly
㉤ there was something weird about it → it was nice

4 ④

해설 This explanation is not supported by the text. George's inability to fully understand or remember what is happening around him is due to the government-mandated handicap radio in his ear, which emits sharp noises every twenty seconds to disrupt his thoughts. This constant interruption prevents him from fully engaging his intellect rather than suggesting inherent intellectual inferiority.

5 ⑤

해설 This option best fits the context as it suggests that George's contemplation on the notion that dancers shouldn't be handicapped was interrupted by another sharp noise emitted by the radio in his ear, causing him to wince and preventing him from further exploring his vague notion.

6 ③

해설 This option accurately reflects the critique of Hazel's similarity to Diana Moon Glampers. It suggests that Hazel's resemblance to the Handicapper General is disturbing because it implies that the country is being run by people who are <u>just as clueless as Hazel</u>. Additionally, it highlights the irony in Hazel's confidence in her understanding of "normal" despite her ludicrous suggestion regarding the government's actions. Therefore, option ③ is the correct pairing of words to fill in the blanks.

어휘 distinction 우수성

7 ⑤

해설 ㉮: This explanation highlights the irony in Hazel's statement, considering her own lack of intelligence and discernible gifts compared to George.

㉯: Hazel이 George를 질투한다는 내용은 없다.

㉰: This explanation emphasizes the disparity in cognitive abilities between George and Hazel, indicating that true equality, especially in terms of intellectual capacity, is unattainable.

8 ④

해설 the forty-seven pounds of birdshot in a canvas bag, which was padlocked around George's neck에서 신체적으로도 뛰어난 사람임을 파악할 수 있다.

Reading Comprehension 2

1 ⑤

해설 There is no indication in the text that Hazel's suggestion is part of a secret scheme to overthrow the government. Her suggestion seems to stem from genuine concern for George's well-being, rather than from any ulterior motive. Therefore, option ⑤ is the correct answer.

2 ①

해설 ⓗ In this context, "a bargain" means *to pay more than you should*.

→ bargain은 "싼 거래"를 의미한다.

Ⓐ George's account of the consequences of law-breaking to Hazel proves that the government attempt of controlling everyone's intelligence is a complete failure.

→ 정부의 통제가 완전한 실패라고 보는 것은 옳지 않다. 오히려 굉장히 효율적으로 통제가 이뤄지고 있다고 봐야 한다.

Ⓞ The fact that Hazel couldn't answer George's question shows why Hazel isn't physically handicapped unlike George.

→ 사이렌 소리에 생각이 흐름의 끊긴 사람은 George이고, Hazel이 오히려 George가 한 질문에 답변을 함.

3 ③

해설 (b): Hazel's statement "he tried. That's the big thing. He tried to do the best he could" emphasizes the value of effort and compassion over intelligence or success.

(c): Hazel's statement "He tried to do the best he could with what God gave him" indicates that <u>she holds a great respect or admiration for the act of putting in one's utmost effort or doing the best one can.</u>

The other options, (a) and (d), are <u>not directly</u> supported by the underlined sentences:

(a): There is <u>no explicit illustration of the absurdity of trying to make everyone equal in Hazel's statement.</u>

(d): Hazel's statement <u>does not indicate a full understanding or discussion of the difficulty in enforcing laws that make everyone equal.</u>

4 ⑤

해설 ㉠ is indeed about Harrison escaping from jail, <u>as indicated by the announcement made by the ballerina.</u> (correct)

㉡ illustrates how the insistence on total equality manifests in citizens modifying or hiding their special attributes, <u>such as the ballerina altering her voice to be uncompetitive.</u> (correct)

㉢ describes Harrison's enormous and hideous appearance, <u>which serves to promote awareness of his danger to the public</u>, aligning with the government's aim to maintain total equality by handicapping those deemed "too exceptional."(correct)

㉣ does indeed reveal that Harrison has exceptional abilities and that the government's attempt to enforce total equality is flawed. <u>Harrison's ability to outgrow hindrances faster than the Handicapper General (H-G) men can impose them suggests his exceptional intelligence or resourcefulness, highlighting the imperfection in the government's control over ensuring total equality.</u>(correct)

5 ④

해설 The photo serves as an intimidating portrayal of Harrison, aiming to suppress any inclination towards rebellion or non-conformity among viewers. It underscores the consequences faced by those who do not conform to societal norms and the handicaps imposed upon them.

① terrifying 무서운 - publicize 선전[공표, 광고]하다
② entertaining 즐거움을 주는 - stifle 숨막히게 하다, 방해하다, 억누르다
③ enlightening 계몽적인 – repress 억누르다, 저지[제지]하다, (반란 등을) 진압하다
④ intimidating 겁을 주는 - suppress 억압하다, (반란 등을) 가라앉히다, 진압하다
⑤ terrorizing 공포감을 주는 – soothe 달래다

6 ②

해설 By removing his own handicaps and those of the ballerina, Harrison demonstrates to the audience <u>what individuals can achieve without the constraints imposed by the government-mandated handicaps</u>. This action briefly reveals <u>the potential for greatness that exists when people are liberated from artificial limitations.</u>

7 ④

해설 ④ Harrison is depicted as an exaggerated alpha male, a breathtakingly strong man, ~~who is somehow reluctant to strive for power~~.

→ In the text, Harrison is not depicted as reluctant to strive for power; rather, he boldly declares himself as the Emperor and demands obedience from everyone. He exhibits a strong desire for power and dominance, which contradicts the idea of him being reluctant in this aspect.

Reading Comprehension 3

1 ①

해설 The narrator's tone can best be described as ① satirical. The text presents a satirical commentary on the idea of enforced equality and the extreme measures taken to achieve it.

2 ②

해설 The effect of the repetition of the phrase "nobody was" is to ② underscore a point. By repeatedly emphasizing that nobody was smarter, better looking, stronger, or quicker than anybody else, the text highlights the extreme nature of the enforced equality in this society.

3 ④

해설 In the first paragraph, the author employs ④ parallel construction. The sentences follow a parallel structure, repeating the pattern "Nobody was [adjective] than anybody else" to emphasize the idea of universal equality in various aspects.
Nobody was smarter than anybody else.
Nobody was better looking than anybody else.
Nobody was stronger or quicker than anybody else.

4 ④

해설 I. This statement is correct. The first paragraph indeed describes how equality is achieved through constitutional amendments and the vigilance of government agents.

II. This statement is incorrect. The passage does not imply that downward leveling made people original and unique. Instead, it portrays a society where everyone is forced to be equal in every way, with any deviations from this equality being suppressed.

III. This statement is incorrect. In ⓛ, it is described how individuals are handicapped to prevent them from taking unfair advantage of their abilities, which suggests that the government aims to maintain control rather than allowing individuals to reach their full potential.

IV. This statement is correct. In ②, the sentence "His thoughts fled in panic, like bandits from a burglar alarm" uses personification (attributing human-like qualities to thoughts) and a simile (comparing the fleeing thoughts to bandits fleeing from a burglar alarm).

V. This statement is <u>incorrect</u>. The statement conveys the character's thoughts about the handicapped ballerinas, which shows George is a lot more intellectual than "normal" Hazel.

5 ④

【해설】 This is correct because <u>the announcer, whose job relies heavily on clear speech, has a serious speech impediment, which is ironic.</u>

6 ⑤

【해설】 And **she had to apologize at once for her voice**, which was a very unfair voice for a woman to use. Her voice was a warm, luminous, timeless melody. "Excuse me—"she said, and she began again, making her voice absolutely ⓓ<del>competitive</del> (→ uncompetitive).

밑줄 친 표현에서 알 수 있듯이 발레리나는 자신의 아름다운 목소리에 대해 사과를 하는 모습이 언급되고 있으므로 자신의 목소리를 의도적으로 "uncompetitive"하게 표현할 것을 파악할 수 있다.

7 ③

【해설】 * Jenny: Based on the underlined part ㉠, I can tell that the person in charge of getting the photo up on the screen may be incapable of performing his task properly, similar to the announcers with a stutter in this fiction.

→ This statement is <u>correct</u>. The underlined part ㉠ describes the erratic display of the photograph on the screen, which implies incompetence on the part of the person in charge.

* Max: Metaphor and alliteration are used in the underlined sentence ㉡ in order to show how scary and grotesque Harrison Bergeron looks.

→ This statement is <u>correct</u>. The use of metaphor ("Halloween and hardware") and alliteration ("Halloween and hardware") emphasizes the frightening appearance of Harrison Bergeron.

* Sophia: According to the underlined sentence ㉢, Harrison Bergeron must be one of the most intelligent inventors who design a variety of handicaps.

→ This statement is <u>incorrect</u>. The underlined sentence ㉢ describes the excessive handicaps worn by Harrison Bergeron, but it does not necessarily imply that he is an intelligent inventor.

* Micheal: Personification and simile are used in common in the underlined sentences ㉣ and ㉤.

→ This statement is <u>incorrect</u>. While there is personification in ㉣ ("The photograph of Harrison Bergeron on the screen jumped again and again"), there is no simile used in this passage. Additionally, simile is not used in ㉤.

* Elizabeth: When Harrison Bergeron yells, like the underlined sentence ㉥, it represents that he is rebelling against authority.

→ This statement is <u>correct</u>. In the passage from "Harrison Bergeron" by Kurt Vonnegut, when Harrison cries out, "I am the Emperor! Everybody must do what I say at once!"

he is clearly rebelling against authority.

8 ②

> 해설 (B) wore → wear
>
> require that S (should) 원형동사 (~해야 한다의 당위적 표현)
>
> (D) must have been → must be

Part 5 Sentence Completion

1 ④

> 해설 A is as 형용사 as B는 A = B이다.

The credit-card cash advance = the automated teller machine

---

the automated teller machine의 특징이 곧 빈칸의 주어인 the credit-card cash advance이다. the automated teller machine의 특징을 가장 잘 드러내는 단어는 선택지 ④ 밖에 없다. 이 문제의 선택지는 전형적인 반의어와 동의어를 제시하는 경우로 일반적으로 이런 경우 반의어와 동의어로 구성된 선택지 중 하나가 답일 가능성이 높다. 즉, 의도적으로 빈칸의 단어와 반의어를 선택지로 구성하는 경우가 많다. 선택지 ③과 ④가 반의어 관계이다.

> 해석 신용카드 현금대출은 자동입출금기계 만큼이나 널리 퍼지고 있다.

2 ④

> 해설 A be B는 A = B임을 활용한다.

---

anxiety about tests = a major _____⊖_____ to strong performance

---

선택지의 단어가 부정인 것을 be동사를 활용하면 쉽게 알 수 있다. 선택지의 단어를 살펴보면,

① incentive 긍정
② impact   문맥에 따라 긍정/부정이 달라진다.
③ spur   동기부여(긍정), 선동(부정) 등 다양한 뜻으로 쓰인다. 문맥에 따라 긍정과 부정을 결정해야 한다. 굳이 하나를 정하라면, 긍정에 조금 더 무게를 싣고 접근한다.
④ obstacle 부정

선택지를 구성한 출제자의 의도를 보자면, 정답의 반의어로 선택지 ①을 준 것을 알 수 있다.

> 해석 많은 학생들에게, 시험에 대한 걱정은 좋은 성적에 방해가 된다. 만약 그렇다면, 당신은 당신의 걱정을 다루기 위한 몇몇 전략들을 세워야 할 필요가 있다.

3 ⑤

> 해설 문장완성의 가장 기본적인 형태이다. 문맥에 가장 적절한 어휘를 선정할 수 있는지 묻고 있다. be동사를 활용하여, A is B는 A = B임을 활용한다. 친절이란 바로 공무원이 지녀야 할 자질이 된다.

$$A(kindness) = B(quality)$$

해석 친절은 공무원이 지녀야 할 가장 중요한 자질이다.

4 ①

해설 첫 번째 문장에서 현상이 드러나고 있다. 이어지는 문장은 이런 현상에 대한 예가 많다는 내용이다. 고로, 빈칸에 들어갈 단어는 바로 앞에서 전개된 '현상'을 나타낸다.

adopt the **accepted** way of thinking = intellectual **dependence**

기존의 방식을 그대로 받아들이는 내용이므로, 이전의 사고에 '의존'한다는 선택지 ①이 가장 적절하다.

해석 많은 사람들은 자신들이 속한 집단의 예의범절을 쉽게 받아들이는 것만큼이나 자신들의 집단 내에서 용인된 사고방식을 쉽게 받아들인다. (따라서) 그들의 지적 의존성의 사례들을 찾아보기는 어렵지 않다.

5 ④

해설 A and B는 A = B임을 활용한다.

not _____ and should be avoided
A   =   B

회피해야 한다는 의미에서 A는 not을 포함해 부정적인 어감의 표현이 되어야 하므로 A는 긍정적인 의미의 표현이 되어야 한다. 즉, 관계대명사 that의 수식을 받는 비판이 어떠하기에 피해야 할지 생각하면 된다. 선택지 ②는 빈칸에 들어갈 품사가 되지 못하고, 선택지 ③은 부정이므로 소거할 수 있다.

해석 개선할 점을 제시하지 않은 채 끌어내리기만 하는 비판은 건설적이 못되며 마땅히 피해야 한다.

6 ①

해설 연설가가 관중을 압도했다는 점에서 관중들이 어떤 반응을 보일지, 그리고 이것이 의미하는 것이 무엇인지 생각해 본다. A indicates B는 A = B임을 활용하여 쉽게 접근이 가능하다.

A	=	B
nodding their heads	indicates	affirmation

해석 그 연설가는 청중을 완전히 압도했다. 관중들은 그의 말 하나하나를 놓치지 않고 듣고자 했으며 고개를 끄덕이며 긍정을 표시했다.

7 ①

해설 사전적 정의를 바탕으로 문제를 만든 고전적 형태로 본문에선 관용어구까지 함께 묻고 있다. if절의 내용을 풀어쓴 부분이 바로 주절이므로 다음과 같이 볼 수 있다.

> If A, B → B는 A를 풀어쓴 내용이므로 결국 A = B이다.

"남의 일을 넘겨받는다"는 'fill someone's shoes'라는 표현을 알아야 한다.

(해석) 당신이 남의 책임을 인계받는다면 남이 과거에 했던 일을 그 사람만큼 잘 하는 것이다.

8 ①

(해설) 전치사구의 동사 수식과 등위의 and를 활용한다.

1) 전치사구 수식

> V   전치사 + 명사

수식하는 내용은 수식받는 내용의 의미를 한정하므로 전치사구와 동사가 같은 맥락의 표현이 되므로 decline into A에서 A의 내용은 부정의 내용으로 채워진다. 그러므로 첫 번째 빈칸이 부정의 뉘앙스를 전달하는 명사임을 알 수 있다.

2) A and B는 A = B임을 활용

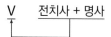

> 부정적 명사 **and** uncertainty

고로 선택지 ①, ③, ④로 답지를 줄일 수 있다. 주어진 문맥상 'uncertainty'와 가장 잘 어울리는 명사는 선택지 ①이 된다.

(해석) 잠 못 이루고 불행한 느낌에 그는 집을 나와 조용히 거닐며, 이 날의 분위기가 더 이상의 불화와 불확실성으로 떨어지지(발전하지) 않기를 희망했다.

9 ③

(해설) 타동사 'observe'에 걸리는 목적어인 strict discipline과 같은 맥락의 빈칸의 단어를 고르는 문제이다. 문장에서 활용된 'strict'란 단어는 학생이 따라야 할 준수사항으로 긍정적인 의미로 파악되고 있다.

> observe strict discipline and <u>decorous</u> behavior

(해석) 모든 학생들에게 학교 내에서나 밖에서나 엄격히 규칙을 준수하고 예의바른 행동을 할 것을 요구하며, 또 그렇게 할 것이라 기대하고 있다.

10 ①

(해설) 'A and B'에서 and는 A와 B라는 같은 성질의 단어를 연결한다. 그러므로 'tedious'와 가장 유사한 단어를 넣은 문제가 된다.

> <u>arduous</u> and tedious
> A   =   B

(해석) 그 일은 정신적/물리적으로 힘들었다.

Part 3 Voca Check

1 1 exemplar　2 clarity　3 interplay　4 apotheosis　5 drape　6 muted
7 depict　8 hemlock　9 embrace　10 fierce

2 1 muted　2 figure　3 tableau　4 vivid　5 executioner　6 stoic
7 commitment　8 ethical　9 monarchy　10 reformer

3 1 install　2 akin　3 antiquity　4 execute　5 unveil　6 commission　7 wildly
8 identify　9 Xanthippe　10 distress

4 1 stage　2 teach　3 echo　4 popularize　5 signal　6 explode
7 re-contextualize　8 idealized　9 position　10 frozen

5 1 lateral　2 gave way to　3 fell out　4 painstakingly　5 terror　6 rigorous
7 betrayed　8 construction　9 blunt　10 render

Part 4 Reading Comprehension

Reading Comprehension 1

1 ⑤

해설 ⑤ ~~three~~ reasons why Socrates was sentenced to death

소크라테스가 사형을 당하는 이유는 두 개가 언급되고 있다.

Socrates had been convicted in Athenian court of failing to acknowledge the gods of the city(이유1) and corrupting the city's youth(이유2) and sentenced to death by drinking hemlocks.

① 근거: So much jumps out at me right away: the clarity of the scene; the fierce gesture of the man in the middle; the interplay of the chalice; and the hand that reaches for it; the angles of the light and the men; the soft draping garments; the bare flat stone wall.

② 근거: Socrates could have escaped into exile, but instead he chooses to die taking the opportunity to teach his final lesson, that death is not to be feared by the philosopher, but embraced as an apotheosis of the soul.

③ 근거: 세 번째 문단

④ 근거: 네 번째 문단

2 ①

어휘 be brought to the fore 유명해지다, 중요한 사람 또는 대상이 되다

3 ④

4 ②

해설 왼쪽에서 오른쪽으로 그림을 이해할 때 아래와 같은 상황임.

The philosopher is thinking back on that fatal day. Behind him the death of Socrates plays out as memory—vibrant, beautiful, and bittersweet.

5 ③

해설 David 작가 자신의 이름을 Crito 아래 적었다는 것은 자신이 강인한 도덕적 이상인 소크라테스보다 신념이 약하지만 그의 다리를 잡고 있는 Crito와 같은 인물로 인식하고 있음을 추론할 수 있다. 그러므로 이를 가장 잘 반영한 선택지는 ③이다.

6 ①

해설 Neoclassical art is much more ornamental and theatrical in style compared to Rococo art.

근거: Neoclassicism, as rendered by David, made its points strongly and severely. This was in direct opposition to the dominant Rococo style that reflected the ornate and hedonistic lifestyles of the monarchy.

7 ④

해설 "he"는 Raphael의 School of Athens에 등장하는 플라톤을 지칭한다.

Reading Comprehension 2

1 ④

해설 muted는 "(색상이) 부드러운"이란 뜻이다.

2 ③

해설 박스에 제시된 문장은 앞에서 전개된 내용을 뒤집는 내용으로 오히려 죽음을 재촉하는 Socrates의 "반항적" 태도를 드러낸다. 해당 내용은 임박한 죽음에 대해서 전혀 신경을 쓰지 않는다는 내용에 이어지는 (다)에 들어가는 것이 적절하다. "David idealizes him."도 박스 안의 제시문에 이어지는 적절한 내용임을 파악할 수 있다.

3 ③

해설 The color of the painting is ~~more softened towards the center and becomes vibrant in the edges~~.

→ 중간으로 갈수록 색이 더 강하다.

4 ④

5 ③

해설 ㉠ This statement accurately reflects the understanding that the painting "The Death of Socrates" by Jacques Louis David represents the Neoclassical style, which emphasizes classical Greek and Roman themes, clear composition, and idealized forms.

ⓒ This is correct. Plato discusses the death of Socrates in multiple dialogues, including "The Phaedo" and "The Crito," as mentioned in the passage.

ⓔ This is also true. While Socrates discusses the immortality of the soul and the idea of an afterlife in Plato's dialogues, he doesn't express certainty about it. However, he does assert that death is not to be feared by the philosopher, as it represents a transition and purification of the soul, as mentioned in the passage.

6 ③, ④

해설 ⓒ had corrupted → corrupting
의미상 had been convicted에 걸리는 것이 아니라 failing에 걸리는 병치구조임.

ⓔ must've escaped → could've escaped
내용상 could've escaped가 옳음.

7 ③

해설 앞 문장에서 언급하고 있는 Socratic method는 자신이 알고 있다는 지식에 이견을 제기함으로 발생하는 모순을 찾으려고 하는 행위다. 즉, 모순을 통해서 증명되는 것은 "내가 아는 것이 없었다"이다. 그러므로 빈칸에 들어갈 표현은 "you know nothing at all"이다.

8 ⑤

해설 ㉠ 근거: For David, Socrates is a symbol of strength over passion, of stoic commitment to an abstract principle even in the face of death.

㉡ 근거: But this is the ethical message David sought to offer the French, two years before the French Revolution, as the monarchy was in decline and reformers ached to install a democracy akin to that of Socrates' own time in Greek antiquity, or the United States which had just executed its own revolution five years prior.

㉢ Thomas Jefferson himself ~~was at the scene of the event,~~ ~~which inspired him to overthrow the government.~~

㉣ 근거: David had already made his names with another severe moralistic canvas, The Oath of the Horatii, which effectively invented the neoclassical style.

㉤ But this is the ethical message David sought to offer the French, **two years before the French Revolution**, as the monarchy was in decline and reformers ached to install a democracy akin to that of Socrates' own time in Greek antiquity, or the United States which had just executed its own revolution five years prior. Indeed, Thomas Jefferson himself was present at the unveiling of this painting at the Salon of 1787.
→ 프랑스 대혁명보다는 2년 전 / 미국의 독립혁명은 5년 전
그러므로 프랑스 대혁명보다는 미국의 독립혁명이 먼저 일어났다.

9 ③

해설 Based on the given content, the most convincing inference about the artist's intention is provided by the opinion of 춘식 (③). He suggests that by placing the elderly depiction of Plato on the left side of the picture, the artist intends for viewers to perceive the events of the time as if they were "recalling" through Plato's point of view. This implies that the artist seeks to reconstruct the events of the past from Plato's perspective through the artwork. While other opinions are plausible, this interpretation best encapsulates the deeper meaning of the artwork.

10 ②

해설 ㉠ failing to acknowledge the gods of the city = impiety

㉢ license의 뜻 주의 할 것.

license 멋대로 함, ; (행동의) 자유

11 ③, ④

해설 Aesthetic austerity의 정의를 하면 다음과 같다.

refers to a style or approach in art <u>characterized by simplicity, restraint, and minimalism</u>. It often involves <u>the use of clean lines, limited ornamentation, and a focus on essential elements rather than embellishment</u>.

위 밑줄 친 정의에 해당하는 보기는 ㉢과 ㉣이다.

㉢ David is renowned for <u>his use of bold, strong lines and minimal ornamentation</u>.

㉣ Stripped of all color, tonality, and treatment of light, this drawing <u>accentuates his simplistic approach to his craft</u>.

12 ⑤

해설 render는 본문에서 "표현하다"의 의미로 쓰이고 있다.

13 ③

해설 ~~Neoclassicism~~(→ Rococo) is characterized by lightness, elegance, and an exuberant use of curving natural forms in ornamentation.

→ This statement is the furthest from the characteristics of Neoclassicism described in the passage. <u>Neoclassical art is known for its emphasis on clarity, restraint, and austerity, often favoring straight lines and simple, balanced compositions over the exuberant ornamentation and curving natural forms typically associated with other styles like Rococo</u>. Therefore, the idea of "lightness, elegance, and an exuberant use of curving natural forms" contradicts the principles of Neoclassicism outlined in the passage.

Part 5 Sentence Completion

1 ⑤

해설 동질의 성격을 드러내는 'and'를 활용한다. 'A and B'에서 A와 B는 서로 같은 의미를 전달하는 단어의 짝으로 구성된다.

> a <u>gregarious</u> animal and tends to <u>associate with others</u>

해석 인간은 근본적으로 사회적 동물로 다른 사람과 어울려 지낸다.

2 ①

해설 'A, B and C'에서 A, B와 C는 같은 성격의 단어로 병렬구성 된다.

해석 경찰견은 특히나 후각이 아주 예민한 종의 개다. 이들은 땅의 흔적을 맡아 사람을 따라가는 능력을 가지고 있다. 때로 경찰들은 실종 아이, 탈옥한 죄수 또는 범죄자의 위치를 알아내기 위해 이들을 사용한다.

3 ②

해설 대조를 이루는 'Unlike'의 활용과 동질의 단어를 연결하는 'and'를 활용한다.

1) 동질의 단어 연결

carefully weighted and <u>planned</u>

→ 바로 앞의 carefully weighted와 가장 근사한 의미를 전달하는 단어가 빈칸에 들어가면 된다.

2) 대조를 이루는 대상

<u>Dante</u> → carefully weighed and planned
↕ 대조를 이룸
<u>Goethe</u> → immediacy and enthusiasm (즉시성 및 일시성)

해석 깊은 생각과 계획적인 단테의 글과는 달리, 괴테의 글은 항상 즉시성과 (순간적) 열정을 담고 있다.

4 ③

해설 동질의 성격/특성을 연결하는 and를 활용한다.

_____ and fewer material goods
A = 적은 물질적 소유

fewer material goods와 같은 맥락의 내용을 담은 선택지는 ③이다.

해석 모든 사람이 거대한 집과 새로운 자동차를 꿈꾸는 것은 아니다. 최근 단출한 삶과 적은 물질적 소유를 향한 세계적인 추세가 이어지고 있다.

5 ④

해설 빈칸에 영향을 미치는 요소는 두 가지이다.

1) 긍정적 주부는 긍정적인 서술부를 이끈다.
   'Christmas gift-giving'을 긍정적으로 해석할 수 있는 근거는 'and' 이후의 동사 'warm'이다.

2) 그러므로 동질의 성격을 연결하는 등위접속사 'and'에 의해 앞의 빈칸도 긍정적인 단어를 골라야 하는 동시에 'the wheels'와 함께 매끄럽게 쓰일 수 있는 동사를 찾아야 한다. 고로, 선택지 ④가 가장 적절하다.

해석 크리스마스 때 선물을 주는 행위는 상업이란 바퀴에 윤활유 역할을 하는 동시에 주고받는 사람들의 마음을 따뜻하게 만든다.

6 ③

해설 동질의 성격을 연결하는 등위접속사 'and'와 앞의 근거로 인해 이끌어 낼 수 있는 결과를 드러내는 'thus'를 활용한다. ' __A__ and __B__ '는 곧 'A=B'인 점과 'connected to the

Internet'의 상황을 고려하면, 선택지 ③이 가장 적절하다.

해석 우리 부서는 몇 개의 온라인 판매상들뿐만 아니라 인터넷에 연결될 것이므로, 전국의 사람들과 더 많이 접근하고 접촉할 수 있을 것이다.

7 ②

해설 동질의 단어를 연결하는 'and'를 활용한다.

<u>veracious</u> and reliable

A　　=　　B

해석 나는 항상 그가 정직하고, 믿음직하다는 것을 알기 때문에 이 직위에 그를 추천할 수 있다.

8 ③

해설 동질의 성격을 나열하는 and와 부연의 코마를 활용한다.

a quiet individual, contemplative and <u>retiring</u>

A　　=　　B

해석 그의 능력이 허락하는 한 완벽에 가까운 책 혹은 이야기의 창작에만 관심이 있는 문예가는 일반적으로, 조용한 개인이며, 사색하길 좋아하고, 그리고 내성적이다.

9 ③

해설 동질의 성격을 연결하는 'A and B(A=B)'를 활용한다.

preferred to be alone = not <u>gregarious</u>

해석 그는 사교적이지 않았고, 그리고 대부분의 시간을 혼자 보내는 것을 선호했다.

10 ①

해설 다음 두 단계를 살펴보면서 풀이에 들어가도록 하자.

1) 'lack of N'은 자주 등장하는 표현이므로 반드시 외워둔다.

lack of <u>긍정적인 표현</u>

즉, 전치사구가 앞의 명사를 수식하는 형태인데, 이 경우 앞의 명사가 'lack'이란 부정을 전달하므로 뒤에 이어지는 빈칸의 명사는 일반적으로 긍정의 명사를 써야 한다. 선택지 ①, ③이 될 가능성이 높다.

2) 동질의 성격의 단어/구를 연결하는 'and'를 활용한다.

A　　and　　B

a large amount of _____ = lack of _____

우선 B의 단어를 먼저 넣으면, 긍정의 뉘앙스를 풍기는 단어가 되어야 하므로 선택지 ①과 ③이 가장 적절하다. 또한 첫 번째 빈칸은 동질의 뉘앙스를 연결하는 'and'에 의해 'lack of _____' 전체가 부정이므로 앞도 부정의 뉘앙스여야 한다. 고로 선택지 ①이 답이 된다.

해석 민족적 집단 특히, 인종적 집단과 같은 범주를 서술함에 있어서는 상당한 차이와 불일치가 있어 왔다.

참고

lack of는 자주 나오는 표현이기에 다음 사항을 기억해 둔다.

1) lack of B
   B는 일반적으로 긍정의 표현이고 전체는 부정의 의미를 전달한다.
2) A and lack of B
   B는 긍정 lack of B는 부정의 표현이기에 A는 당연히 부정의 의미를 전달하는 표현이다.

Unit 4

Shelley and Romanticism and Ozymandias

Part 3 Voca Check

1 1 prominent   2 emerge   3 a reaction against   4 rationality   5 celebrate
6 antique   7 expelled   8 lyrical   9 sublime   10 gifted

2 1 meditation   2 transformative   3 advocate for   4 be reflected in   5 fierce
6 call for   7 tyranny   8 short-lived   9 advocate   10 boating

Part 4 Reading Comprehension

1 ④, ⑤

해설 ⓓ His poem "The Masque of Anarchy," written in response to the Peterloo Massacre of 1819, **calls** for non-violent resistance to tyranny and injustice.

ⓔ His work continues to inspire and challenge readers today, as it **did** during his own time.

2 ①

해설 objective → subjective

아래 내용을 보면, Romanticism은 이성과 합리성을 강조하는 계몽주의(the Enlightenment)에 반대하여 나온 운동으로 "개인의 상상적과 감정, 그리고 (주관적) 경험을 추구"하는 경향이므로 objective는 적절하지 않다.

... the Romantic movement, which emerged in the late 18th century as <u>a reaction against the Enlightenment's emphasis on reason and rationality</u>. Romanticism <u>celebrated the power of imagination, emotion, and nature, and sought to express the individual's experience</u>.

3 ①

해설 II. One of Shelley's writings, such as "The Masque of Anarchy," convey his belief in ~~standing up against~~ tyranny and injustice, emphasizing ~~the need for violent reform~~.

→ This statement is not correct. "The Masque of Anarchy" by Percy Bysshe Shelley does not emphasize the need for violent reform. On the contrary, the poem advocates for non-violent resistance to tyranny and injustice. It calls for peaceful protest and civil disobedience as a means to bring about social and political change.

III. Moving to London and associating with radical writers and intellectuals further solidified his role as an activist, encouraging the public to conform to ~~established institutions~~.

→ This statement is incorrect as Shelley's association with radical writers and intellectuals in London actually strengthened his role as an activist challenging established institutions, rather than encouraging conformity to them.

4 ③

해설 Shelley describes a crumbling statue of Ozymandias as a way to portray the ~~permanence~~ of political power and to praise art's ability to preserve the past.

→ In fact, the poem "Ozymandias" by Percy Bysshe Shelley portrays the impermanence of political power and the transience of human achievements. The crumbling statue of Ozymandias serves as a symbol of the inevitable decline of even the most powerful rulers and their legacies. Therefore, it does not praise art's ability to preserve the past but rather highlights the fleeting nature of human endeavors.

5 ④

해설 ⓓ shows that time **hasn't** been kind to the statue. (⑤의 같은 맥락에서 이해할 것.)

→ In fact, ⓓ expresses the opposite sentiment. It conveys the idea that nothing remains of the once-great statue except for its decaying remnants in the desert, emphasizing the relentless passage of time and the eventual decay of even the most grandiose human creations. Therefore, interpreting it as time being kind to the statue would be inappropriate.

6 ④

해설 The traveler informs the narrator that the statue bears an inscription on its pedestal, ~~though not declaring~~ the identity of the figure.

→ The traveler does inform the narrator about the inscription on the pedestal, explicitly stating the identity of the figure as Ozymandias, king of kings. Therefore, the statement that it does not declare the identity of the figure is incorrect.

7 ⑤

해설 V. The tone of the poem ~~stays the same~~ throughout the poem, aiding in conveying the underlying message of the transient nature of power and empire.

→ The poem invites us to reflect solemnly on our mortality and the transience of human power. Moreover, the tone shifts from awe-inspiring to ironic and mocking, emphasizing the downfall of Ozymandias and the vanity of his grandeur.

8 ⑤

해설 The poem ~~praises the humility of the ruler~~ who believes his empires and achievements ~~will eventually wither away.~~

Part 5 Sentence Completion

1 ④

해설 A and B는 A = B임과 역접의 양보 though를 활용한다.

1) A and B는 A = B이다. 두 번째 빈칸을 먼저 채운다. 주어는 the man이다.

> the man allowed his associates <u>no such privacy</u>
> and (=)
> was constantly _____ information about what they intended to do next

그 남자는 자신의 동료의 사생활을 전혀 허용하지 않는다고 했다. 그럼 그는 자신의 동료들이 항상 무엇을 할지 알려고 하는 내용이 전개되도록 빈칸을 채우면 된다. 선택지 ③과 ④가 이에 해당한다.

2) 양보의 though를 활용한다.

자기 자신에 대한 태도	↔	남에 대한 태도
<u>reticent</u> about his own plans		allowed his associates <u>no such privacy</u>

해석 자신의 계획에 대해 아주 과묵하지만, 그는 자신의 동료에게 어떠한 프라이버시도 허용하지 않고 지속적으로 다음에 무엇을 할 것인지에 대한 정보를 요구한다.

2 ②

해설 첫 번째 빈칸은 A and B는 A = B임을 활용하고, 두 번째 빈칸은 양보의 despite을 사용한다.

1) A and B는 A = B이다.

> single-minded and uncompromising
> (=)

첫 번째 빈칸은 single-minded의 동의어를 고르는 문제가 된다. 선택지를 보면, 답과 반의어 관계를 형성하는 선택지는 ①과 ⑤이다. 이렇게 선택지에 반의어 또는 동의어 관계가 형성되어 있으면 둘 중 하나가 정답일 가능성이 높다.

2) 대조의 despite를 활용한다.

> her <u>compassionate</u> nature ↔ her <u>strict adherence</u> to the letter of the law

해석 대법원의 새로 지명된 사람은 자비로운 성격을 가졌지만, 법조문을 엄격하게 지키는 타협 없는 일관성 있는 마음만을 가지고 있었다.

3 ③

해설 A and B는 A = B이다.

> <u>vindicate</u> her client and <u>prove him innocent</u> on all charges

선택지의 성격을 둘로 나누어 묶는다면, vindicate와 나머지로 나눌 수 있다. 한 쪽은 무죄를 증명하는 것(vindicate)이고, 나머지는 모두 상대를 고소/기소하거나 협박하는 내용이다.

해석 그 변호사의 목표는 그녀의 의뢰인을 변호하고 모든 혐의에 대해 그가 죄가 없다는 것을 증명하는 것이었다.

4 ③

해설 역접의 while을 이용하여, 의미상 정답을 골라낼 수도 있지만, A and B가 A = B임을 활용하면 좀 더 손쉽게 답을 이끌어 낼 수 있다.

> a _____⊕_____ and concerned leader
>
> A   =   B
>
> 백성을 근심하고 _____하는 지도자

선택지 ③이 답이다. 나머지 선택지를 볼 경우,

① vicious   부정
② languid   부정
③ benevolent 긍정
④ treacherous 부정

선택지 중 하나만이 긍정이다. 이런 경우 빈칸에 들어갈 일순위로 생각하고 문제에 접근한다.

해석 그는 자비롭고 이해심 많은 지도자의 이미지를 투사하려고 노력하지만, 그를 잘 아는 사람들은 그의 성격의 나쁜 면에 대해 말한다.

5 ③

해설 빈칸은 try에 걸리는 to부정사이다. A and B가 A ↔ B의 역접의 기능이 있음을 반드시 기억하자. 일반적으로 역접으로 해석되는 and에는 대상이 두 개가 나오는 경우가 많다. 위 문제에선 a few와 other가 대조를 이룬다. **Thomas Paine had many enemies**라는 문장에서 토마스는 많은 적이 있다는 내용을 알 수 있다. 이와 같은 맥락에서 이후 전개되는 내용을 따라가야 한다.

> a few tried to simulate grief ↔ other continued to slander him
> 단지 몇 사람만이 슬픔을 애도하고, 나머지 많은 이가 그를 죽은 후에도 비방했다

해석 토마스 패인은 적들이 많아서, 그가 죽었을 때, 소수는 애도를 흉내 냈고, 또 다른 이들은 지속적으로 그를 욕해댔다.

6 ①

해설 재진술을 이끄는 in other words는 A in other words B일 경우 A = B이다. 고대 종교는 선과 악이 공존하고 있다고 가르치고 있다. 고로 빈칸에 들어갈 표현은 선뿐 아니라 악이 함께 존재하고 있다는 내용의 ①이 가장 적절하다.

해석 어떤 고대 종교에서는 인간은 악을 무시하지 말고 이 세상에서 선을 지켜야 한다고 가르치고 있다. 다른 말로 말하면 선을 구하라, 그러나 악도 이 세상에 존재한다는 것을 명심하라.

7 ④

해설 A similarly B가 A = B임을 활용한다. 첫 번째 문장의 내용은 어떤 사건의 부차적인 면이 주된 면보다 더 많은 관심을 이끈다는 내용이다. 이와 같은 맥락에서 '책의 경우 본문(text)보다 주석이 더 흥미를 끈다.'이므로 선택지 ④가 가장 적절하다.

해석 어떠한 일의 부차적인 면이 종종 그 부차적인 면이 따르는 본래의 사건보다 더 우리의 관심을 사로잡는다. 마찬가지로 (책의) 각주가 본문보다 더욱 흥미를 끄는 책이 많이 있다.

8 ②

해설 순접등위의 and를 활용한다. A and B는 A = B이다.

preserve a calm and peaceful mind =

never to allow passion or a transitory desire to disturb his tranquility

해석 성숙된 인간은 항상 침착하고 평화로운 마음을 유지해야 하고, 격정이나 일시적 욕망이 그의 평온을 방해하도록 해서는 결코 안 된다.

9 ②

해설 1. 비유적 표현을 근거로 답을 이끌어 낼 수 있다.

United States = mosaic (a picture made of many different pieces)

= diversity

2. 순접병렬의 A and B는 A = B임을 활용하여 답에 접근할 수 있다.

its _____ and the contributions made by people of many different cultures

A(diversity)　　　　　　　　　=　　　　　　　　　　　B

해석 오랫동안 미국은 용광로, 즉 다른 말로 하면 전 세계에서 온 사람들이 미국 문화를 자신들의 문화로 받아들이는 그릇이었고 그릇이어야 한다고 생각되어 왔다. 보다 최근에 몇몇 사람들은 미국을 여러 개의 서로 다른 조각이 모여서 하나의 그림을 이루는 모자이크에 비유하기도 했다. 그들의 주장에 의하면 미국의 힘은 다양성과 수많은 다양한 문화를 가진 사람들을 통해 이루어진 공헌들에 있다는 것이다.

10 ①

해설 첫 번째 문장과 두 번째 문장은 인과로 연결되어 있다. 두 문장 사이에 'because'를 삽입할 수 있다. 빈칸에 들어갈 표현에 대한 직접적인 힌트는 A, B, C and D의 관계이다. 접속사 and로 명사가 연결될 경우 A = B = C = D이다. 즉, and로 연결된 모든 단어는 같은 부류의 표현이어야 한다. 해당 경우는 앞에서 열거된 표현을 모두 포괄하는 단어이다.

bonuses, stock, summer vacations = benefits

해석 봉급만으로는 사람이 자기 고용주부터 얼마를 받고 있는지 알 수 없다. 많은 회사에서는 그들의 근로자들에게 상여금과 주식과 회사소유의 휴양지에서의 하기휴가와 그리고 다른 혜택을 제공하고 있다.

Why Leaves Turn Color in the Fall

Part 3 Voca Check

1 1 stealth 2 unaware 3 perch 4 close up shop 5 keen-eyed 6 squint
7 barbed 8 a string of 9 distant 10 lighted

2 1 dawn on 2 macabre 3 spectacular 4 cringe 5 roll up
6 in clenched fists 7 fall off 8 rattle 9 gushing 10 confetti

3 1 edict 2 solstice 3 pare 4 choke off 5 slender 6 petiole
7 undernourished 8 photosynthesis 9 cease 10 migrate

4 1 hibernate 2 fragile 3 splotch 4 vein 5 define 6 dissolve 7 replaced
8 pigments 9 camouflage 10 vivid

5 1 glowing 2 odd 3 be predisposed to 4 shimmer 5 tawny
6 shuddering 7 adaptive 8 haphazard 9 sizzling 10 thrilling

6 1 fragile 2 disintegration 3 bloom 4 sublime 5 mummify 6 radiate
7 radiant 8 vanish 9 sublime 10 mute

7 1 leafy 2 abundance 3 wither 4 simmer 5 whine 6 unruly 7 figment
8 never-never 9 sheer 10 conceal 11 awkward 12 fade 13 airborne
14 glide 15 swoop

Part 4 Reading Comprehension

1 ②

해설 밑줄 친 내용은 첫 번째 문장의 내용(The stealth of autumn catches one unaware.)의 사례를 통한 부연에 해당한다.

① The realm of nature beyond human perception 인간의 인식을 넘어선 자연의 영역

② Secretive attributes of Autumn 가을의 숨겨진 속성

③ The piercing eyes of leopards 표범의 날카로운 눈

④ The nature of Autumn that never ceases to stimulate human curiosity 인간의 호기심을 끊임없이 자극하는 가을의 속성

⑤ Capriciousness of nature 자연의 변덕스러움

2 ④

해설 ㉠ (나): Visual and auditory imagery is maximized through figurative descriptions.

→ In the underlined section (나), the author uses vivid language to create strong visual and auditory imagery. For example, phrases like "cringing on the trees"

34

and "clenched fists" evoke rich visual images, while "dry seedpods will rattle like tiny gourds" appeals to the auditory senses. This figurative language enhances the reader's experience by painting a vivid picture of the autumn scene.

   Ⓛ (다): It emphasizes how agilely trees relocate for the winter.

     → This interpretation is not correct. The sentence "Animals can migrate, hibernate, or store food to prepare for winter" does not relate to trees relocating for the winter. Instead, it refers to the various strategies that animals employ to survive the winter season, such as migrating to warmer climates, hibernating in burrows or dens, or storing food to sustain themselves during periods of scarcity. The correct interpretation would be that the sentence highlights the adaptive behaviors of animals in response to seasonal changes, contrasting with the discussion of how trees prepare for winter in the surrounding text.

   Ⓒ (라): It explains why the leaves keep wearing green clothes during the summer.

     → In section (라), the author explains why leaves remain green during the summer despite the presence of other colors within them. The explanation revolves around the role of chlorophyll, the green pigment responsible for photosynthesis. During the summer, chlorophyll is continually replaced as it breaks down, maintaining the dominant green coloration of the leaves. However, as the days shorten in the fall, chlorophyll production ceases, revealing the other pigments present in the leaves that were previously masked by the green chlorophyll. This explanation clarifies why leaves appear green during the summer months and why their true colors become visible in the fall.

3 ④

해설 camouflage는 여기서 엽록소에 의해서 만들어지는 녹색(chlorophyll's shocking green)이다.

4 ⑤

해설 ⓜ splotch: a mark or spot that has a ~~regular~~(→ irregular) shape

5 ④

해설 The underlined sentence in [A] contains the literary device of personification. The sentence attributes human-like qualities or actions ("staggering in") to the season of fall, which is a non-human entity.

   ① Simile 직유

   ② Alliteration 두운(頭韻)《What a tale of terror now their turbulency tells!의 [t]음 따위》

   ③ Allusion: something that is said or written that is intended to make you think of a particular thing or person

   ⑤ hyperbole 과장법

6 ③

해설 (다) Undernourished, we see the leaves stop producing the pigment chlorophyll, and photo-synthesis ceases.

   → Undernourished, the leaves stop producing the pigment chlorophyll, and photosynthesis ceases. ← dangling participle

undernourished의 주어가 we가 아니라 the leaves임에 주의할 것.

7 ④

(해설) 제시된 문장은 아래 밑줄 친 내용에 이어지는 것이 가장 적절하다.

They shimmer with the colors of sunset, spring flowers, the tawny buff of a colt's pretty rump, the shuddering pink of a blush. Animals and flowers color for a reason—adaptation to their environment—but <u>there is no adaptive reason for leaves to color so beautifully in the fall any more than there is for the sky or ocean to be blue</u>. It's just one of the haphazard marvels the planet bestows every year.

밑줄 친 문장의 내용은 하늘과 바다가 파란 이유에는 특별한 진화 또는 기능적 이득이 없는 것과 같이 나뭇잎이 아름다운 색을 띠는 것도 마찬가지란 의미다. 박스의 내용은 해당 내용에 자연스럽게 이어진다.

> **보충**
>
> there is no adaptive reason for leaves to color so beautifully in the fall any more than there is for the sky or ocean to be blue.
>
> → This statement suggests that there is no evolutionary or functional advantage for leaves to change color so vividly in the autumn season, similar to how there is no specific adaptive reason for the sky or ocean to appear blue. It implies that these phenomena are not directly linked to survival or reproductive advantages for the organisms involved, but rather are incidental features of nature that arise from physical or chemical processes.

8 ⑤

(해설) ㉣ Dry seedpods = the leaves (rolled up in clenched fists)

9 ⑤

(해설) ㉑ enlighten → dupe(deceive)

이어지는 문장의 아래 밑줄 친 내용을 보면 다음과 같다.

We find the sizzling colors thrilling, and in a sense they ㉑＿＿＿＿ us. **Colored like living things, they signal death and disintegration**.

문맥 상 밑줄 친 분사구문의 접속사 Although를 살려 적으면 다음과 같다.

Although they are colored like living things, they signal death and disintegration.

그리고 겉과 속이 다른 측면에서 빈칸에 들어갈 단어로는 dupe 또는 deceive가 적절하다.

10 ②

11 ⑤

(해설) ⑤ The author ~~deplores~~ on the moodiness of the changing seasons and on life and death.

→ 변화하는 계절의 변덕을 "한탄[개탄]"하는 내용은 없다.

① allusion: An indirect reference to something that originates from outside the text (or something from earlier in the text). (다른 텍스트에서 나오는 표현을 간접적으로 지칭.)

→ 본문에서 성경의 이야기

③ Alliteration is a literary device that reflects repetition in two or more nearby words of initial consonant sounds. (둘 또는 그 이상의 가까운 단어의 첫 자음 소리가 반복되는 현상.)

→ ⓒ summer is when we simmer, and winter is when we whine from the cold.

Part 5 Sentence Completion

1 ③

해설 인과의 기능인 'and'를 활용한다. 본문은 'as a result'라는 단서를 쉽게 던져주고 있지만, 그것이 없다 하더라도 인과의 기능을 가진 'and'를 활용하여 풀 수 있다. 결과적으로 지명이 확정되었다는 내용에 걸맞은 빈칸의 표현을 고르면 된다.

> 근거 : His qualifications for the diplomatic job were impeccable
>
> 결과 : as a result his nomination was confirmed

이 문제의 경우 빈칸에 들어갈 단어가 긍정이라는 점을 파악할 경우 선택지에서 부정의 내용은 먼저 소거하고 풀이를 할 수 있다.

① terrible   부정
② stingy   부정
③ impeccable   긍정
④ simple   부정
⑤ retroactive   부정

선택지 ③만이 주어인 His qualifications와 긍정의 의미를 형성한다.

해석 외교관의 업무를 위한 그의 자격은 완벽했기에 그의 지명은 확정이 되어, UN의 대사가 되었다.

2 ②

해설 'A(원인) ~, and B(결과)'를 구성하는 'and'를 활용한다. 즉, A가 원인이 되어 발생할 수 있는 가장 적절한 결과를 빈칸에 넣으면 된다.

> 원인 : Human activity wipes out a thousand plant and animal species
>
> 결과 : species are pushed to the edge of extinction

부정적인 원인은 부정적인 결과를 가져온다. 선택지에 부정적 의미를 직접적으로 전달하지 않는 선택지 ①과 ③은 소거한다.

해석 인간의 활동으로 천 여 종 이상의 동식물이 매년 사라지고 있다. 그 결과 많은 종이 멸종의 위기에 몰려 있다.

3 ④

해설 인과의 역할을 하는 'and'를 활용한다.

not _____ and should be avoided if possible
원인(부정)   →   피해야 한다(결과적으로)

빈칸에 긍정적인 단어가 들어가야 [not + _____]의 전체 내용이 부정이 됨으로 선택지 ①, ②는 들어갈 수 없고, 나머지 선택지에서 문맥에 맞는 단어를 선정해야 한다.

해석 향상의 기미가 보이는 영역에 대한 지적 없이 논박하는 비판은 건설적이 못하기에 최대한 피해야 한다.

4 ③

해설 빈칸 앞의 'and'를 활용한다. 앞 내용에 추가적인 정보를 전달하는 기능(점층 강조)을 하는데, 내용상 'its reduction'보다 강한 어조의 'elimination'이 더 적절하다.

해석 폭력을 싫어하는 사람이 많고 이들은 이것을 줄이기 위해 가능하면 인간사에서 이것을 없애는 것을 위해 일하는 가장 중요하고 동시에 가장 희망적인 일 중 하나라고 확신한다.

5 ④

해설 인과의 and를 활용한다. A and B는 인과의 관계이다.

religious ardor was diminishing and church building was consequently declining
원인   →   결과

해석 서구세계의 나머지 지역에서 종교적 열정은 줄어들고 있으며, 교회 건축은 따라서 쇠퇴하고 있다.

6 ①

해설 '원인 + V + 결과'를 이끄는 동사 'result in'과 동일한 성질의 단어/구를 연결하는 등위접속사 'and'를 활용한다.

1) 노동조합의 힘을 약화시키는 서비스 산업으로의 전환이므로 제시된 문장에서 주어가 부정이다. '부정의 원인은 부정의 결과를 이끈다'는 원칙을 활용한다

부정적 주어 + result in + 부정적 결과

2) 두 빈칸의 연결사 'and'는 동질의 성질을 가지므로, 단순논리로 다음과 같이 볼 수 있다.

_____A_____ = _____B_____ (A와 B는 동질의 성격)

부정적 단어로 구성된 선택지가 답이 된다.

해석 제조 산업에서 서비스 산업으로 전환은 낮은 봉급의 직업과 노동조합의 힘을 약하게 만들었다.

7 ④

해설 인과의 and를 활용한다.

Change means disorganization, and many groups tend to view it with suspicion
변화는 부정적 의미 ———————————→ 부정적 관점

빈칸에 들어갈 단어가 부정적 표현임을 안다면 선택지 접근도 쉬워진다.

해석 변화에 저항하는 것이 많은 집단들의 특징이다. 왜냐하면, 그들은 변화란 것이 반드시 더 나은 쪽으로의 변화인 것은 아니고 오히려 더 나쁜 쪽으로 변화일 수도 있다고 주장하기 때문이다. 변화는 기존 질서의 해체를 의미하고 많은 그룹들이 변화를 의심의 눈으로 바라보는 경향이 있다.

8 ③

해설 인과의 and를 활용한다. 과학자는 자신의 연구를 열렬히 옹호한다고 했다. 그녀가 제시하는 이에 대한 가장 적절한 근거가 무엇인지를 생각한다.

> 주장 : vehemently defended her research practices
>
> 근거 : her results were indubitable

해석 과학자들은 격렬하게 그녀의 조사실행을 방어했고, 그리고 그녀는 자신의 연구결과가 의심할 나위 없는 것이라고 주장했다.

9 ③

해설 인과의 'and'와 결과를 이끄는 부사 consequently를 활용한다.

> conducted its second nuclear test → contended with the U. N. members
>   부정적 원인   부정적 결과

해석 북한은 5월 두 번째 핵 실험을 실시했고, 결과적으로 한국과 미국을 포함한 UN회원국들과의 사이가 나빠졌다.

10 ②

해설 인과의 and와 역접의 접속사 however 및 전체문장에 부정적 영향을 미치는 부사 unfortunately를 활용한다.

1) 인과

> 원인 : The president's secretary and his chief aide adored him,
>
> 결과 : both wrote obsessively devoted personal memoirs about him

2) 역접

> The president's secretary and his chief aide adored him
>
> ↕ however
>
> idolatry does not make for true intimacy

즉, 대통령 장관과 보좌관이 그를 높이지만 사실 그런 숭배는 진실한 친밀함을 형성하지 못한다는 대조적 내용으로 전개되고 있다.

해석 대통령 비서실장과 그의 핵심 참모진은 그를 아주 좋아했다. 그리고 둘 다 그에 관한 강박적으로 헌신적인 개인적 기억에 관해서 작성하였다. 그러나 불행히도, 우상숭배는 진실한 친밀에 도움이 되지는 못한다.

The Tell-Tale Heart

Part 2 Text Reading

Quick Quiz

1 ① True ② False ③ True ④ True ⑤ False ⑥ False

해설 ② Edgar Allan Poe's mother, Elizabeth Arnold, was ~~a mediocre actress~~ who deserted him when he was a baby.

→ Elizabeth Arnold was a talented actress, and it was David Poe, his father, who deserted him.

⑤ John Allan ~~formally adopted~~ Edgar Allan Poe as his son.

→ John Allan did not formally adopt Edgar.

⑥ Frances Allan, ~~Edgar's foster mother~~, disapproved of his literary ambitions.

→ The passage mentions John Allan's disapproval, not Francees Allan's.

2 ⑤

해설 직접적 근거: For his gold I had no desire.

Throughout the passage, there's no indication that the protagonist desires the old man's wealth. Instead, the protagonist's motivation for contemplating the murder seems to stem solely from his aversion to the old man's eye, particularly the pale blue eye with a film over it, which fills him with dread whenever it falls upon him.

3 hyperbole, hyperbolic

해설 The common literary device used in both underlined sentences from the passage is hyperbole. In both sentences, exaggeration is employed to emphasize the slow passage of time or the stillness of the protagonist.

Part 3 Voca Check

1 1 mediocre 2 talented 3 desert 4 charitable 5 self-righteous
   6 idleness 7 indifference 8 moody 9 resentful 10 meager 11 bitter
   12 quarrel 13 in despair 14 intercede 15 recognition

2 1 heir 2 dismiss 3 intuitive 4 ghastly 5 peopled 6 distraught
   7 grotesque 8 deranged 9 doomed 10 convincing 11 likeness
   12 frighten 13 unsettling 14 considerable 15 body

3 1 humiliating 2 senseless 3 agonizing 4 elude 5 pursue 6 delirious
   7 raging 8 relentless 9 delirium 10 dreadfully 11 sharpen 12 dull

13 acute   14 haunt   15 wrong

4 1 insult   2 pale   3 proceed   4 caution   5 foresight   6 creak   7 vex
8 boldly   9 hearty   10 inquire   11 profound   12 sagacity   13 contain
14 deeds   15 fairly

5 1 startle   2 groan   3 mortal   4 terror   5 grief   6 stifled   7 arise
8 overcharged   9 awe   10 deepening   11 dreadful   12 distract
13 causeless   14 supposition   15 stalk

6 1 mournful   2 unperceived   3 patiently   4 resolve   5 crevice
6 stealthily   7 dim   8 furious   9 gaze upon   10 distinctness   11 dull
12 hideous   13 veil   14 chill   15 acuteness

7 1 dull   2 envelop   3 fury   4 refrain   5 motionless   6 tattoo   7 seize
8 shriek   9 gaily   10 deed   11 muffled   12 vex   13 cease   14 remove
15 corpse

8 1 stone dead   2 trouble   3 precaution   4 concealment   5 wane   6 hastily
7 deposit   8 cunningly   9 stain   10 wary   11 suavity
12 with perfect suavity   13 suspicion   14 foul play   15 lodge

9 1 depute   2 premises   3 undisturbed   4 fatigue   5 wild   6 audacity
7 beneath   8 repose   9 corpse   10 definitiveness   11 vehemently   12 trifle
13 gesticulation   14 fury   15 agony

Part 4 Reading Comprehension

1 ⑤

해설 I. The unnamed narrator is called crazy by someone.
→ This is evident from the narrator's statement, "True!—nervous—very, very dreadfully nervous I had been and am; but why will you say that I am mad?" The narrator acknowledges that someone is accusing him of being mad.

II. The person calling the narrator crazy is also unknown just like the narrator himself.
→ The identity of the person calling the narrator mad is not revealed in the text, mirroring the anonymity of the narrator.

III. The narrator clearly distinguishes between "being nervous" and being crazy.
→ The narrator asserts that being nervous doesn't equate to being mad. He claims that his senses have been sharpened rather than dulled by his condition.

IV. The narrator thinks he knows better than "you."
→ The narrator asserts his superiority in understanding his own mental state over the judgment of the person accusing him of madness.

V. The words such as "dreadfully nervous" and "how healthily or how calmly" are contradictory, which reveals the narrator's mental status.

→ This statement suggests that the contradictory language used by the narrator, such as being "dreadfully nervous" yet claiming to tell the story "healthily" and "calmly," indicates a potential inconsistency or instability in the narrator's mental state. This contradiction could imply that the narrator's perceptions and behaviors are not entirely reliable, providing insight into his mental condition.

2 ①,②,③,④,⑤ all of them

어휘 dubious 의심스러운, 불안한

3 ⑤

해설 나레이터가 죽은 남자의 낮은 심장박동 소리가 자신의 것임을 확신하는 내용은 없다. 나머지는 본문을 통해서 추론할 수 있는 내용이므로 적절하다.

① The narrator's heightened sensitivity, leading to his inability to distinguish between real and imagined sounds, is evident in the passage. He hears what he believes to be the beating of the old man's heart, which is likely imagined due to his heightened state of anxiety and paranoia. (○)

② The narrator's belief that he hears the dead man's heart beating demonstrates his disturbed mental state and descent into madness. (○)

③ The narrator's focus on the sound of the man's heart, while showing little concern about his loud shriek, suggests a distorted prioritization of sensory stimuli, further highlighting his derangement. (○)

④ The sound of the heart drives the narrator to greater agitation and ultimately to revealing his crime out of guilt. (○)

어휘 overcome(= overwhelm) 압도하다

4 ③

해설 남자의 심장박동을 시계 소리에 비유한 것은 맞지만, 해당 소리가 벽시계라는 것을 나타내려는 뜻은 아니다.

5 ③

해설 어두워서 소재파악의 어려움으로 죽이지 못하는 것이 아니라 노인 자체에 대한 감정보다는 감은 눈꺼풀 뒤에 보호되고 있는 눈(his Evil Eye) 때문이다.

The narrator does not mention the darkness of the room as a reason for not being able to kill the old man. In fact, the darkness of the room is not presented as an obstacle in the story. The narrator's inability to carry out the act is attributed to his emotional conflict and fixation on the old man's eye rather than any external factors like darkness.

6 ②

해설 ㉣ 바로 앞의 내용은 다음과 같다.

I fairly chuckled at the idea; and perhaps he heard me; for he moved on the bed suddenly, as if startled.

나의 웃음으로 노인의 뒤척이는 모습을 묘사하고 있다. 해당 내용에 이어 Now you may

think that I drew back—but no. 로 전개되는 것이 자연스럽다.

7 ②

해설 (B) His room was as black as pitch with the thick darkness ← simile
→ The phrase "black as pitch" is not a metaphor; it is a simile, as it directly compares the darkness of the room to pitch. Therefore, this explanation is not accurate.

어휘 brag about ~에 대해서 자랑하다

8 ④

해설 He had been trying to fancy them causeless, but could not. He had been saying to himself—"**It is nothing but the wind in the chimney—it is only a mouse crossing the floor,**"or "**it is merely a cricket which has made a single chirp.**" 해당 문장의 밑줄 친 내용 모두가 다음 문장에 이어질 박스 안의 "these suppositions"에 해당한다.

Yes, he had been trying to comfort himself with **these suppositions**; but he had found all in vain. All in vain;

9 ⑥

해설 the damed spot = the eye of the old man

어휘 soft spot 허술한 곳, 약점 have a soft spot for something ~에 약하다(~을 너무 좋아하다)

10 ②

해설 I knew that sound well too. It was **the beating of the old man's heart**. It increased my fury, **as the beating of a drum stimulates the soldier into courage**.
비유적 표현을 통해서 마치 군인이 용감하게 진군하도록 부추기는 드럼소리와 같이 남자의 심장박동 소리가 실제 살인행동에 옮기는 결정적 자극을 한다.

11 ②

해설 * Intelligence에 대한 본문의 근거

"Never before that night had I felt the extent of my own powers—of my sagacity."
"I fairly chuckled at the idea; and perhaps he heard me; for he moved on the bed suddenly, as if startled."
"I knew what the old man felt, and pitied him, although I chuckled at heart."

* Patience에 대한 본문의 근거

"Upon the eighth night I was more than usually cautious in opening the door."
"I kept pushing it on steadily, steadily."
"For a whole hour I did not move a muscle, and in the meantime I did not hear him lie down."

12 ③

해설 ⓐ were → was (도치 확인할 것)

ⓓ laid → lay (lie - **lay** - lain)

13 ④

해설 I. False: The story doesn't begin with a conversation in progress. It starts with the narrator reflecting on his mental state and his actions.

II. True: The narrator explicitly states, "I loved the old man," indicating that he harbors no feelings of hatred or resentment towards him.

III. False: The narrator states that he was kind to the old man and interacted with him normally until he decided to kill him.

IV. True: The narrator expresses conflicting emotions of sympathy and amusement while observing the old man's terror in the dark room.

14 ①

해설 dissimulate (감정·의사 따위를) 숨기다; 모르는 체하다, 시치미떼다
dissimulate fear 무섭지 않은 체하다.
dissimulation (감정을) 감춤; 시치미뗌; 위선; 〖정신醫〗 질환(疾患) 은폐

② ⓛ sagacity 총명함: wisdom 지혜, discernment 분별
③ ⓒ contain 억누르다: restrain 제지하다, control 통제하다
④ ⓔ stifled 억압된, 질식하는: suppressed 억압된, smothered 질식하는
⑤ ⓜ suppositions 가정: assumptions 가정, speculations 추측

15 ⑤

해설 The figure of speech used in "the unperceived shadow" is oxymoron, which juxtaposes contradictory terms.

① "Is she at home?"Jack asked with careful carelessness.
→ This is an example of an oxymoron as it combines two contradictory terms.

② All your perfect imperfections give yours all to me.
→ This is also an oxymoron, as it pairs opposites to create emphasis.

③ The silence was deafening.
→ This is an example of an oxymoron, which combines the contradictory terms "silence" and "deafening" to emphasize the overwhelming and oppressive nature of the silence.

④ Parting is such sweet sorrow.
→ This is another example of an oxymoron, combining two contradictory terms to convey complex emotions.

⑤ That piece of chocolate cake is calling my name.
→ This is an example of personification, as it attributes human-like qualities (the ability to call someone's name) to an inanimate object (the chocolate cake).

16 ⑤

해설 Readers know the old man is buried under the floorboards while the police search the house without knowing anything. It is called ~~situational irony.~~(→ dramatic irony)

Dramatic irony is a literary device in which the audience or reader knows something that a character does not, creating a sense of tension or suspense in the narrative. It occurs when the reader or audience has more information about a situation than the character or characters in the story.

Situational irony is a literary device that occurs when there is a contrast between what is expected to happen in a story and what actually happens. It involves a discrepancy between what is anticipated and what actually occurs.

17 ④

18 ⑤

(해설) And still the men chatted pleasantly, and smiled. Was it possible they heard not? Almighty God!—no, no! [They(= the men) heard!—they suspected!—they knew!—they were making a mockery of my horror!—this I thought, and this I think.]

Part 5 Sentence Completion

1 ①

(해설) 인과의 with를 활용한다.

---

with delineations arbitrary → Proposals for appellations seem capricious
자의적으로 보이는 서술로 인해 명칭에 대한 제안은 변덕스러워 보인다

(해석) 명칭에 대한 제안들은 자의적으로 보이는 서술로 인해 종종 변덕스러워 보인다. 정부가 승인한 영업상 표가 존재한다는 것은 최소한의 고려만을 한 것으로 보인다.

2 ②

(해설) 부대상황의 as와 인과의 so ~ that을 활용한다.

---

the name became so common → generic

(해석) 아스피린은 원래 바이어 제약회사(Bayer Company)에 의해 사용된 상표명이었으나 제품의 사용이 급속히 퍼지면서 그 이름이 일반화되어 일반적인 용어로 받아들여졌다.

3 ②

(해설) 인과를 이끄는 부사절의 내용을 근거로 선택지에 접근한다.

---

time was limited → read the lengthy novel War and Peace in an abridged edition
근거   A ←————————————→ B

즉. '시간적 제약이 있어, 긴 책을 요약본으로 읽었다'의 내용이 전개되도록 선택지를 고르면 된다.

(해석) 시간의 압박 때문에 Weng은 긴 소설인 전쟁과 평화의 축소판을 읽어야 했다.

4 ①

(해설) 'so 원인 that 결과'를 활용한다.

drowsy(원인) → could not stay awake(결과)

해석 그 아이는 너무 졸려서 깨어 있을 수가 없었다.

5 ①

해설 이유의 'since'를 활용한다.

no cure for AIDS → palliative at best
치료제 없음   기껏해야 고통을 경감시키는 정도

해석 AIDS에 대한 치료제는 아직 발견이 되지 않았기에 이에 대한 치료란 기껏해야 병의 고통을 경감하는 정도다.

6 ④

해설 인과를 이끄는 'because'를 활용한다. his의 어떠한 언급이 embarrassing 했을지 생각해야 한다. because of 이후에 그 이유가 언급되고 있다. frankness에 해당하는 단어를 찾아 넣는 문제인데 선택지 ③을 쓸 경우 단어중복으로 옳지 못하기에 선택지 ④가 가장 적절하다.

해석 그의 꾸밈없는 말로 너무 있는 그대로를 드러내서 종종 당황스럽다.

7 ④

해설 인과를 이끄는 'Now that(Because)'를 활용한다.

realize his brother's chicanery (원인)   → 'impossible for me to trust his brother sincerely (결과)

해석 내가 그의 형의 속임수를 알아차렸기에, 앞으로 그의 형을 진심으로 믿는 것은 거의 불가능할 것으로 생각된다.

8 ②

해설 동사 'prevent A from V-ing'에 영향을 미치는 주어가 부정(flames and extreme heat)의 의미를 담고 있기에 부정적 상황을 이끈다. 즉,

S(부정적 요소) prevent A(주체) from B(부정적 결과)
부정적 원인 ————————→ 부정적 결과의 행위

그러므로 선택지 ②가 가장 적절하다.

해석 불길과 높은 열기로 인해 그는 아파트에 다시 들어갈 수가 없다고 주민들은 나에게 말했다.

이런 문제를 쉽게 푸는 방법 중 하나는 빈칸의 주체가 'he(him)'라는 점에서 다음과 같이 볼 수 있다.

'him from _____ the apartment'

     S   V   O

선택지 ① → He(him) seizes the apartment.

선택지 ② → He(him) re-enters the apartment.

선택지 ③ → He(him) constructs the apartment.

선택지 ④ → He(him) rents the apartment.

그러므로 문맥적 상황에서 선택지 ② 밖에 답이 되지 않는다.

9 ④

해설 일반적으로 A↔B인 not because A but because B와 인과의 so ~ that을 활용한다. 두 번째 빈칸부터 채운다.

1) so ~ that 구문을 활용한다.

_____ prepared her cases → she failed to bring the expected number to trial

부정

두 번째 빈칸에 들어갈 단어는 부정의 표현이다. 선택지에서 부정의 의미를 전달하는 단어는 선택지 ③ 밖에 없는 듯하다. 만약 ③으로 설정했을 때, 첫 번째 빈칸에 들어갈 단어가 congenial이 되는데, 문맥상 적절하지 못한다. 선택지 ④는 '세세한'이란 뜻의 minutely인데, 지나치게 세세하기 준비하다보니 법정이 요구하는 수치를 가지고 오지 못했다는 의미를 전달한다.

2) not because A but because B를 활용한다.

앞에서 이끌어낸 minutely와 함께 본문의 주인공인 she가 비난을 받은 것은 열심히 일하지 않아서가 아니라 너무 꼼꼼히 하다 보니 그 정도가 지나쳤기 때문이다. 쉽지 않은 문제이다.

해석 그녀는 자신의 동료 변호사에게 비판을 받았는데, 이것은 그녀가 일을 열심히 하지 않아서가 아니라 자신의 사건을 지나치게 세세하게 준비하다 보니 법정에 기대한 수치를 가져오지 못했기 때문이었다.

10 ⑤

해설 인과를 활용한다. 부정적인 원인은 부정적인 결과를 가진다.

A(원인) → B(결과)라 했을 때, 부정의 원인은 부정의 결과를 가진다.

그러므로 답은 같은 뉘앙스의 단어를 짝으로 한 선택지 ⑤가 된다.

해석 그녀는 계획이 잘 안 풀려 마음이 혼란스러웠다.

MEMO